NIGHTS IN FAIRYLAND

NIGHTS IN FAIRYLAND

Gossip, Blackmail, and the Many Lives of *Broadway Brevities*

WILL STRAW

McGill-Queen's University Press
Montreal & Kingston • London • Chicago

ISBN 978-0-2280-2659-4 (paper)
ISBN 978-0-2280-2660-0 (ePDF)
ISBN 978-0-2280-2661-7 (ePUB)

Legal deposit first quarter 2026
Bibliothèque et Archives nationales du Québec

Printed in Canada on acid-free paper that is 100% ancient-forest-free, containing 100% sustainable, recycled fibre, and processed chlorine-free.

This book has been published with the help of a grant from the Federation for the Humanities and Social Sciences, through the Awards to Scholarly Publications Program, using funds provided by the Social Sciences and Humanities Research Council of Canada.

Funded by the Government of Canada | Financé par le gouvernement du Canada | Canada | Canada Council for the Arts | Conseil des arts du Canada

We acknowledge the support of the Canada Council for the Arts.
Nous remercions le Conseil des arts du Canada de son soutien.

McGill-Queen's University Press in Montreal is on land which long served as a site of meeting and exchange amongst Indigenous Peoples, including the Haudenosaunee and Anishinabeg nations. In Kingston it is situated on the territory of the Haudenosaunee and Anishinaabek. We acknowledge and thank the diverse Indigenous Peoples whose footsteps have marked these territories on which peoples of the world now gather.

Library and Archives Canada Cataloguing in Publication

Title: Nights in fairyland : gossip, blackmail, and the many lives of *Broadway Brevities* / Will Straw.
Names: Straw, Will, 1954- author
Description: Includes bibliographical references and index.
Identifiers: Canadiana (print) 20250225646 | Canadiana (ebook) 20250225697 | ISBN 9780228026594 (paper) | ISBN 9780228026600 (ePDF) | ISBN 9780228026617 (ePUB)
Subjects: LCSH: Clow, Stephen G. | LCSH: Sensationalism in journalism—New York (State)—New York. | LCSH: Celebrities—Press coverage—New York (State)—New York. | LCSH: Celebrities in popular culture—New York (State)—New York. | LCSH: Extortion—New York (State)—New York. | LCSH: American periodicals—New York (State)—New York. | LCSH: Gossip in mass media. | LCSH: Celebrities in mass media. | LCSH: Journalism—Social aspects—New York (State)—New York.
Classification: LCC PN4888.S46 S77 2026 | DDC 302.2309747/1—dc23

This book was designed and typeset by studio oneonone in Adobe Garamond 11/14.
Copyediting by Eleanor Gasparik.

McGill-Queen's University Press
Suite 1720, 1010 Sherbrooke St West, Montreal, QC, H3A 2R7

Authorized safety representative in the EU: Mare Nostrum Group BV, Mauritskade 21D, 1091 GC Amsterdam, the Netherlands, gpsr@mare-nostrum.co.uk

This book is dedicated with love to two people. To Johanne Sloan – art historian, deltiologist (look it up!), and the person with whom I have the good fortune to share my life. She has had to listen to me talk about *Broadway Brevities* for twenty years. And to the memory of my brother Christopher Straw – radio broadcaster, proud father, and environmental activist – who was killed in a tragic construction accident on Gabriola Island, British Columbia, in 2021. One of my fondest memories is of us all with Chris's family, my siblings Patrick and Sarah, and my late mother walking through the graveyard in Murray Harbour, Prince Edward Island, looking for the Clow family gravesites. (We found them.)

CONTENTS

FIGURES

FIGURES

PREFACE

I can trace my interest in *Broadway Brevities* and its editor, Stephen G. Clow, to the day, back near the turn of the millennium, when I entered a second-hand bookstore in an out-of-the-way location in Toronto. I was in that city on sabbatical leave from McGill University, working on a big interdisciplinary, inter-university research project called "The Culture of Cities." In my off-hours I frequented second-hand bookshops and research libraries, pursuing a side-project interest in Canadian pulp magazine publishers of the 1940s. Near the front of the store, boxes holding several dozen Canadian true crime, romance, and humor magazines from the 1940s caught my eye. All were in near-perfect condition – probably from the publishers' original stocks – and while the owner believed they were rare and valuable, it seemed he was also in need of money. I told myself that, because I was "working" on crime magazines at the time, I needed them. I bought the whole collection.

All these magazines, I discovered, were published by a Toronto company called Superior, one of those Toronto publishers that rose to prominence during World War II when various kinds of magazines from the United States could no longer be imported into Canada. As I began tracing the history of this company, searching for information in the digitized editions of old Toronto newspapers, I came across references to a Canadian magazine called *Broadway Brevities*. I learned of the arrest in 1939 of a man involved in launching the magazine in Toronto, a Stephen G. Clow. From further searches I learned that *Broadway Brevities* had been the name of a magazine published in Manhattan from 1916 to 1925 and then, in a revived version, in the early 1930s. Its editor, during much of this time, was the same Stephen G. Clow.

All of this led to several dozen automated eBay searches running over two decades, a half-sabbatical leave spent in New York City reading court records, and visits to a dozen or more libraries and archives across the United States and Canada. This work continued despite all the distractions confronting me as a mid- then late-career Canadian academic. I chaired my department on a few occasions, directed a research institute for six years, supervised more than sixty doctoral students, and pursued other interests (on music scenes, true crime magazines, Canadian cultural policy) that often had little to do with my work on *Broadway Brevities*. Nevertheless, I continued to move that project ahead, little by little. I told myself that I would complete it once I had finally acquired all thirteen instalments of the "Nights in Fairyland" series, which appeared in *Broadway Brevities* in 1924 and 1925. (I met that objective in 2019.)

The greatest impediment to this research was the scarcity of the magazines I wanted to study. Historian George Chauncey, one of the first scholars to acknowledge the importance of *Broadway Brevities*, had already commented, in his book *Gay New York*, on the rarity of issues of the magazine. The New York Public Library, when I began looking, believed it had no copies of the magazine from its 1920s incarnation, but I found four of them in a "clipping" file under the name of its editor. Issues of the 1930s tabloid *Brevities* were easier to find, largely because the Kinsey Institute at Indiana University collected them for what they said about sex, and other archives acquired them for collections devoted to the histories of comics and cartooning. The greatest surprise in the entire research process came in the early 2000s. When visiting a repository of criminal records in New York City, I was handed a box of materials related to the suit between the publishers of the 1930s *New Broadway Brevities* and the Warner Bros. film company. I expected to find little more than lawyer briefs and courtroom documents, but the box contained dozens of issues of the magazine, all in perfect condition and probably unseen or untouched since 1932. (I assume they are still there.) Other important sources, particularly for the Canadian version of *Broad-*

way Brevities, were gay, lesbian, and queer archives in their various incarnations and institutional homes.

In Toronto, the ArQuives, formerly the Canadian Lesbian and Gay Archives, was one of the only repositories holding issues of the Canadian version of *Brevities*, which was launched in 1937. These were sought and saved in large part because they recycled, in fragmentary and rewritten form, some of the content of the "Nights in Fairyland" series published in the original New York magazine in 1924 and 1925. The Thomas Fisher Rare Book Library at the University of Toronto had significant runs of these and other relevant Canadian materials, evidence of their devotion to documenting the history of Canadian sensational tabloids and magazines.

Mostly, though, my research has depended on the slow appearance of these magazines on eBay and other collector sites. While I have still not seen every issue of the original *Broadway Brevities* magazine, I now own fifty-eight and have others in full or partial scans. My collection of the 1930s tabloid *Brevities*, and of the weekly tabloids it inspired, is closer to being complete. (If you have the first issue of *Broadway Tattler*, from 1932, let's talk!) Large numbers of issues of the 1930s tabloids discussed here turn up for sale with the upper half of their front-page covers stripped off because that's how vendors returned unsold copies to distributors. I would buy these, then wait patiently for full issues to turn up and buy those as well. Whenever dealers offered *Gems of Brevities* – cheap, stapled compilations of multiple back issues of the 1930s tabloid *Broadway Brevities* – I bought them just in case they contained an issue I was missing. The absences that continue to intrigue me are those of magazines announced, but seemingly impossible to find and probably never even published. These include a magazine of the early 1930s called *Personals* or *Gotham Gossip*, which Stephen G. Clow was supposedly going to co-edit with a young man named Noel Meadow. Or the "spicy" magazine that the editors of the tabloid *Brevities* announced in 1934 as they faced bankruptcy.

The absence of the kinds of magazines studied here from libraries and archives meant that I had to build a large collection from across the broader field of 1920s and 1930s periodicals to make sure I was not missing important pieces of the puzzle. As the research unfolded, I amassed a greater collection of the magazines published by Joseph "Cap'n Joey" Burten than I ever imagined I would.

These proved invaluable for understanding the worlds I was trying to reconstruct and intersected with the main throughlines of this book at several points. Conversely, I spent long periods pursuing dead ends or going down rabbit holes that turned up little that was relevant to this project. In particular, I bid online (successfully, alas) for a great many issues of magazines like *Jim Jam Jems* or *Film Fun*, which filled in only the haziest of contexts. A two-day trip to Saratoga, New York, to track down information on the tipsheet racket involving Theodore Epstein – a man deep at the heart of many of the publishing ventures described here – led me to a great deal of information that was fascinating but ultimately beyond the scope of this book. As this project got underway, I began amassing a collection of books published between 1902 and 1915 by Clow's Broadway Publishing Company, stopping only when I had about sixty of these and realized that this was probably sufficient. (Many others are available on Google Books and in the holdings of the HathiTrust. In twenty years of searching, I only ever found one BPC book in a second-hand or antiquarian bookstore.)

I have spent a great deal of time in flea markets in Canada, the United States, Mexico, and France. It became clear that, while print culture treasures might turn up on dealer tables in most of those countries, almost everything in the United States had moved to eBay. In twenty years, I never saw a single issue of *Broadway Brevities* or the other magazines discussed here offered for sale in an in-person market. In the time I've spent on this project, I've watched with fascination as the few publicly available issues of *Broadway Brevities* moved through different media supports. For the last fifteen years, twelve issues of the original magazine, from the years between 1919 and 1923, have been available for download as PDFs from the Internet Archive. These are the same issues that, for years, dealers have gathered on CD-ROMs for sale on eBay and other sites (as they have for other magazines of the period, like *Film Fun* or *10 Story Magazine*). These same scans may be purchased in book form through Amazon, AbeBooks, or eBay, or from publishers in the UK, India, and elsewhere who will print single issues and bind them in leather covers. This erratic, artisanal kind of republishing is typical of magazines like those studied in this book, which fall into no obvious category and are not the focus of organized fandoms and collector subcultures. In contrast, for those interested in old comic books or pulp fiction magazines, there is an abundance of well-organized information online and coordinated attempts to offer full runs of scanned titles.

The scarcity of issues of *Broadway Brevities* led me to ponder whether I could perform a service by simply reproducing lots of the magazine's content in this book. In particular, the "Nights in Fairyland" series of 1924–25 has been much sought after, as assumptions have grown about its usefulness for writing queer histories of New York during this period. I have written this book in a way that I hope balances my own commentary and historical detail with enough of the original material to be useful, though this has not always been easy. (External reviewers have had contrasting ideas about the extent to which I should be quoting original text or commenting upon it.) As this book goes to press, I am already consulting with university libraries and other archives about a digital site that would make most of these materials available to the public.

In the last few years, much of my scholarship has unfolded in the young interdisciplinary field known as "night studies." While it was not intended as such, I am happy to offer this book as in some way a contribution to that field.

ACKNOWLEDGMENTS

Twenty years of research for this book have left me owing thanks to a great many people. Sarah Brouillette and Travis DeCook invited me to present very earlier versions of this research to the History of the Book program at the University of Toronto in 2004, an opportunity that was both intimidating and rewarding to me. They did so, I suspect, at least partially on the urging of David Galbraith and Heather Murray, dear friends and colleagues who have supported this work since its inception. Jaleen Grove, Susan E. Houston, Don Wallace, Michael Feldman, Susanna Paasonen, Robert Hambrecht, Charles Acland, Keir Keightley, and Ed Dimendberg, each of them experts in areas germane to this book, were very generous with their time and ideas in different stages of my writing and research. Christine Bourolias of the Archives of Ontario, John Bell of the National Archives of Canada (now Library and Archives Canada), Sandra Alston of the University of Toronto Libraries, and staff at the Toronto Metropolitan University Libraries Research rare books room, the Thomas Fisher Rare Book Library of the University of Toronto Libraries and the New York Public Library were all very helpful despite my regular demands on their time. Don McLeod of the Canadian Lesbian and Gay Archives was particularly generous in providing a photocopy of an issue of the Canadian *Broadway Brevities*. Collectors (or dealers) of vintage magazines, like George Flye and Beau Collier, have been generous in sharing materials and knowledge.

Other thanks go to Donna Johnston Collings and Paulette Edwards, both from Prince Edward Island, whom I have never met, but who sent photos and information in the early days of this project. And I am indebted to the late, great Canadian lawyer Clayton Ruby, who responded promptly to my request for any memories about his uncle, publisher Morris Ruby.

As I slowly moved into the field we call "print culture studies," many accomplished scholars made me feel welcome, by inviting me to speak at conferences or seminars and to publish my work. Their warmth calmed my sense of being an imposter in a field with such a distinguished history. Love and thanks to Vanessa Schwartz, Faye Hammill, Michelle Smith, Darren Wershler, Susanna Vargas, Jean-Philippe Imbert, Patricia Garcia, and Nora Ramtke. For many years I have followed, with great admiration, overlapping networks of francophone scholars who move with great skill between literary studies and periodical studies. In France, Marie-Ève Thérenty and Mathieu Letourneux, among many others, have produced work that has inspired me and that, in a perfect world, would all be translated into English. In Canada, Micheline Cambron, Mélodie Simard-Houde, Rachel Nodon, Adrien Rannaud, and Marie-Pierre Luneau have all welcomed me into contexts where I might speak and write about sensational tabloids. A special thanks to Graciela Martin-Zalce for helping me to develop some of these ideas in a Mexican context, and for everything else. And to Jess Reia, close collaborator and dear friend, who pushes me to think about media and the culture of the night.

I am lucky to have worked on this project with some of the very best research assistants available. Many of these are now successful, published scholars or archivists in their own right. Thank you to Danielle Schwartz, Lucia Bell-Epstein, Caylin Smith, Molly Kass, Robert Read, Blaire Martis, Nathan Richard-Velinou, and others whose names may have slipped away from me.

At McGill University, I have been inspired by a group of smart, supportive, and adorable colleagues. I cannot name them all, but I will single out Darin Barney, Jenny Burman, Nathalie Cooke, Mary Hunter, Lynn Kozak, Marc Raboy, Carrie Rentschler, Ipek Tureli, and Jonathan Sterne, who passed away as this book was being copyedited and was a model of generosity and intellectual integrity.

ACKNOWLEDGMENTS

The skilled professionals at McGill-Queen's University Press were a pleasure to work with, and I hope this is not the last of our collaborations. Warm thanks to Jonathan Crago, Eleanor Gasparik, Kathleen Fraser, Elena Goranescu, Jacqueline Davis, Catherine Bienvenu, and others at the press.

Financial support for much of this research came from the Social Sciences and Humanities Research Council of Canada and McGill University's James McGill Professor program.

Three previous publications were based in part on the research presented in this book:

"Traffic in Scandal: The Case of Broadway Brevities." *University of Toronto Quarterly* 73, no. 4 (2004): 947–71.
"Constructing the Canadian Lowbrow Magazine: The Periodical as Media Object in the 1930s and 1940s." *Journal of Modern Periodical Studies* 6, no. 2 (2015): 112–33.
"The Sporting Pornographer." *Media History* 23, no. 17 (2017): 4–27.

NOTE FROM THE AUTHOR

Derogatory Language

This book reproduces many instances of writing that use derogatory terms to name sexual inclinations and identities. Many of these terms, like "queer," have been subject to different kinds of reclamation (ironic or not) in recent years and have lost most of their derogatory force. Others, like "fairy," simply appear antiquated in the present time. In parts of this book, but especially in chapter 3, I have quoted a great many passages that contain harsh, even disturbing descriptions of queer people and, in some cases, call for collective violence against them. I have omitted some of these passages when their very number began to seem overwhelming. Nevertheless, it seemed to me necessary to reproduce some of this writing here, if only to temper a present-day sense that the coverage of queer life in the publications discussed in this book was merely quaint and caricatural.

Magazine Titles and Digital Sources

The title of the magazine known as *Broadway Brevities* was modified several times over the course of its various incarnations. As well, within individual issues, there might be variation between the title on the cover (typically "Broadway Brevities") and the title running along the tops of pages or used within editorial references to the publication (often simply "Brevities"). In this book I move regularly between using the full title and calling the magazine *Brevities*, largely to avoid cumbersome repetition by using the longer title exclusively.

Many of the newspaper sources quoted here were accessed using online archives and repositories, such as newspapers.com, newspaperarchive.com, ProQuest Historical Newspapers, and the online newspaper resources made available by the New York Public Library, the Library of Congress, and other institutions. In cases where I quote newspaper articles or columns that were syndicated or carried by wire services across the United States, I have tried, whenever possible, to cite the version appearing in a New York City newspaper, on the assumption that this would be the version "closest" to the news organization producing the item, and because it would likely have been the first version published. In some instances, and particularly with Stephen Clow's syndicated series "How I Blackmailed the Stars of Society and the Stage," there is no obvious original place of publication. In these cases, I have chosen to reference versions most easily available online and with highest quality reproduction. (For the Clow series, then, this meant using the version of the series published in the *Orlando Sentinel*, though I consulted many other versions for comparison and an image from the [Shreveport, Louisiana] *Times* turned out to lend itself best to reproduction here.)

Misspellings and Slang

The quotes from gossip columns and other writing have been left intact, even when they contained what were misspellings. This kind of writing often played with language and relished slangy ways of speaking, particularly in some of the later attempts by Stephen G. Clow to convey the character of gay male speech. With this understanding, and to avoid cluttering and disturbing the flow of quoted text, I have not used the interjection "[*sic*]" for most cases of wrong or fanciful spelling.

NIGHTS IN FAIRYLAND

INTRODUCTION

In November 1925, New York City's *Daily News* was briefly fascinated with the life of a young criminal named Jackie Rogers. Headlines called her a "girl car thief," and though she lived in Greenwich Village, her arrest on 30 October was based on accusations she had stolen as many as forty automobiles from the streets of New Jersey. The novelty of a female car thief was newsworthy enough, but Jackie was deemed a curious figure in other ways. Reporters referred to her "mannish attire" and noted that friends called her the "Prince of Wales," because of her uncanny resemblance to the man who would one day be Britain's King Edward VIII.[1] In a brief memoir published in the *Daily News*, Jackie told readers that, after finishing her studies at the University of Chicago, she had moved to Greenwich Village, to live among the "effeminate men, the masculine women" she found there. On her first visit to the Village, she had gone with a "girl chum" to a restaurant she had learned about in a series of magazine articles titled "Nights in Fairyland." Inside, she remembered, they had been warmly welcomed, as if "everyone had known us all our lives."[2]

"Nights in Fairyland" was a thirteen-part series of exposés of queer life in Manhattan published in the magazine *Broadway Brevities* in 1924 and 1925. The restaurant in which Jackie Rogers found a queer haven was almost certainly Paul and Joe's, located at the time of Rogers's visit on 19th Street in Chelsea. *Broadway Brevities*' reporter had called Paul and Joe's "a Nest of Carousing Androgynes,"[3] and his elaborate description of goings-on inside the establishment was intended to elicit shock and revulsion. In fact, Jackie Rogers wrote, the magazine's exposure of the restaurant had given it a "sudden increased popularity."[4] In a pattern observed in so many big cities in the twentieth century, journalism intended to uncover and denounce queer gathering places often provided credible guidance for those looking to find them.[5]

Broadway Brevities had turned its attention to Manhattan's queer night life in 1923, after six years of offering gossip about the moral transgressions of personalities from the worlds of business, theatre, and cinema. "In the history of Broadway," journalist Jim Bishop remembered, looking back from the vantage point of 1952, "no other paper has ever aroused so much fear and hatred … it exposed every dirty secret it could uncover."[6] When it launched its "Nights in Fairyland" series, in 1924, *Broadway Brevities* appeared to be trying to move away from reporting the gossipy secrets of individual lives, toward a broader concern with the moral condition of New York City as a whole. Celebrities were pushed to the sidelines, ceding attention to the unnamed queer men and women who frequented places like the Childs Restaurants of midtown or the basement clubs of Greenwich Village, all described in detail in the magazine's pages.

In 1924, *Broadway Brevities*' owners and staff were charged with running the publication as the basis of a blackmail and extortion racket. For at least five years, the charges read, the magazine had collected information on the intimate lives of the rich and famous, then threatened to publish it if payment (usually disguised as the purchase of advertising) was not made. In 1925, when the magazine and its staff went on trial, the *New York Sunday News* called the proceedings "the greatest show on earth."[7] In a later recounting of his misdeeds, *Broadway Brevities*' editor, a man named Stephen G. Clow, described himself as "the most famous and wicked blackmailer in world history," a claim that *Time* magazine was happy to repeat.[8]

This book is the story of a magazine and its many lives, and of the preoccupation with nonconforming sexualities that ran through its different versions. The first incarnation of *Broadway Brevities*, launched in 1916, would be forced by courts to stop publication in 1925, but other revivals, imitations, and spinoffs would continue over the next two decades. These include a later resurrection that

Gershon Legman, a scholar and collector of American pornography, called "the fabulous tabloid newspaper of the 1930's, Broadway Brevities."[9] The original *Broadway Brevities* had concealed its sensational tales of sex and sin behind glamorous covers featuring smiling stars of the theatre. In contrast, the tabloid *Brevities* of the 1930s moved its sensations to the cover, with lurid front-page headlines like "Sapphic Sisters Scram" or "Queers Seek Succor." While the first version of *Broadway Brevities* had whispered its gossip on its inside pages, with a coyness typical of earlier society magazines, the tabloid version that followed shouted out its promises of scandal and sensation, with graphic layouts and an exclamatory tone borrowed from the daily tabloid newspapers that had come to dominate print journalism in New York City.[10] There would be other incarnations of *Broadway Brevities* as well – a short-lived attempt in 1930 to replicate the sophistication of the *New Yorker* magazine and a revival of the title in Toronto, in the late 1930s, aimed at the Canadian market.

In its different versions, *Broadway Brevities* drew together minor figures of early twentieth-century New York literary culture, fringe members of Greenwich Village bohemia, and journalists deeply involved in political work for progressive causes. Eccentric show business figures and aspiring downtown artists, from Evelyn Nesbit, "The Girl in the Red Velvet Swing," to Juanita Clivette, the "Sappho Poetess of Greenwich Village," moved in and out of the different versions of *Broadway Brevities* and circulated through the larger publishing networks in which they were produced. Delving into the lives of these people serves here as a means of entry into some of those worlds of New York periodical publishing of which little has thus far been written. These worlds took shape at some distance from the innovative little magazines and coteries of modernist print culture that have made New York a rich terrain for those studying periodicals of the 1920s and 1930s. Arguably, though, the writers, artists, publishers, and hucksters associated with *Brevities* – and its various imitators or offshoots – were engaged in their own transformation of expressive forms, in elaborating new relationships between the printed press and those other media, like radio and the cinema, that were rising around them.

The Life of Stephen G. Clow

The life of *Broadway Brevities'* most long-lasting editor, Canadian-born Stephen G. Clow, runs through this book as a thread connecting the different incarnations of the title and the circles in which they were produced. From the early 1900s through the late 1930s, Clow's professional trajectory in New York took him from a position as critic and book publisher, on the edge of Manhattan's literary worlds, to notoriety as the scandal-mongering editor of *Broadway Brevities* in three of its incarnations.

In *The Longest Street*, a memoir by leading New York entertainment journalist Louis Sobol, Clow is remembered for having once been "the top chronicler of Broadway's romances, tragedies and scandals in the era preceding the gossip columnist of the newspapers."[11] Sobol is referring to the years before 1925, when gossip about the worlds of show business was most easily found in weekly or monthly magazines (like *White Way*, *The Tatler*, or Clow's own *Broadway Brevities*). The nightlife columnists for daily newspapers, who would redefine and popularize the genre – journalists like Walter Winchell, Mark Hellinger, and Sobol himself – came to prominence just as the first incarnation of *Broadway Brevities* was forced by court order to cease publication.

Following his trial in 1925 and subsequent imprisonment, Clow was reduced to working in the tawdry realms of the sensational weekly tabloid newspaper and the low-brow "spicy" magazine. In all these roles, he pursued his preoccupation with queer Manhattan, promising one day to write a book-length treatment of the subject and regularly brandishing the vision of a New York in which, at some point in the near future, everyone would be queer. Clow's fixation on queer life was matched only by his resentment at all those forces that he believed had kept him from achieving the stature and respectability he craved. His writings for *Broadway Brevities* and other publications were full of attacks on established critics of literature and theatre whose support of modernist experimentation repelled him and whose cozy intimacies, at the Algonquin Hotel and elsewhere, confirmed his belief in a conspiracy of "log-rollers" secretly controlling cultural life in New York. In the early 1930s, when the gossip columns of daily newspapers had usurped the function of monthly gossip magazines, like the one that had brought him fame, Clow wrote bitterly of having invented virtually all the stylistic devices of modern celebrity gossip journalism. He denounced pre-eminent columnist Walter Winchell as little more than a "parasite" who had stolen from him.

Clow makes fleeting appearances in many of the memoirs or biographies of figures central to New York entertainment journalism in the decade following World War I.[12] In almost all, he is painted as a talented but unscrupulous destroyer of reputations whose eventual disgrace was largely deserved. Typically, as in Jim Bishop's *The Mark Hellinger Story*, Clow's fall from grace parallels the biographical subject's own climb to fame and prosperity. Hellinger would acknowledge Clow's role in setting him on the way to success as a high-profile New York columnist, first at the *Daily News* and then at the *Daily Mirror*. Even after he had established himself in Hollywood as a successful screenwriter and producer – co-writing Frank Capra's *Broadway Bill*, for example, and producing Raoul Walsh's *The Roaring Twenties* – Hellinger continued to send handouts to Clow. Finally, in 1941, Hellinger paid for Clow's funeral.[13]

Thinking about Gossip

In a broader sense, this is a book about gossip and its place within a stratum of New York–based print media of the 1920s and 1930s that made it a key basis of their appeal. The many lives of *Broadway Brevities* allow us to capture at least two of the significant ways in which modern life has transformed our understanding of gossip. If gossip was once imagined as fundamentally oral – overheard in moments of interpersonal intimacy and made to travel through the viral repetition of whispered speech – it would, with time, come to be fixed in printed media, in the carefully etched phrase of the nightlife column or the blaring headline of the tabloid newspaper. The fluid virality of oral gossip would persist, of course, but journalistic creativity would find ways of freezing rumour and innuendo, giving them permanence in the grammatical and typographical forms that had evolved over time to accommodate them.

The movement from oral slipperiness to typographical fixity, then, marks one of the significant changes in the historical life of gossip. The other change makes gossip, long associated with small villages and tightly knit family circles, a characteristically urban form. If, as Richard Jean So has suggested, gossip is "words in motion,"[14] we may see it as one of the vehicles that carry information through the space of cities. More fancifully, we might follow Clive Scott's suggestion that, while mainstream newspapers function like the main throughfares of cities, showing us urban life in its most ordered and public forms, the gossipy magazine or tabloid scandal sheet is analogous to a city's side streets and alleyways, leading readers to barely overheard secrets and unexpected connections.[15]

It is common, in scholarly reflection on gossip, to endow it with positive social functions. Many of the first sociologists to study gossip took pains to find useful purpose in something so easily dismissed as inconsequential. In one of the foundational academic works on gossip, Patricia Spacks efficiently summarized the claims of such work: "Gossip, they tell us, is a catalyst of social process. It provides groups with means of self-control and emotional stability. It circulates both information and evaluation, supplies a mode of socialization and social control, facilitates self-knowledge by offering bases for comparison, creates catharsis for guilt, constitutes a form of wish-fulfillment, helps to control competition, facilitates the selection of leaders, and generates power."[16]

Recent scholarly treatments of the gossip of earlier periods are likely to find, in even the most blatantly retrograde exposés of people's intimate lives, resources for rescuing the experiences of those typically left out of conventional histories.[17] As with all gossipy media content, *Brevities*' observations of moral transgression were also ways of cataloguing moral alternatives, of noting the many ways in which people might be married or share living quarters or perform sexual identities. This liberating variety was visible through the haze of condemnation with which *Brevities* reported on it. While the magazine's accounts of non-conforming lives regularly concluded with horrific fantasies of individual downfall or civilizational collapse, the obsessive interest that drove such accounts left in its wake an abundance of valuable detail about alternative ways of living and loving.

ONE

STEPHEN G. CLOW

His Early Years and Literary Ambitions

The man whom newspapers would one day call the "Wolf of Broadway" was born in the small fishing village of Murray Harbour, in the Canadian province of Prince Edward Island, on 5 June 1873.[1] Stephen G. Clow's parents, James and Lucy, were well-to-do, prominent citizens of Murray Harbour, variously described as farmers, shipbuilders, and merchants. On James's death in 1901, newspapers in Charlottetown, the island's capital and largest city, paid tribute to his civic and political career, noting that he had been justice of the peace, member of the Legislative Council, and – until his defeat after one term – Conservative member of the House of Assembly (the provincial parliament).[2]

Little information remains concerning Stephen's childhood, but we know that, in his adolescence, his ambitions came to centre on literature and journalism. Proof of his erudition and precocity survives in a paper he wrote at the age of eighteen for presentation to the 1891 annual meeting of Prince Edward Island's Teachers' Provincial Institute. In a summary read to the meeting by the institute's secretary (and printed in its entirety in Charlottetown's *Daily Examiner* newspaper), Clow – already identifying himself as "Stephen G." – took up the question of what sorts of literature might be appropriate for youthful (male) minds: "The school-master has it in his power to wield the finest corrective influences over a boy's studies," Clow observed. "Not a few teachers, however, flounder in the greatest error in dealing with this matter. They frequently mistake the text-books for true literature. It is cruel that a boy should be scared away from the

Figure 1.1 Family photo, Stephen G. Clow, *c.* 1885.

great masterpieces which are the glory of our age. It is high time to rectify this mistake."[3] The circumstances under which this young man's pronouncements on literary matters might serve as counsel for local members of the teaching profession are a mystery, but the Teacher's Provincial Institute would move to take up the report's recommendation in a subcommittee formed for that purpose.[4]

The scale of Clow's other youthful accomplishments would be clouded by his tendency to exaggerate them later in life. An entry on Stephen G. Clow in the 1909 edition of *Who's Who in New York City and State*, which Clow seems to have written himself, claims he had been a member of the Parliamentary Press Gallery in Ottawa "for several years" and had "written widely for newspapers and magazines in Canada and the U.S."[5] In 1904, when the Prince Edward Island–based *Guardian* newspaper reported on Clow's launch of a new publishing company in New York, it noted proudly that he had once been city editor of the *Guardian* and occasional contributor to the "Poet's Corner" of a local weekly.[6] Clow was listed as a stenographer in the Prince Edward Island census of 1901,[7] though by this point he had relocated to New York City. In a column of reminiscences published in the magazine *Broadway Brevities* in 1917, Clow stated that he "came to New York in 1898," a claim confirmed by the US Census of 1910.[8]

In response to queries about Clow's Prince Edward Island family, a descendant of his parents passed on (unsolicited) family lore that Stephen had been shipped off to Boston (where the family had relatives) for showing homosexual tendencies.[9] Whether or not this was the principal cause of his move to the United States or merely one among many factors – including his obvious literary ambitions – queerness would hover around Clow for the rest of his life and career. As we shall see, Clow's writing, from the late 1910s onward, seemed driven by a preoccupation with non-conforming sexualities, with exposing gay gathering places in New York, and with venomous denunciations of lesbians and their allegedly predatory behaviours. Of his own personal sexuality, we have only the partial clues left by his short-lived marriage, his accounts of journeys through queer Manhattan nightlife, and his claim in the 1930s that he was devoting much of his intellectual energy to the study of gay and lesbian lives.

If, as seems likely, Clow relocated to New York via Boston, he was part of a broader migration. As Nick Mount has shown, the years 1880–1900 saw the highest levels of Canadian resettlement in the United States of any period before or since, and people of literary accomplishment or inclination were represented disproportionately in this migration.[10] Literary historian Dean Irvine notes that ex-patriate Canadian writers living in Boston and New York at the turn of the twentieth century "were extensively integrated into periodical cultures – both commercial and non-commercial, mass-market and cenacle."[11] One of those who did not make this move to the United States was Lucy Maud Montgomery, author of the Anne of Green Gables books, who was born one year after Clow and no more than one hundred kilometres from Murray Harbour.[12]

Clow in New York

By 1900, Clow was apparently working in a clerical position for the law firm of W.P. & R.K. Prentice, at 52 Broadway in New York City.[13] He would soon insert himself into New York's literary worlds, contributing to the letter columns of newspapers and other venues in which questions of cultural value were debated. Clow intervened several times in an ongoing dispute in the pages of the *New York Times Saturday Review of Books* over the future of poetry in the modern age. In long letters, he argued that the conditions of modern life made true poetry impossible and that those contemporary poets deemed to possess talent (like Edwin Markham) excelled only in what he called the "mechanics" of writing, while lacking the "magic spirit" of poets of earlier ages.[14] Observing this debate from another coast, the San Francisco magazine *Town Talks* identified Clow as "the critic of the New York Times" and claimed he was "ranked as a great critic in the East."[15] Clow's appearances in the *New York Times Saturday Review of Books* seemed to have been restricted to letters, however, and there is scant evidence, beyond his own claims and the *Town Talks* article, of any widespread recognition of his stature as critic. The crusty anti-modernism that would mark most of Clow's later pronouncements on culture, and that could be glimpsed as early as his report to the Prince Edward Island Teacher's Provincial Institute, found its fullest expression in letters to newspapers.

In his memoir *The Longest Street*, journalist Louis Sobol claimed that, for much of his later life, Stephen G. Clow wallowed in memories of his early days in New York City, when he had been at the very centre of the city's cultural sensations:

> Clow was always promising to write about fin-de-siècle Manhattan, about Allen street when it was, in his words, "the port of missing nymphy, in the full penumbra of 40 cents lubricity." Of Fourteenth Street, as he put it, "when Tom Sharkey hung over the bar of his saloons." Of Luchow's and its "sacrosanct odors of Pilsner where Frank Harris used to berate the waiter about his delayed amontillado while eating buns from an ambulatory cardboard box."
>
> He told me he was present when Harry K. Thaw sent three bullets into the body of Stanford White at Madison Square Garden in 1906. He claimed to have been a friend of Bat Masterson and Alfred Henry Lewis, often sitting with them in the little side room at Stanley's on Forty-second Street, draining the glass-bottom mugs of their ale.[16]

If, indeed, these were some of the people with whom Clow associated after his arrival, he was well integrated within the tavern-centred life of many of Manhattan's most prominent personalities. Of those named here, Tom Sharkey was a well-known, Irish-born boxer of the late nineteenth century. Frank Harris, also Irish-born, was a journalist who would achieve his greatest fame later, with a memoir of his sexual past, *My Life and Loves*. Harry Thaw, heir to an industrial fortune, would be convicted of killing prominent architect Stanford White in 1906, after accusing White of an affair with his wife, the performer and model Evelyn Nesbit. Arguably the best known among these people, Bat Masterson was a legendary figure of the Old West who, in his later years, came to New York to work as a journalist. Journalist Alfred Henry Lewis was respected for his coverage of corruption in New York City and pursued a secondary career as the author of popular novels in various genres, notably Westerns.

In 1904, a flattering portrait of "Stephen G. Clow, the Poet-Publisher" appeared in the magazine *Broadway Weekly*, a short-lived offshoot of the better-known *Broadway Magazine*. The latter title would soon be edited by Theodore Dreiser and (after several changes of title) would become known for publishing fiction by prominent writers like O. Henry and Jack London. *Broadway Weekly*, however, was devoted almost exclusively to the personalities and fashions of New York's theatrical worlds. The pretext for its article on Clow was his recent launch of a book publishing firm, the Broadway Publishing Company. In fact, the name

STEPHEN CLOW, THE POET-PUBLISHER.

By HELEN KENNEY.

PROBABLY the youngest publisher of prominence in New York to-day is Mr. Stephen G. Clow, proprietor of Broadway Publishing Co., at No. 835 Broadway. Mr. Clow is a Canadian by birth, a native of Prince Edward Island, and has gradually, but steadily, risen from the post of reporter on a small Canadian daily to his present position. He still feelingly refers to the time when he was a persevering contributor to the "Poet's Corner" of the country weekly.

Some of these "pathetic compositions," as he now calls them, were, of course, at that time regarded by idolizing friends as efforts of genius. Mr. Clow says that if he can resurrect these pieces he will publish them—some day—as a terrible warning to young poets.

While engaged in newspaper work in Canada, Mr. Clow was a member of the famous Press Gallery of the House of Commons at Ottawa. It is not very many years since he came to New York, but during this time he has been associated with several well-known publishing houses. About two years ago he founded the Broadway Publishing Company and has quickly made the name of this house familiar throughout the country.

STEPHEN G. CLOW, THE POET-PUBLISHER.

His new catalogue contains a list of nearly one hundred titles, many of a notable character, which have had large sales and attracted widespread attention from readers and reviewers, including "A Girl and The Devil," by Jeannette Llewellyn Edwards.

Two of the best novels of the year, "Zebadiah Sartwell" and "By the King's Command," have been published by Mr. Clow. and about the middle of March he will issue another notable work entitled "Shakspere: Personal Recollections," from the pen of the well-known wit and poet, Colonel John A. Joyce, of Washington.

Mr. Clow's literary idols are Tolstoi and Hardy, whom he considers immeasurably the greatest of living novelists.

Mr. Clow is a man who has made his own way and believes that every one can make a certain success of life, at the same time admitting that that success may not be the result of the first effort, however sincere that effort may be.

In other words, he believes that each man has a vocation, and that sooner or later he will find his special place in life.

The secret of the undoubted success of Mr. Clow is: he fully understands a subject, and then lives up to his word.

Figure 1.2 "Stephen Clow, the Poet-Publisher," *Broadway Weekly*, 17 March 1904.

of Clow's new company was the same as that of the firm that had published *Broadway Magazine* until it went bankrupt around 1901. Clow appears to have taken up the name for his own venture.[17]

In the *Broadway Weekly* profile, Stephen G. Clow, who had just turned thirty, is shown sitting in a high-backed chair, a magazine in hand, elegantly dressed, and serious in demeanour. Clow's several pronouncements in the piece include the judgment that Tolstoy and Hardy were the greatest of living novelists. Of his own early poetry, Clow admits that these were "pathetic compositions" and suggests that their future publication would be useful only as "a terrible warning to young poets."[18] His new publishing house, the article notes, had quickly become known throughout the country, with one of its first titles, Jeannette Llewellyn Edwards's *A Girl and the Devil*, reaching significant levels of success with critics and buyers.

The Broadway Publishing Company

The fullest account of Clow's life as a book publisher appears in an unexpected source. *Lord Broadway*, published in 1941, was a biography of Simon "Sime" Silverman (1873–1933), who founded and served as long-term editor of the show-business trade periodical *Variety*. The book's author, Dayton Stoddart, spends several pages of *Lord Broadway* recounting the sleazy adventures of a Canadian-born book publisher he calls "Arthur Drew," who met Sime during *Variety*'s early years.[19] Drew is described as a vain, ruthless man, busy exploiting would-be authors through the vanity book publishing company he had purchased with an inheritance. As *Variety* grows in circulation and influence, Arthur Drew weaves his way in and out of the story. In 1918, with his book publishing business bankrupt and his family money squandered, Drew finds new success as editor of a widely read Broadway gossip magazine that would soon be exposed as the basis of a blackmail racket. With this highly unflattering portrait of Arthur Drew, Stoddart was really recounting the life of Stephen G. Clow, who died in 1941, the year in which *Lord Broadway* was published. While Clow is thanked in the book's acknowledgments, he is spared posthumous humiliation by appearing in the book under an invented name. Nevertheless, the trajectory of Arthur Drew's life offered in *Lord Broadway* is identical to that of Stephen G. Clow in every detail. We learn from Stoddart that Clow started the Broadway Publishing Company (BPC) with $40,000 from the estate of his father, James, who had passed away in 1901.[20]

The first book published by Clow's company was probably *Sketches in Ebony and Gold*, by Mary Cochran Thurman. It carried a claim of copyright for 1902 on its interior pages but was entered for registration with the Library of Congress only in November 1903. Described in one listing of newly published books as centred on "striking pictures of home life and the devotion of the negro mammy to her white family,"[21] *Sketches in Ebony and Gold* has the distinction of being among the holdings of the Charles L. Blockson Afro-American Collection in Temple University Libraries. It is also, like several Broadway Publishing Company titles, currently available in digital form from the HathiTrust and Google Books, and in hard-bound editions offered by print-on-demand publishers (in India and elsewhere) who base their reprints on these publicly available scanned versions.

Clow's Broadway Publishing Company would go on to publish over two hundred books before its final dissolution in 1915. While few of these seemed of lasting merit, they were nevertheless advertised in mainstream publications and featured in lists of new books in newspapers across the United States. The firm maintained a single address – at 835 Broadway – throughout its entire existence. Its 1904–05 catalog offers large numbers of poetry collections and memoirs, genres one might expect to find in the lists of a publisher whose mode of operation involved charging authors for publication.

Stoddart claimed that the Broadway Publishing Company was a vanity press, and it is clear, from the ways in which the company presented itself to potential authors, that it presumed most of these were seeking publication for the first time. A 1909 advertisement by the firm in the *New York Times* promised authors with book manuscripts that they could have their works published "for just about one-half the sum demanded by other houses."[22] *Lord Broadway* offers numerous accounts of Clow flattering would-be authors even as he mocked them in private, returning their manuscripts with the judgment that they could be made right with just a little editing (which Clow would happily undertake for a fee). Stoddart reveals Clow's contempt for these victims: he apparently referred to their manuscripts as "*excrementa vanitatum*." Stoddart adds: "Occasionally a good script would come his way, but Mr Drew [Clow] accepted such mishaps with philosophical fortitude. It was a hazard any publisher must face." A good manuscript was not one for which Clow could charge his standard $100 for "editorial advice."[23]

One of the most intriguing scenes in Stoddart's book has Arthur Drew going to the apartment of Aimée Crocker Gouraud, a bohemian heiress and enthusiast of mysticism, to accept the commission to publish a book of her poetry. As Clow launches into praise for Gouraud's manuscript, which bore the title *Moon Madness and Other Fantasies* (and was published by the BPC in 1910), the author silences him by making it clear that the opinions of any readers were of no interest to her.[24] Stoddart's biography of Sime Silverman also recounts, at length, negotiations between Clow and the management of the White Rats, an organization formed in 1900 to protect the rights of vaudeville performers. George Fuller Golden, who had founded the White Rats, was gravely ill with tuberculosis – he would die in 1912 – and the organization had raised funds to pay for the publication of his history of the group. The $3,500 fee that Clow requested for publishing the book was higher than other bids, but his offer nevertheless prevailed. Golden's *My Lady Vaudeville and Her White Rats* appeared as a Broadway Publishing Company book in 1909, with forty-seven pages of testimonial advertisements following Golden's text. These were presumably solicited to help defer the publication costs that Clow had negotiated.[25]

Clow's efforts to convince potential authors of the scale of the Broadway Publishing Company extended to claims that the firm had offices outside of New York. The frontispieces to BPC books from 1903–04 announced that the publisher's operations were located in "Montreal – New York – London." By 1905, references to branches in London and Montreal had disappeared, and from 1909 until the firm's demise, BPC books would claim branches in various combinations of Baltimore, Chicago, Atlanta, Des Moines, Florence (Alabama), Washington, and Norfolk. The most solid of these outposts seems to have been in Baltimore, whose "branch" was managed for a time by the prolific editor and critic Eugene L. Didier (1838–1913), best known as an authority on the work of Edgar Allan Poe.[26]

Clow's Broadway Publishing Company ceased operations at some point in 1915. In the serialized memoirs he published in 1928, Clow claimed that his book publishing venture had been "snuffed out by the war."[27] The latter years of its history, in any case, seem to have been rocky. A *Certificate of Incorporation of the Broadway Publishing Company, Inc.*, deposited in 1912, suggests that Clow restructured the company in that year, with capital of $10,000.[28] Little more than one year later, the dissolution of the company was announced, on the grounds that it had "done no business."[29] Nevertheless, the BPC continued to issue books, albeit in small numbers, until 1915.

Stephen G. Clow as Author and Critic

Clow's own critical, literary, or dramatic works were few and generally of little consequence. His entry in the 1909 *Who's Who in New York City and State* claimed he had authored a work with the title *The Decay of Poetry*, and the trade magazine *Bookseller, Newsdealer and Stationer* listed that title, with his authorship, among new books appearing in November 1907.[30] Later, in 1924, a theatrical sketch by Clow, "The Hat Shoppe," was performed with two other short works (including F. Scott Fitzgerald's "Porcelain and Pin") at New York's Triangle Theatre. The *New York Tribune* critic called Clow's contribution to the evening "very bad."[31]

Even after he had ceased being a literary publisher, Clow would jump into newspaper or magazine debates over a question that seemed to preoccupy him and arouse his vitriol: the future of culture in the modern age. These letters were especially frequent in the 1910s, perhaps because Clow saw his career as an author or literary publisher slipping away during these years and sought to reclaim his authority in other ways. With time, Clow's pronouncements on literary and artistic matters would find him increasingly outside the realm of level-headed debate, as he adopted a voice that was more and more that of the rigidly anti-modern (and misogynistic) crank. A lengthy letter published in the New York *Sun* newspaper on 10 December 1917 finds him denouncing signs of decline across a wide range of cultural and social fronts:

> Painting has become a laughing stock in the crazy arabesque of the cubists; poetry almost a name in the foolish hands of the vers libre humbugs; the theatre a temple of slang and claptrap, with one extreme at buffoonery and the other at dilettantism; in politics a league of women and male gastritics have the supreme effrontery to legislate the majority of their fellow beings out of a drink; in our courts juries will not convict women of felonies; in sculpture a ridiculous caricature of Lincoln has been put forth as a marvellous interpretation; to crown it all, moving pictures and "dancing," the two stupidest and dullest of all forms of human entertainment, have overrun the public and are doing their deadly work upon the small quota of sanity and soberness we have left among us.[32]

At the time these words were published, Stephen G. Clow was beginning to find a new role and voice for himself as editor of *Broadway Brevities*, a monthly magazine quickly gaining a reputation for its irreverent treatment of New York's social and theatrical elites. By 1920, Clow would be known as an unscrupulous trader in personal secrets and a skilled practitioner in the rhetorical arts of gossip. With *Broadway Brevities*, Clow came to adopt a lively, of-the-moment persona that almost – though never completely– displaced the stuffy pedantry of the earnest man of literary ambitions who had come to New York two decades earlier.

"A magazine typical of Broadway"

The first issue of *Broadway Brevities: A magazine typical of Broadway* was entered for copyright on 20 April 1916, with a cover date of May.[33] (The subtitle did not appear on the cover and was quickly dropped.) "It was at that time," Clow remembered in 1928, a small "sheet of 16 poorly printed pages, issued from a dingy office in the New York Times building."[34] By the end of its first year, the number of pages in issues of *Broadway Brevities* often reached fifty-two. Its newsstand price at the time of its launch was ten cents, climbing steadily to thirty-five cents in 1920, and remaining there until the magazine's demise. Though its first offices were at 1070 Madison Avenue, the magazine moved, in 1919, to the Knickerbocker Theatre Building, at 1400 Broadway, where it remained until it ceased publication in 1925.

Clow apparently had nothing to do with the magazine in its first few months. The original copyright registration for *Broadway Brevities* was attributed to a Melvin Gutman of New York.[35] Gutman stayed with the publication until the following year, when it was announced that he had moved into the photo-engraving business, though he continued to write a feature called "Broadway Flashes" for a few issues after his departure.[36] In December 1916, the firm publishing the magazine, "Broadway Brevities, Inc.," was registered as a corporation, with a capitalization of $12,000. The three officers named were Homer R. Mallow, Oscar H. Cacciola, and C. Nicholas Reinhardt.[37] Mallow's career had mostly unfolded in the hotel industry, and he had been charged by police in 1915 for giving theatrical performances without a licence in his Hotel Wallick.[38] Cacciola served as director of various business ventures, in such fields as outdoor advertising; in 1915 he had been appointed a commissioner of deeds in New York.[39] Different versions of Reinhardt's name pop up in the historical record, but he appears to have spent his early years in newspaper work.[40] Popular New York columnist O.O. McIntyre, plugging the arrival of *Broadway Brevities* in a 1917 column, referred to Reinhardt as "a young man of journalistic ability" and noted

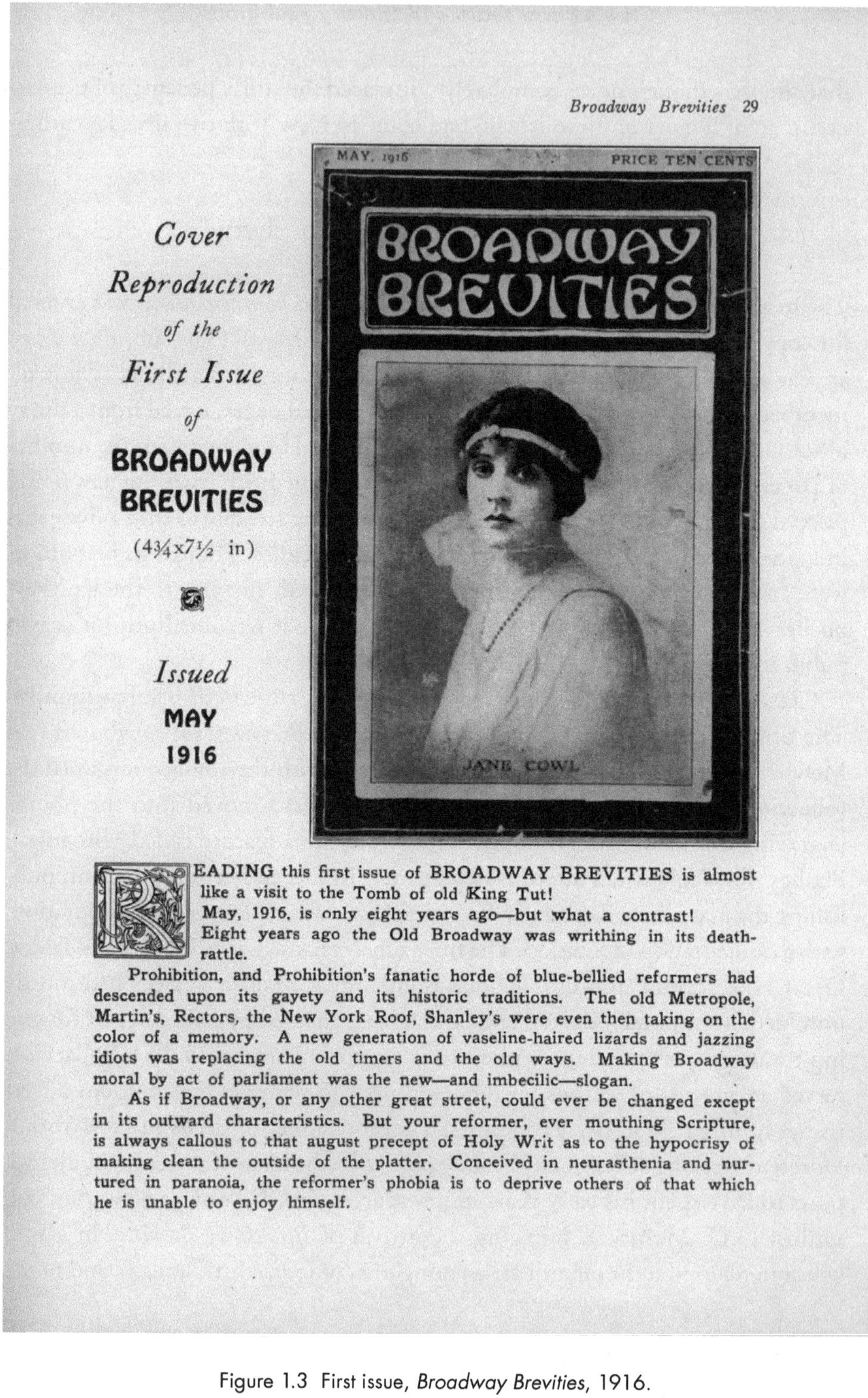

Broadway Brevities 29

Cover Reproduction of the First Issue of **BROADWAY BREVITIES** (4¾x7½ in)

Issued **MAY 1916**

MAY, 1916 PRICE TEN CENTS

BROADWAY BREVITIES

JANE COWL

READING this first issue of BROADWAY BREVITIES is almost like a visit to the Tomb of old King Tut!

May, 1916, is only eight years ago—but what a contrast!

Eight years ago the Old Broadway was writhing in its death-rattle.

Prohibition, and Prohibition's fanatic horde of blue-bellied reformers had descended upon its gayety and its historic traditions. The old Metropole, Martin's, Rectors, the New York Roof, Shanley's were even then taking on the color of a memory. A new generation of vaseline-haired lizards and jazzing idiots was replacing the old timers and the old ways. Making Broadway moral by act of parliament was the new—and imbecilic—slogan.

As if Broadway, or any other great street, could ever be changed except in its outward characteristics. But your reformer, ever mouthing Scripture, is always callous to that august precept of Holy Writ as to the hypocrisy of making clean the outside of the platter. Conceived in neurasthenia and nurtured in paranoia, the reformer's phobia is to deprive others of that which he is unable to enjoy himself.

Figure 1.3 First issue, *Broadway Brevities*, 1916.

that the new magazine contained "all of the spicy gossip of Flash Alley in a bright and breezy style." McIntyre added that the magazine "has a way of presenting the salacious talk of the White Way by letting the reader read between the lines."[41]

The visual appearance of the original *Broadway Brevities*, from the first issue in 1916 to the last, in 1925, was remarkably consistent. Like all issues of the magazine, the first featured a theatrical performer (actress Jane Cowl) on its front cover, in what was almost certainly a publicity photograph. Across the nine-year lifespan of the magazine, the vast majority of its cover images were of female performers. Some are barely remembered Broadway stars or aspirants, like Yvette Rugel (June 1921) or Emlee Haddone (October 1921). Others are people whose fame or notoriety has woven its way through histories of American show business or celebrity: Hope Hampton (August 1921), Mae Murray (April 1922), Mae West (August 1922), Helen Lee Worthing (July 1923), Marilyn Miller (October 1924), Evelyn Nesbit (December 1920), Pola Negri (May 1923), and Marion Davies (several covers.) The few men granted cover appearances included the team of Willie and Eugene Howard (April 1921), Tommy Lyman (May 1924), and, for the magazine's last issue, Harry Richman (January 1925). Publication of these photographs often coincided with plugs for the same performers in the magazine's various features. In his 1928 memoirs, Clow admitted that he would often sell the cover space for $500 to amorous men anxious to promote lovers who were pursuing show business careers.[42]

The written content of *Broadway Brevities* was dominated by one- or two-page assortments of miscellany (such as poetry and jokes) and compilations of short bits of news about Broadway personalities. These bits were sometimes gathered under umbrella titles, like "Along the Line," or left to wind their way around advertisements and boxes containing plugs or brief reviews. The vicious innuendo for which *Broadway Brevities* would eventually become known was largely absent from the first few issues, not emerging until the early months of 1918, when Stephen G. Clow assumed control over the magazine. Indeed, some of the content of *Broadway Brevities*' earliest issues recalls that of society magazines, like the Waldorf Astoria's *Tavern Topics*, aimed at readers with an interest in luxuries available to those of appropriate means. The fourth issue of *Broadway Brevities* (September 1916), typical of the magazine in its first year, contains a long account of roadster trips to out-of-town restaurants and a feature by the unnamed art editor on "Villa

Beatrice: John Hoagland's Estate in Westchester." A column of restaurant reviews devotes over two pages to the Astor Roof, then moves on to the Hunter Island Inn on Long Island before returning to Manhattan and the Deoch an Doris restaurant in midtown.

Elsewhere, however, this issue looks ahead to the preoccupation with Broadway scandal for which the magazine would soon be known. An editorial, long by the standards of *Brevities*' future issues, bears the title "Broadway and Blackmail" and warns readers of racketeers who will extract money from men by setting them up as violators of the Mann Act (known on its passage as the White-Slave Traffic Act of 1910), which criminalized the transportation of women across state lines for immoral purposes. References to a few "cases" of this blackmail feature no names, however, and the piece is free of even the mildest of hints as to any real persons whose experience might have prompted the warning.

In the earliest issues of *Broadway Brevities*, the names of Broadway personalities are in abundance, but their presence in New York's public life is simply observed or used as the basis for light promotional mention. From 1916 to 1919, the magazine's principal section devoted to Broadway life was called "Along the Line," a compendium of items ranging in length from two lines to short paragraphs like the following: "At the Orange Fizzade Tea in the Hawaiian Room at Reisenweber's last week, the millionaires and leaders of the younger social set who compose this exclusive organization, cheered when Walter Kingsley walked in at the head of six resplendent beauties, namely: Dorothy Leeds, Ethel Sykes, Gladys Sykes, Dorothy Foster, Mildred Gaylord and Lucille Cavanagh."[43]

Kingsley, the man at the centre of this incident, was a major vaudeville press agent and sometime journalist who would later be accused of furnishing the editors of *Broadway Brevities* with some of the backstage gossip that filled such columns.[44] He was one of those, close to the magazine, whose minor public appearances *Broadway Brevities* would celebrate in its early years, particularly if these provided the pretext for the stringing together of other names. Indeed, "Along the Line," which captured the personality of the magazine better than any other feature of its first two years, often seemed little more than a useful banner under which, in each issue, two or three dozen names could be scattered.

Lists of names had for some time been the principal currency of the society or social columns found in newspapers and magazines, and the significance of an event was usually a function of the number and stature of those in attendance.[45] In *Brevities*, we glimpse a shift that would become more pronounced with the spread of so-called nightlife columns in newspapers in the 1920s. More and more, strings of names would convey the sense of urban sociability in motion, of people observed in brief glances as they moved from one festive place to another. Rather than the simple enumeration of people assembled in circumscribed, static gatherings. these lists served to map the criss-crossing paths of people out on the town.

In its January 1917 issue, *Broadway Brevities* announced a change of staff. C.N. Reinhardt replaced Melvin Guttman as editor (and the copyright passed between the two). H. Edwin Keller was now listed as associate editor, and, while Homer Mallow remained on the masthead as president and treasurer of the firm, his name would soon disappear. Rapid changes in the magazine's administration, editorial staff, and frequency of publication took place throughout much of 1917. In September, after having published on a monthly basis since its launch, the magazine announced that "Broadway Brevities is now a weekly."[46] News was arriving so quickly, the announcement explained, that more frequent publication was necessary if the magazine was to keep up with other more frequent publications in offering information that was fresh.[47] Noting this change, *Vanity Fair* glibly suggested that frequent publication was now necessary in a world (i.e., that of Broadway) in which people were divorcing as quickly as readers were learning about their marriages.[48]

The magazine's switch to weekly publication may also have been prompted by the ongoing spread of show business gossip through the specialized and general interest press. While the glory period of the daily newspaper's nightlife columnist was still a decade in the future, weekly show business trade magazines like *Billboard*, the *New York Clipper*, *Zit's Theatrical Weekly*, and *Variety* increasingly featured columns of backstage rumour and gossip alongside the itemized lists of factual information that were their principal currency. In any event, *Broadway Brevities*' experiment with more frequent publication did not last long. In 1918, the magazine briefly switched to biweekly publication and, in 1919, returned to monthly.[49]

There were other signs of the magazine's fragility during this period. In October 1917, *Broadway Brevities* was investigated for the first time by New York authorities. *Variety* reported on 5 October that the magazine's "business editor," Edwin Keller, had spent "an uncomfortable period" being questioned by Assistant District Attorney Rittenberg.[50] The interrogation of Keller was in response to a complaint made by "an estimable young woman of irreproachable character" who felt that an item in the magazine's "Impertinent Questions" feature had cast aspersions on her character. The woman in question was probably Broadway actress Florence Webber who would soon launch a suit against the magazine for having libelled her in the column of that name.[51] *Variety*'s report on the assistant district attorney's visit to the *Brevities* offices noted that ADA Rittenberg had come accompanied by a man identified as "Frederick Sumner, of the Vice Society." This was most likely John S. Sumner, executive secretary of the New York Society for the Suppression of Vice (NYSSV), who had replaced Anthony Comstock (the society's founder) in 1915 and would remain in this role until 1950. Sumner threatened to "suppress the paper" if it did not clean itself up in one week. While the NYSSV's cozy relationship with New York legal authorities in this case was hardly unprecedented, the society appeared to be using a Broadway performer's complaint about her injured reputation as a pretext for going after the magazine for more general violations of moral standards.

The visit by Rittenberg and Sumner caught the magazine just as its staffing was disrupted by the United States' entry into World War I. *Variety*'s report noted that Keller, under questioning by the assistant district attorney, had evaded responsibility by claiming that no copy flowed through his hands or passed his eyes. A week later, Keller left the magazine, heading north to join the Canadian Aviation Corps. Soon after, in January 1918, *Vanity Fair* reported that all five of *Broadway Brevities*' editors had quit the magazine to join the military, in what was the last year of World War I.[52] These departures made it possible for Clow to assume ownership and editorial control of *Broadway Brevities*. Guttman and the other founders or executives of the magazine would soon disappear from most accounts of its history.

Clow in Control

In his memoirs, published in 1927–28, Stephen G. Clow claimed that he had attached himself to *Broadway Brevities* in 1918, following the departure of Charles G. Reinhardt (who went to Montreal to join the Royal Flying Corps). Clow suggested that the magazine was in dire financial straits at this point, unable to pay its bills or secure advertising. With his book publishing business having collapsed, Clow recounted, he entered into partnership with Harry Edwin Keller to continue the magazine and set about solidifying its financial situation. He did so, he claimed, by cutting costs and "getting advertisements in droves from former cafes and business houses on the strength of their memory of the thousands of dollars I had once spent with them in my former years as a Broadway boulevardier."[53] Clow further explained that, when Reinhardt returned from military duty in 1919, both he and Harry Keller had lost interest in the magazine. They turned over full ownership to Clow in return for a promise of $5,000 worth of advertising for their own ventures – a compensation they do not appear to have claimed in full.[54]

In fact, the first appearance of Clow's writing in *Broadway Brevities* came not in 1918, but in its May 1917 issue, which featured the first in a series of Clow's reflections on "Broadway Yesterday and Today." Though he was only forty-four – but already shaving five years off his age – Clow positioned himself as one of the few survivors able to remember the glories of "Old Broadway." In this article, one of the few to which he signed his name, he assumed a persona to which he would occasionally return throughout the rest of his life and career – that of the aging chronicler of an earlier, more wondrous Broadway:

> Into the gray antiquity of eighteen years I would peer to contrast the Old and New Broadway. I shall try to compress in a small folio its Bohemian Baedeker. …
>
> So, to the old-timer – with whom in my hoary thirty-nine years I may possibly align myself – there never again will be a Broadway like the old one. For him there is no duality of affection. He loved the old names, the old faces, the old places. He tolerates the "cabaret" days. Very likely, as myself, he hates dancing and moving pictures in the degree that the devil

> hates holy water. He is uncomfortable in the gorgor of the new eating places. There will never again, for him, be a slice of roast beef such as watered his mouth at the old Astor Hotel on lower Broadway, and never again mugs of ale such as washed it down.[55]

Clow would regularly indulge in maudlin reminiscences of the lost Broadway of his early New York years, but these obscured the extent to which he was also making himself a man of the moment. By early 1918, Stephen G. Clow was clearly the dominant editorial influence on *Broadway Brevities* and the author of a great deal of its content. From this point, until the magazine's demise in 1925, articles and features in *Broadway Brevities* were almost never signed. Celebrities like George Jessel would claim, later in their lives, to have written for the magazine, but the lack of bylines makes these contributions impossible to identify or verify.[56] That the magazine's principal voice was Clow's is confirmed in the commentary of others on his role in the magazine, and by his own willingness, in later personal reminiscences, to describe his methods and identify some of his targets.

In the early years of Clow's editorship (1918–21), we find *Broadway Brevities* extending its influence in two ways. One was by regularly promoting people, events, and places. Typically, editorial plugs bolstered people or businesses whose paid advertisements appeared in close proximity. Favourable mentions of retail outlets like Adela Hats and nightlife venues like the Palais Royal, Moulin Rouge, Café de Paris, Folies Bergère, and The Aristocrat could usually be found just a page or two away from space purchased by these interests to promote themselves. The more blatant exercise of the magazine's power, however, was rooted in its willingness to inflict damage on people's reputations. By 1918, as Clow's involvement in the magazine solidified, voluminous quantities of gossip wound their way through its pages. Bits of innuendo in some cases expanded to paragraphs rich in detail or shrank to brief phrases full of suggestion. "Impertinent Questions," which had prompted the visit from the New York District Attorney's Office, continued as the most sensational of the magazine's features in the first years of Clow's editorship. An early version began with the disingenuous disclaimer that "Questions are never indiscreet: answers sometimes are."[57] But the feature, which often ran to over two pages of short items, became brazenly suggestive in the questions it asked, in a manner far from the coy curvature of the gossipy paragraphs in society magazines like *Town Topics*, which let suggestion hang, unspoken, in the air. Here, for example, are some of the "Impertinent Questions" bluntly posed in the 1 July 1918 issue of *Broadway Brevities*:

> Why is Marion H. so interested in Frankie Fay?
>
> Did Dolores cut out Margie Cassidy with Joe Whitehead? And Why?
>
> Who was the middle-aged woman the wife of Francis Bushman mentions in her suit for divorce against the movie hero and former wrestling champion?[58]

Romantic interest, betrayal, or retribution provided the gossipy substance conveyed in such questions. In other gossip-filled features, like "Gum-shoeing along the Old Street" (April 1921), suggestive questions would alternate with short paragraphs richer in information:

> Where does Eugene Sullivan dig up the new beauties he is springing along Broadway these days? But why the Astor supper club?
>
> So Ruth White and Janet McGrew are to give up that cute apartment in old 57 West and no less a cutie than Louise Stafford is to move in. Give a housewarming, Louise, and invite dear old Mr. Fleischmann whose proposal of honorable marriage you are said to have scorned. "Back to Cincy!" you cried. Perhaps you spoke in error for wonderful tunes are often played on ancient Stradivari.[59]

Four years later, it would become clear that the item about Cincinnati-born "yeast king" Julius Fleischmann, whose marriage had ended in 1920, laid some of the groundwork for *Brevities*' effort to extort money from the man in return for the magazine's silence about his personal life. The trial of *Broadway Brevities* in 1925 – the focus of chapter 5 – showed that Fleischmann had paid $500 to the magazine for advertising space he never used, presumably in an effort to block further publication of items like this one, which revealed his unsuccessful proposal of marriage to Broadway performer Louise Stafford.

One issue from the middle years of *Broadway Brevities*' first incarnation is notable for an abundance of gossip it can scarcely contain. The cover of the August 1921 issue features a photograph of Hope Hampton, a film star since her appearance in the Metro movie *A Modern Salome* in 1920. Above her image, a banner announces that this is a "Ziegfeld Pictorial Number" of *Broadway Brevities*, though only one of the photographs inside (of "Miss Geneva Mitchell") is linked by any text to the then-current edition of Ziegfeld Follies. Full-page advertisements – for the Long Island restaurant Pavillon Royal (where Paul Whiteman was playing), fashion retailer Gilman's Gowns, Millinery and Lingerie, and the Hotel Commodore – precede any editorial content. Just below the magazine's masthead, on page 6, a lengthy paragraph plugs the newly opened Café de Paris, for which an advertisement can be found on the facing page. The overall tone of these early pages is one of bemused and innocent observation of life in and around Broadway.

Several pages later, however, under the title "Rhymes of a Broadway Bum," gossip explodes across sixty lines of densely packed and inconsistently rhyming couplets. The feature opens with wistful reminiscences of an earlier Broadway before moving on to dozens of pointed inferences targeting people of the moment:

> Where is the gang I held so dear when Broadway was Broadway!
> I'm sitting here wondering whether I'll ever see you again
> . . . .
> Dot Green's been a gay little bounder, since she and her hubby split
> The way Owen Moore hung around her gave Kathryn Perry a fit
> Peggy May has disappeared, I know because I phoned her
> But Wallace Reid still wears the ring that Arthur Swanstrom loaned her.[60]

Several pages of short gossipy items follow, then "The Nuts in a Nutshell: Or Vamps and Vampesses Viciously Versified," running over two pages, offers another compendium of one-line bits of gossip, written once again as rhyming couplets, though this time in a self-consciously stilted and old-fashioned style:

Figure 1.4 *Broadway Brevities*, August 1921.

We thought his awful pop and he had all the records beaten
They now describe as a "Dead Map" the phiz of Buster Keaton
We hear that Theda Bara, who so long has had 'em conned
Was ev'n in long past childhood days a vamping, dizzy blonde[61]

Of the names mentioned in these two features, most (Owen Moore, Wallace Reid, Theda Bara, and Buster Keaton) were stars of the cinema. (Arthur Swanstrom was a composer and musical arranger.) Even as it indulged in nostalgic returns to "old Broadway," *Broadway Brevities* in 1921 had joined *Variety* and other show business periodicals in expanding its coverage beyond Broadway and the vaudeville stage to encompass the world of films. While it appeared to relish, above all else, the slippery state of show business marriages and romantic entanglements, *Broadway Brevities* also took delight in hinting at the hidden backgrounds, past indiscretions, or real ages of film stars, as in these two-line items from "The Nuts in a Nutshell":

Dolores Cassinelli now swims gaily in our ken,
A Contest *populare* she won out west, me boys – but when
. . . .
Now, promise not to giggle, and a secret we'll tell thee,
Dear old Bev Bayne avers that nex' month she'll be twenty-three.[62]

Even as more and more of its gossipy bits and feature articles were focused on the film industry, *Broadway Brevities* continued to treat the cinema as a shallow fad, the centre of a world full of talentless hacks with falsified pasts waiting to be exposed.

Clow's "Regency"

In 1919, *New York Tribune* reporter Harriette Underhill wrote in her "At the Cabarets" column of going to the opening of a new restaurant called the Little Club: "Almost as soon as we got inside we met 'Steve' Clow and Carolyn Hart, and they asked us to have supper with them. Millions of people were being seated and millions more were being turned away ... Of course 'Steve' is more amusing than anybody else on earth and 'Carrie' is so pretty it's a pleasure to look at her and then we had lobster and ice cream and altogether we quite forgot that this was our night for renouncing the world and its allies."[63]

Underhill, who suffered serious injuries in a 1919 automobile crash and died in 1928 of tuberculosis, is remembered today as one of the most skilled and well-respected of early film reviewers and a strong supporter of work by female directors.[64] While writing lengthy features on the film industry for the *New York Tribune*, in 1919 and 1920, she also signed two regular features in that newspaper, "At the Cabarets" and "At Hotel and Restaurant." In their lightly narrativized accounts of the author's visits to nightlife venues, these anticipated the more full-blown on-the-town columns of the decade that followed. Although items in *Brevities* repeatedly mocked Underhill's age, and accused her of lacking journalistic talent, she was one of those whose journeys through Manhattan nightlife regularly crossed Clow's own paths.[65]

Clow would later remember these as years in which he was part of an unofficial "Night Club Patrol,"[66] of people, presumably like Underhill, whom he encountered on an almost nightly basis. In the memoirs he published in 1928, Clow spoke of the period 1919–22 as his "regency" – the years when he felt that he ruled Broadway, before descending into what he would later call "the 'dirty work' of blackmail and extortion":

> The paper was doing splendidly, jumped in pages to 40 and sometimes 48, while, like the Village Blacksmith, I "owed not any man." I was "the whole works," for a clever attorney had put through a dummy corporation, a feat not unusual with the most legitimate enterprises. Circulation was always increasing, and it was safe always, in the case of "Brevities" to count ten to fifteen readers per copy. Chorus girls had begun in force to cut down their gin and delicatessen outlay to buy copies; the newsstands in the 40's and 50's, those barometers of printing popularity, ran buys of four or five hundred copies an issue, trailing only the best sellers.[67]

As proof of its expanding reputation, *Broadway Brevities* would lend its name to a theatrical revue. *Broadway Brevities, the Gossip of 1920* was produced by Rufus

Lemaire and written by his brother George; it featured music by George Gershwin, Irving Berlin, Bert Kalmar, and Harry Ruby. The Broadway production bore little thematic relationship to the magazine or its preoccupations, but it joined a list of Broadway shows taking their names from magazines. (Other such borrowings included the show *Jim Jam Jems*, which also opened in 1920, and *Ned Wayburn's Town Topics* of 1915.) *Broadway Brevities* magazine began promoting the theatrical production in 1919, claiming that its title referenced "the most famous magazine of its kind in the world,"[68] but an actors' strike delayed the show's opening until 29 September 1920, when it had its premiere at the Winter Garden. If, as trade papers suggested, "Broadway Brevities of 1920" was meant to initiate an annual series of theatrical revues, this did not happen.

The theatrical version of *Broadway Brevities* starred the Bahamian-born Black performer Bert Williams alongside Eddie Cantor, a Jewish-American star who had debuted on Broadway in the *Ziegfeld Follies of 1917*. Williams and Cantor had worked together regularly as a blackface act, and the *Brevities* production featured them both as a team and in separate numbers. Reviews for the show leaned toward the negative. Heywood Broun of the *New York Tribune* called it "the worst musical show we ever saw," while Jack Lait, in *Variety*, damned it with faint praise by predicting that it would "get money on the road," presumably from audiences less sophisticated than those of Broadway.[69] For the most part, reviewers made no connection between the show and the magazine. The show's producers acknowledged the source of their title and compensated the magazine by letting it run a contest to choose a select number of chorus girls who would appear in the production at higher salaries than were the norm. As *Variety* reported, "the first prize winner will receive $150 weekly and will be programmed 'The Brevity Girl.' The next five girls will be paid $75 per week and the third five will receive $50 per week."[70] This contest seems to have received little publicity.

On 20 November 1920, at 203 West 56th Street in New York, Stephen G. Clow married, for the first and only time. His bride was Janice A. Carson, described on the marriage certificate as twenty-seven years of age, white, and of Swedish birth.[71] Clow's age, the certificate said, was forty-one. (In fact, he was forty-seven.)[72] Of two witnesses at the wedding, one was Harry Keller, who had been Clow's partner when the latter assumed control of *Broadway Brevities* in 1918.[73]

Janice Carson's hometown newspaper, the *Kane* [Pennsylvania] *Republican*, ran a lengthy account of the marriage, and of the circumstances behind it, on its front page: "When his best friend and colleague eloped with a girl about six months ago to get married, Stephen G. Clow, editor of Broadway Brevities, went along and made a vain attempt to dissuade the couple from their contemplated act. Clow has been an opponent of marriage for many years ... The wedding was the result of a romance that began three months ago. Mr Clow said last night that all of his antipathy toward marriage vanished when he met Miss Carson at the home of a friend and gazed into her blue eyes and caught sight of her dimples."[74]

Later, in his 1925 trial, Clow testified under questioning that the marriage had ended in 1923. "Janice Clow" would be identified as the magazine's treasurer on *Broadway Brevities*' masthead between June 1921 and May 1923, and then, in a return to her original name, as "Janice Carson." With the September 1923 issue, she disappeared entirely from the magazine's list of officers. Carson's 1967 obituary noted that she had worked as a stenographer at the *New York Herald Tribune* but had spent the last twenty years of her life in Kane, Pennsylvania.[75]

Critical Cliques

Clow's sense of accomplishment during the period he called his regency does not appear to have been complete. The disdain for modernist experimentation in the arts that had fuelled so many of his letters to newspapers in the 1910s would, in the 1920s, manifest itself as hostility and resentment toward those he saw as controlling critical opinion in New York City. In the August 1921 issue of *Broadway Brevities*, Clow published a mean-spirited, full-page attack on the group of theatrical critics he called "The Clique of Craps." The article denounced many of the most widely read New York–based theater reviewers of the time: "Aleck [Alexander] Woolcott [*sic*], The Pembertons, Hey Broun, [Robert] Benchley (of Life), Geo. Kaufman (of the Times), Mark Connolly (at Liberty)." This "Snobocracy of Criticism" was condemned for their disinterest in the classics. (Marc Connelly, whose name Clow misspelled, was singled out for having once laughed at a performance of *King Lear*.) The harshest of his accusations involved the suggestion of corruption: "BREVITIES has not the records to prove it, and can only hazard the guess and the rumor that much of the superlative publicity given certain plays arose from the fact that one or more of the Dauntless Six held shares in them."[76]

More than a year later, in its December 1922 issue, *Broadway Brevities* ran a lengthy article with the title "The New York Log-Rollers, Inc." Like most of what appeared in the magazine, the feature was unsigned, but one may assume, from its focus and tone, that it was written by Clow (and references to the controversy published outside *Brevities*' pages confirm this).[77] The "Log-Rollers" in question were a handful of critics whom Clow accused of collaborating to bring about a general decline in cultural standards in New York, largely through their embrace of new literary fashions and their eagerness to jettison the values of a classical canon. The article's subtitle made clear Clow's feelings about the composition of this log-rolling group: "A Conglomeration in Restraint of Trade in the Classics Consisting of Young Intellectuals, Cubist Daubers, Anemic Play Critics, Moronic Columnists, Never-Will-Be Playwrights, Imbecile Vers Librists, Pigeon-Toed She-Journalists, Subnormal Professionals and Dirty-Necked Coryphees, Whose Principal Rendezvous is the Soup and Prune Dept. of the Hotel Algonquin."[78]

Among the purported officers of this imagined coterie, Clow listed, as its president, Burton Rascoe, "Sophomoric Parasite of the 'Tribune.'"[79] The Log-Rollers as a body, and Rascoe in particular, were accused of promoting each other's work, and of laying waste to the literary monuments and standards of the past.[80] Their preferred meeting place, the Algonquin Hotel, had been a favourite target of Clow's magazine even before the hotel's literary Round Table had assumed the legendary status for which it is still remembered.[81] A one-line item in *Brevities*' October 1921 issue had asked, "Why is the Algonquin Hotel called 'The Indoor Sporting Club'?" presumably in reference to the sexual activity known to transpire there.

The following chapter looks at how *Broadway Brevities*' preoccupation with the supposedly lesbian coterie known as the "Horsewomen of the Algonquin" wove its way into the homophobic and misogynistic excesses of the magazine's final years. That Burton Rascoe and his circle met regularly at the Algonquin seemed only to confirm, for Clow, that the hotel was a breeding ground for all those forces engaged in tearing down the values he claimed to hold dear. It is not difficult to see, in Clow's vision of a closely knit coterie supporting shifts in literary value he opposed, the frustrations of someone whose own literary ambitions had floundered. While he had arrived in New York with the aim of becoming a respected poet and arbiter of taste, by the early 1910s Clow found himself at the low end of the city's literary institutions, bilking would-be authors of their money and finding his own pronouncements of literary matters more and more reduced to cranky contributions to the letter columns of newspapers and magazines. Turning fifty in 1923, Clow may have attempted to wield his own nineteenth-century erudition against the purported faddishness of youthful post–World War I modernism, but there is no evidence that anyone in his professional circles joined him in this struggle.

In 1922, *Broadway Brevities* fell more and more under the sway of another preoccupation that would consume it until it ceased publication in 1925. While the magazine's well-entrenched concerns – the fragile state of theatrical marriages and cronyism among corrupt critics – continued to generate both brief gossipy items and lengthy articles, the magazine seemed more and more fixated on the lives of New York's gay men and lesbian women. This focus emerged slowly, first revealing itself in bits of innuendo accusing show business celebrities, most of them women, of same-sex dalliances. Then, at the end of 1923, *Brevities*' coverage of queer Manhattan life would detach itself from specific personalities and take, as its purview, the city as a whole. Brief items about gay or lesbian liaisons gave way to lengthy "reports" recounting investigative journeys to the meeting places of the city's homosexual subcultures. The fullest expression of this obsession was the thirteen-episode "Nights in Fairyland" series, which ran through all of 1924 and concluded in the very last issue of this incarnation of *Broadway Brevities*, that of January 1925. This fixation on queer lives, which had a significant impact on the ways in which the magazine is remembered today, is the focus of the next two chapters.

TWO

QUEER COTERIES
New York and Hollywood

If all this excitement, that circles and swirls
O'er Hollywood causes a bust,
Miss Alla Nazimova's queer school for girls
Will get some attention, I trust.

Unsigned, "Rhymes of a Broadway Bum," *Broadway Brevities*, October 1921, 36

The first hints of what Stephen G. Clow would later call the "dirty work" of *Broadway Brevities* could be sensed in the magazine's pages in 1921 and 1922, when gossipy items about individuals often assumed a nasty tone and seemed unchecked by any concern for people's privacy or well-being.[1] By "dirty work," Clow was referring to the practice of extorting money from people in return for silence about their personal secrets, the crime that would eventually lead to the closure of the magazine and his own imprisonment. Arguably, however, *Broadway Brevities'* descent into dirty work was also apparent in the magazine's new assaults on the people and places of queer New York. The place given to such assaults expanded between 1922 and 1925 as short items targeting individuals gave way to lengthy "investigations" of queer gathering places. These two sides of *Broadway*

Brevities' dirty work seem to have had little to do with each other. The many instances of blackmail or extortion uncovered later by federal prosecutors involved none of the people targeted by *Brevities* for their allegedly queer behaviour or inclinations.[2] The magazine's denunciations of gay and lesbian people seemed to be driven exclusively by a moralistic fervour that did not lead to the exploitation of such people's secrets for financial gain. The dirty work of blackmail and the unsavoury attacks on queer New York were parallel strands running through the history of Clow's editorship of *Broadway Brevities.*

Over this and the next three chapters, we look at each of these two kinds of dirty work separately, devoting two chapters to each. We begin here with an account of *Broadway Brevities'* ever-expanding focus on queer lives in New York, then move, in the next chapter, to an examination of the "Nights in Fairyland" series, whose thirteen episodes explored places of gay and lesbian socializing in Manhattan. Attention then shifts, in chapter 4, to the magazine's other form of dirty work: the cases of blackmail or extortion that prompted a judicial investigation into the magazine and the laying of federal charges of mail fraud in 1924. Chapter 5 follows these charges into the trial itself, a sensational event that resulted in the closure of the magazine and prison sentences for Clow and members of his staff.

The Horsewomen of the Algonquin Hotel

Brevities' preoccupation with queer life first gathered momentum in items attacking the coterie of allegedly lesbian show business figures who socialized (and, in some cases, lived) at New York's Algonquin Hotel on 44th Street. The most frequent target of these items was Tallulah Bankhead, the film actress from Alabama who would soon depart for England to work in the theatre. In its February 1922 issue, *Brevities*, hinting at Bankhead's failing relationship with an unidentified woman, posed this question: "Is it true that the rapid fading of Tallulah Bankhead's beauty is due to the revolt of the little red-headed flapper, causing Tallul' to lose pride in her clothes 'n ever'thin'?"[3] Later that year, another item wielded one of the many names *Brevities* would attach to the coterie of queer women to which Bankhead supposedly belonged: "TALLULAH BANKHEAD: Known familiarly as 'Toots,' of the famous 'Five Horsewomen of the Apocalips.'"[4]

In his biography of Tallulah Bankhead, Joel Lobenthal notes that *Brevities'* original term, "Four Horsewomen of the Algonquin," was inspired by Rudolph Valentino's popular 1921 film *The Four Horsemen of the Apocalypse.*[5] In the magazine's usage, "Apocalypse" was sometimes replaced by "Algonquin," but just as often rewritten as "Apocalips," presumably to add a suggestion of sexuality. Between late 1922 and mid-1924, *Brevities* would brandish the term "Apocalips" at least a dozen times in gossipy items about Bankhead and her circles. In January 1923, a short feature titled "Discord Among the Horsewomen" showed the magazine relishing any news of conflict within the group: "Well, the expected has happened. There's a rupture among the Five Horsewomen of the Algonquin! It is said that Estelle Winwood, the well-known 44th Street Cockneye [*sic*] who lived with 'Toots' Bankhead at the Webster, recently invited 'Toots' to vacate in the recent ides of December ... 'Toots' was down to Atlantic [City] to see Stelle's opening, but it is whispered that the greeting between the two noted equestrienne had icicles hanging on it."[6]

"Equestrienne," which referenced the Horsewomen label, would join the rich lexicon *Brevities* used to designate show business lesbians and their behaviour. In its June 1923 issue, under the heading "Initiations," *Brevities* claimed to have established a membership list for the Horsewomen of the Apocalips, It included theatre artists Eva Le Gallienne (or La Gallienne, as she was also known), Blyth Daly, Estelle Winwood, and Bankhead herself. Recognition of this coterie extended beyond the pages of *Brevities* and continued long after the magazine's demise. The women named would come to be known as "The Four Riders of the Algonquin" in later theatrical gossip and histories of queer Hollywood.[7] On *Brevities'* list as well, as an occasional fifth member, was Zoe Akins, who would win a Pulitzer Prize in 1935 for her stage play adaptation of Edith Wharton's *The Old Maid.*

The networks of female friendship and sexual intimacy mapped by *Brevities* moved outward from the New York worlds of Broadway theatre and the Algonquin Hotel to encompass Hollywood. In the August 1923 issue of *Brevities*, a paragraph-length item proposed two film actresses for membership: "They do say that of all the pals in filmdom Bebe Daniels and Betty Compson take the large red apple. In fact, BREVITIES has received by wire from Hollywood a round robin requesting that Bebe and Betty be at once submitted for membership in the Horsewomen of the Algonquin. Bebe is a sumptuous brunette, Betty a flabbergasting blonde – and as contrast is of the very essence of attraction, what are you going to do about it?"[8] That *Brevities* had sources of information on lesbian coteries in Hollywood became clear in its treatment of the scandal surrounding a woman named Florence Beery.

"For Love of Women" – The Case of Florence Beery

One of the fascinating, forgotten women targeted in *Broadway Brevities*' crusade against queer lives was Florence Beery. Although she appears to have been a relatively minor figure in the lesbian subcultures of both American coasts, Beery became the focus of a New York scandal in 1924 that *Broadway Brevities* did much to magnify. Florence Beery first received press attention in 1921 while living in Los Angeles, when she accused her husband, Benjamin Beery, of beating her and imprisoning her in the house they shared.[9] Florence sued Benjamin for divorce and child support, and these were granted in December 1921. In 1923, Florence Beery wrote and published a slim book bearing the title *For Love of Women*. For this, she used the masculine pen name "François Beerié," though she appears to have made little effort to conceal her own authorship. *For Love of Women* was written as a memoir of its narrator's string of romantic-sexual affairs with women, lightly fictionalized and using invented names for its characters.[10] Shortly after its publication, Florence was once again the focus of newspaper coverage after her new husband, a tax collector named George Lyons Merrick, returned to their Los Angeles home one day to find her drinking with several friends. Merrick apparently called the police and arranged for Beery to be arrested on charges of intoxication and disturbing the peace. The charges were dropped, and by September 1923, Florence had filed suit for divorce against Merrick, accusing him of physical violence. A Los Angeles newspaper reported in the same month that Beery had then gone East "for treatment."[11]

The unspecified "treatment" was to take place in New York City, and by early 1924 Beery was at the centre of a minor scandal there. She had come to the city, the *Daily News* reported, to deliver a lecture titled the "Psychology of the Intermediate Sex."[12] The real controversy, however, erupted when Beery mailed copies of *For Love of Women*, with no warning, to a number of women in the New York area. Households receiving the volume were expected to make payment for the book upon delivery. One of its recipients, described as "Miss Alice Bush, a wealthy society woman of 10 Monroe Place, Brooklyn," was given the book by her maid, who had paid the charges when it arrived.[13] Bush was scandalized by the book, and all the more incensed to learn that several of her acquaintances had also been sent copies. She made a complaint to the District Attorney's Office, which set about investigating the matter.

The New York scandal over *For Love of Women* was not front-page news in the city, but wire services carried the *Daily News* reporting to newspapers across the country. The greatest attention to Beery and her New York troubles, however, came from *Broadway Brevities*, which published a five-page article in its February 1924 issue with the title "'Insides' on the life of Florence Beery: The Hollywood Girl, Whose Youth and Beauty Have Led Her To Fate's Murky Morass." An "Editor's Note" framed the piece by suggesting that the magazine's own recent series "exposing Broadway perversion" was born of the same moral impulses that had led the district attorney to go after Florence Beery and her obscene little book. This reference was to the "Nights in Fairyland" series, introduced in the previous issue of *Brevities* (and the focus of the next chapter in this book).

The opening sentence of *Broadway Brevities*' first-person "investigation" of the Beery affair offered an image more typical of the private eye fiction slowly taking form elsewhere in mid-1920s American culture: "I found her at the Brevoort – that gloomy and weather-beaten pile on lower Fifth Avenue, once the rollicking, pre-Prohibition haunt of Broadway spenders and spoofers." The article recounts Beery's arrival in New York at the beginning of the year, bearing with her "three dozen volume *de luxe* of a little book of fifty pages, titled 'For Love of Women.' … Believing with an almost childish simplicity in the right of homogeneous love she had trustingly mailed copies of the small work to certain fashionable ladies in the far-distant province of Brooklyn."[14] Whether the author had sent *For Love of Women* to Alice Bush on the basis of prior knowledge of the woman's inclinations or simply targeted persons of elevated social stature remains unclear. In any event, *Brevities* explained, a newspaper item reporting that law enforcement agents were on her trail compelled Florence Beery to leave the Cumberland Hotel in Manhattan – where she had gone after arriving in the city – and move into the much less conspicuous Brevoort. This did not stop two men from the District Attorney's Office from finding her, but Beery so charmed these men, *Brevities* suggests, that they dropped any action against her in return for a vague promise from the author to cease promoting her book.

While its account of the New York controversy over Beery's book ended here, *Brevities* nevertheless spent another three pages denouncing the author. The level of detail here suggests that *Brevities* had an abundance of information on Beery's earlier life in Los Angeles and on queer coteries both there and in New York to which she had belonged. It became clear, as well, that the magazine had in its possession one of the rare copies of *For Love of Women*. In that book, *Brevities* tells us, "names are fictitious, but veil the identities of women well known in the private and professional circles of San Francisco, Los Angeles, Hollywood, and New York – even Paris is represented."[15]

Brevities offered a paragraph excerpted from the novel,[16] informing the reader that "Billy," the novel's central character, was a stand-in for the author:

> One never to be forgotten night Jean met Billy. One day, dressing feverishly, Jean hurries to her apartment. The atmosphere was exotic – Billy, lazily inclining among the thousand cushions, put aside her book and offered both her hands to the visitor. As their hands touched, the spark of love was lighted; they looked long in one another's eyes; as Jean leaned near to Billy the love-spark flamed into the white heat of passion, and Jean's mouth closed over Billy's in one long tremulous embrace – They slept in each other's arms, shutting themselves from all the world, dwelling in their loves. Their only companions were the two books, "Aphrodite" and "The Songs of Bilitus."[17]

Jean, *Brevities* tells us, was Billy's first lesbian lover and "believed to be a noted figure in motion picture circles." Leaving the excerpt and book behind, the *Brevities* article goes on to paint a picture of Florence Beery as a key player within Los Angeles queer life: "When Florence Beery married her palatial bungalow in Hollywood became open salon for men and women of every type, dominated by aberrants of all hues and conditions. Among those who were frequent visitors at her monage [*sic*] were A_____ N_____, G_____ D_____, G____ H _____, M______ M______, and a lot of the smaller fry of the cinema colony, including Arthur J ______, who played in support of 'Salome,' Julia H______, George F______ and others of like feather."[18]

The Internet Movie Database tells us that Arthur J_____ was the actor Arthur Jasmine. We might guess that A____ N____, the first person mentioned, was actress Alla Nazimova, whose own "8080 Club" was one of the most high-profile salons at which Hollywood lesbians and gay men were known to congregate.[19] Whether Florence Beery's queer Los Angeles circles overlapped significantly with those at the higher end of film industry society remains to be uncovered, but her name is nowhere to be found in the published histories of queer Hollywood during this period.

The rest of the astonishingly detailed "'Insides' on the life of Florence Beery" offers up stories of women obsessed with Beery and given to sending her poetic expressions of love even as Florence rebuffed them. These included Lillian Bret Harte (daughter of the writer Bret Harte and herself an author), Helen Hammond Sterling,[20] and two others partially identified as Beatrice M_____ and "well-known newspaper woman G____ S_____." The *Brevities* piece pauses at this last name to quote and mock the latter's poetry, then indulges in an apocalyptic vision in which the magazine gives full rein to its preoccupation with the lesbian circles allegedly meeting at the Algonquin Hotel: "Pretty good, eh wot! If BREVITIES ever succeeds in securing a complete collection of the poetical works of the talented G_____ S_____, we may make a pyramid of them in the Algonquin lobby and, while a balalaika orchestra croons *Valse Mauve* and the merry Horsewomen dance like furies, we shall set the match and have a bonfire par excellence."[21]

Having revelled in the details of Florence Beery's life over a dozen paragraphs packed with the outlines of names and incidents, *Brevities* quickly returns, in the article's final lines, to a denunciation of the broader climate of perceived degeneracy of which this was all somehow a symptom. In what was becoming a familiar pattern, *Broadway Brevities*, having displayed its obvious taste for the deliciously intimate details of other people's lives, wraps this up in the language of moral crusade. What the Beery case laid bare, the article concludes, was the "appalling moral turpitude that seethes under and behind the apparently placid exterior of the Broadway apartments, cafes and hotels."[22]

It is unclear whether Beery was able to deliver her lecture on "The Psychology of the Intermediate Sex," in New York or elsewhere. Nevertheless, the January–February 1924 issue of the New York–based *Medico-Legal Journal* ("devoted to medical jurisprudence and forensic medicine") published an article, authored by Florence Beery, with an almost identical title: "The Psyche of the Intermediate Sex."[23] The *Medico-Legal Journal* was edited by Vienna-born Dr Alfred W. Herzog, a medical doctor and surgeon who, in 1918, had published (and introduced) Earl Lind's *Autobiography of an Androgyne*, recognized today as a landmark of transgender writing.[24]

Florence Beery's article, running just short of six pages, is a serious plea for understanding those whose "soul distinctions in relation to sex" do not correspond to "the outer bodily sex development." Beery insists on the variety of personality types produced by this non-correspondence: "The truth is, that there are good and bad; high and low; worthy and unworthy; – and while some exhibit through their double temperament a rare and beautiful flower of humanity, others show us perverse and tangled ruins."[25] Beery goes on to invoke Havelock Ellis's claim that "every normal being is bi-sexual," then offers a rebuttal of arguments by the Freudian psychologist Wilhelm Stekel asserting environmental causes of homosexuality. She bases her disagreement with Stekel on her own knowledge of "the different anatomical appearance we often find in pronounced homo-sexuals, which surely cannot be ascribed to environment or circumstance."[26] Beery refers, as well, to the German sexologist Otto de Joux, attributing to him the claim that homosexuals are a race apart, "Uranians" (a notion more commonly credited to the German gay activist Karl Heinrich Ulrichs).

In 1998, an academic study by Margaret Gibson of early medical approaches to lesbianism quoted several lines of Beery's article, identifying her as one of the most forceful defenders of lesbianism to speak from the edges of the medical profession in this period.[27] Until more is known of Florence Beery's education or possible professional training, we can only speculate as to whether her wide-ranging exploration of homosexuality was that of the autodidact or formed in more collective fashion in the social circles and communities in which, on the basis of the limited evidence available, she seemed to move.

Society Gossip and "The Mirrors of Mayfair"

On the editorial page of its January 1923 issue, *Broadway Brevities* announced that the magazine would hereafter be known as *Broadway Brevities & Society Gossip*. The editor's explanation noted that a growing part of the magazine's readership was now to be found among the "socially elect" and that, in addition to the name change, it seemed "no more than fair to institute a department devoted solely to their own personalities, fads, and fashions."[28] The name of this new feature was "The Mirrors of Mayfair," and it would report on the lives of people at some social distance from the theatrical worlds to which the magazine was otherwise devoted. In his memoirs, written and serialized after his release from prison, Clow claimed that the idea for "Mirrors of Mayfair" had come from his "chief of staff," Andrew S. Brown, later a co-defendant in the 1925 *Brevities* trial.[29]

By 1924, *Brevities*' "Mirrors of Mayfair" feature was a key vehicle for gossipy innuendo concerning the nonconforming sexual behaviour of the city's social and financial elites. Much of the time, the column's style mimicked the wordier, somewhat musty prose of the society columns appearing in older magazines like *Town Topics*. This tone seemed more suited to conveying gossip in a manner that circled around revelation and dabbled in euphemism, rather than laying out its claims in brief, punchy items, as was typical of *Brevities*' treatment of contemporary show business personalities. As well, the style of "Mirrors of Mayfair" seemed appropriate for a feature whose subjects were very often figures of the past, remembered in the present or observed in their final days.

The April 1924 instalment of "Mirrors of Mayfair" shows this tone in its full flowering. It also manifests the tendency, common in society magazine coverage of the monied classes, to find evidence of same-sex intimacy in travelling habits and vacation preferences – in the familiar rituals of the well-to-do. A central target of this issue's column (and one to whom the magazine would turn on other occasions) was Clyde Fitch (1865–1909), one of the most popular playwrights of the turn-of-the-century American theatre. Fitch was also, it was claimed, a one-time lover of Oscar Wilde.[30] The following passage, quoted at length, conveys something of the crafted wit and sly innuendo that distinguished the "Mirrors of Mayfair" feature:

> Poor Clyde Fitch! He was, for long, known as "the American Oscar Wilde" probably because of his bizarre demeanor and writings, which caused him to be surrounded by a coterie of sympathetic souls. Most have passed to that bourne whence no epigram returns, but a conspicuous survivor is Martin Birnbaum, at present working union shifts with a Fifth Avenue art-dealer, and who has written essays on art and artists. Mr Fitch was a friend of an English playwright, Cosmo Gordon-Lennox, described as "a bird of the same feather," and there was still another, a product of our own soil, who hung about Fitch in his later years, eventually writing a memoir of him – Archie Bell, now critic on a Cleveland sheet …
>
> Another English playwright, mentionable in this strange company, is Somerset Maugham, who wrote "Rain" for little Zhon E-Gal. Also add Robert Hichens, the novelist, whose solitary masterpiece was "The Garden of Allah." Hichens, Maugham and Fitch, it is tres thrilling to recall, used to winter together at Taormina, Italy, described by one who knows, as "a modern Sodom and Gomorrah." Americans in that ill-omened spot were Reginald J——, of New York and Bermuda, likewise Alfred P——, banker.[31]

In this movement from person to person, worlds of queer affiliation are etched. It is worth noting that the memoir of Clyde Fitch attributed to journalist Archie Bell had been published by Clow's own Broadway Publishing Company in 1909.[32]

Queerness wove its way through almost all episodes of *Brevities*' "Mirrors of Mayfair" feature. Item after item spoke of "smart bachelors," of artistic or temperamental men and their proteges, of women given to wearing masculine attire. Among the latter, a regular target of the column was Elisabeth Marbury. One of the most elaborate and wide-ranging of *Brevities*' assaults on the lives of Manhattan's queer women was an item on Marbury in the "Mirrors of Mayfair" column of one of the magazine's last issues. It began: "A veritable cyclone of protest has thundered upon the heels of Elizabeth [*sic*] Marbury's attack on the domestic virtues of Mrs Coolidge. That the attack was ill-advised in the extreme no one now probably realizes more keenly than that gargantuan spinster who gave it utterance."[33]

The Worlds of Elisabeth Marbury

Elisabeth Marbury (1856–1933), who appeared briefly in the item on Clyde Fitch already excerpted, was a prominent figure in several of New York's worlds. As a successful theatrical and literary agent, she is credited with having modernized those professions, negotiating the rights to plays and novels on an international scale and setting in place the cross-media exploitation of properties that would characterize agentry in the twentieth century. She represented both Oscar Wilde and George Bernard Shaw, and negotiated deals with major managers and impresarios, like Lee Shubert. Marbury was also host of a popular salon held over many years in the Union Square house she shared with her long-time partner, the interior decorator Elsie de Wolfe.[34] Known for her expensive tastes and lifestyle, Marbury owned a chateau in Versailles and reputedly had friends across the highest social strata of European society. As a prominent philanthropist with a home in France, Marbury was close to those women of elite New York families, like Anne Morgan and Anne Vanderbilt, who eschewed conventional lifestyles and devoted themselves to such causes as the care of wounded French soldiers during World War I. Her various worlds were also key points of entry for young women into important Manhattan lesbian coteries of the 1910s and 1920s. The Russian-born actress Alla Nazimova, for whom Marbury became a professional mentor at a crucial turning point, was one of those whose connection to Marbury gave her access to these circles.[35] (From 1921 onward, Nazimova herself was a regular target of brief items in *Broadway Brevities* hinting at her same-sex attachments.[36])

Later in her life, Elisabeth Marbury's interests turned toward politics, and she served as a representative of New York state on the Democratic Party's National Committee. In October 1924, at a party dinner honouring the wife of the defeated Democratic presidential candidate, John W. Davis, Marbury gave a speech that amounted to an attack on Grace Coolidge, the spouse of the recently elected Republican president. Marbury ridiculed Grace's early life on a Vermont farm and her insistence on talking about it in public. Her remarks took offence at Grace Coolidge's public claims that, in her early life, she had done her own sewing and baking. Such activities, Marbury suggested, were "milk pail stuff."[37] Marbury's widely reported remarks were received by broad segments of the American population (cutting across party lines) as filled with disdain for traditional gender roles and fuelled by elitist contempt for those without wealth and servants.

Brevities seized on this incident to mount a vicious attack, dressed up in populist offence, on all those New York women of unconventional sexuality who seemed to show little interest in sewing and baking: "Rather paradoxical was it that Miss Marbury's fine scorn should direct itself at the domestic virtues of cooking biscuits, making shirt-waists and milking cows. For it goes without saying that such vocations are not especially esteemed in Sutton Place, where the backyards overlook Blackwells Island." The author then added that "the kitchen and the sewing room have never been an obsession of the Misses Marbury and de Wolfe, through all the long years they have lived together."[38]

The *Brevities* article moved on to attack other targets within Marbury's worlds, obscuring the identity of the first and then exploding in a torrent of names that once again returned to the Algonquin Hotel and its Horsewomen: "Another dweller in that East Side nirvana is Miss A_____ M_____, who, although she may not cook biscuits herself, nor make shirtwaists, has long taken an interest in the poor working gel who must, of necessity, possess such ability … What, for example, does Eva Le Gallienne think of ladies who cook and sew, and Blyth Daly, and Estelle Winwood, and Julie Lentilhon, and Adele Colgate, and Eleonara Sears, and Mrs Tommy Pierce – and the Poillon Sisters?"[39]

The "A_____ M_____" mentioned here is clearly Anne Morgan, the youngest child of banker John Pierpont Morgan and an important contributor to the development of the Sutton Place community in which Elisabeth Marbury and other women of her circle came to live. The Poillon sisters mentioned here, Charlotte and Katherine, were notorious personalities of early-twentieth-century New York, known in the 1920s for bilking rich men of large sums of money and for launching lawsuits against prominent society figures. Later treatments of their lives have been more sympathetic to the ways in which their various schemes laid bare the economic basis of sexual relations, and to the subversive qualities of the "Amazonian" persona they inhabited and performed.[40] Press coverage of Charlotte regularly mentioned her "mannish attire" and the fact that she had studied boxing under the heavyweight champion James J. Corbett. In 1933, Stephen G. Clow spent a night in jail when the Poillon sisters sued him for libel and he was unable to pay for his bail. (The charges were soon dropped.)[41]

Fairies and Fairylands

A shift in *Broadway Brevities*' treatment of queer lives, from brief innuendo directed at specific individuals to longer pieces recounting investigations of queer meeting grounds, first became apparent in 1923. At this time, we see a sharpening of the vocabulary used by the magazine to name sexual identities or dispositions. "Fairyland," in the magazine's usage, ceased being a description of fancifully designed restaurants or nightclubs – like the Palais Royale on West 48th Street[42] – and served more pointedly to identify places of gay or lesbian congregation. A change in the magazine's uses of the term "fairy" was less abrupt, but we may observe a slow slide from a vision of fairies as magical, wispy creatures of no explicit sexual orientation to a sense of them as a distinct social and sexual subculture.

Evidence of these shifts was abundant in the two-page fantasy "Alice in Fairyland: A True Story of Alice's New Adventures" (May 1923). This piece does double duty at this moment in the magazine's history: it enacts, in the story it tells, *Broadway Brevities*' broader shift in attention from the fairylands of theatrical fantasy to those of queer intermingling and, in doing so, serves as a trial run for many of the extended "investigations" of queer life that would follow over the next year and a half. We follow the fictional Alice as she flees the "wonderland" of the Broadway theatre for the explicitly queer "Fairyland" assembling at the corner of Broadway and 46th Street ("the favorite meeting place of the fairies at nightfall"). Alice gazes with wonder at the spectacle:

> Young men, of wasp-waisted figure, smoking Fatimas, their eyes phosphorescent from belladonna, their lashes coal-black and carrying little canes on their arms, ran hither and thither in a state of feverish excitement. They seemed to fly, rather than run, which – to little Alice's mind – established them truly as the fairy tribe of the vast, bewildering forest of skyscrapers into which her tiny feet had ventured, and of which Yellow Tassel had told her such enchanting tales.[43]

In fits and starts, over the rest of 1923, *Brevities* developed a fascination with observing the spectacle of queer people in the urban habitats in which they might be found. Five months after "Alice in Fairyland," an isolated one-sentence item in the October 1923 of *Broadway Brevities* asked a question: "Is Childs at 59th Street now known as 'The Home of the Fairies'?"[44] The Childs chain of popular, economically priced restaurants had grown from a single location in 1899, at 41 Cortland Street in New York's Financial District, to several branches in the city by the early 1920s. With its question, *Brevities* began its assault on the night-time spaces of New York gay life, a project that would carry the magazine through the remaining months of its existence.

Stephen G. Clow would have been familiar with the 59th Street branch of the restaurant chain, but we know from another source that the 42nd Street Childs served as a place in which he gathered some of the theatrical gossip that filled his magazine. In the memoirs of her years as a Ziegfeld Follies dancer, completed before her death in 1955 but unpublished until 1999, Marcelle Earle writes of at least one chorus girl who would meet Clow at the 42nd Street Childs and feed him backstage gossip:

> Secrets, that were not supposed to go beyond the dressing room walls, were beginning to appear in print in Broadway Brevities, a despicable little publication. No one was safe until the tattler was finally caught. Her method was to enter the dressing room early, hide behind racks of costumes, and listen to exchanged confidences. She would go to Child's [*sic*] restaurant after the shows to meet Steve Clow, publisher of the Brevities, and blabber all. Clow became so brazen threatening well-known people if they refused to take an ad in Brevities that he was convicted of extortion and sent to federal prison. The exposed tattler's punishment was ostracism, the silent treatment, administered by the rest of the cast.[45]

If the 42nd Street Childs was a popular hangout for Broadway chorus girls, the question of whether the branch of Childs on 59th Street was the "home of the fairies" would dominate the first of *Brevities*' extended examinations of gay life – a two-page article in the November 1923 issue with the breathless title "Startling Revelations of Broadway Perversion: An Epidemic of Homosexuality, Unparalleled in the City's History." The opening lines claimed that the simple question about Childs posed in the previous issue had elicited an "anonymous" communication laying out in detail the full extent of the debauchery transpiring

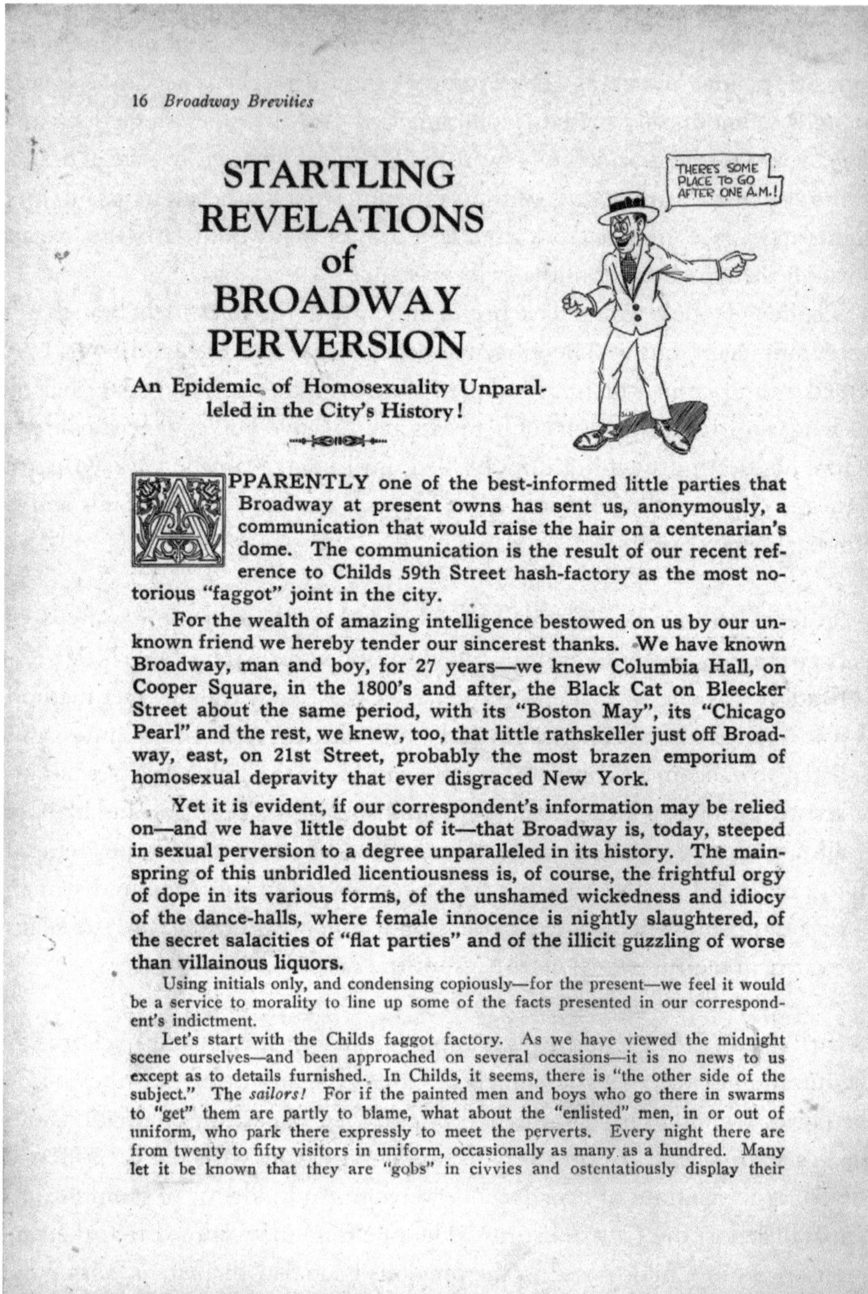

16 *Broadway Brevities*

STARTLING REVELATIONS of BROADWAY PERVERSION

An Epidemic of Homosexuality Unparalleled in the City's History!

APPARENTLY one of the best-informed little parties that Broadway at present owns has sent us, anonymously, a communication that would raise the hair on a centenarian's dome. The communication is the result of our recent reference to Childs 59th Street hash-factory as the most notorious "faggot" joint in the city.

For the wealth of amazing intelligence bestowed on us by our unknown friend we hereby tender our sincerest thanks. We have known Broadway, man and boy, for 27 years—we knew Columbia Hall, on Cooper Square, in the 1800's and after, the Black Cat on Bleecker Street about the same period, with its "Boston May", its "Chicago Pearl" and the rest, we knew, too, that little rathskeller just off Broadway, east, on 21st Street, probably the most brazen emporium of homosexual depravity that ever disgraced New York.

Yet it is evident, if our correspondent's information may be relied on—and we have little doubt of it—that Broadway is, today, steeped in sexual perversion to a degree unparalleled in its history. The mainspring of this unbridled licentiousness is, of course, the frightful orgy of dope in its various forms, of the unshamed wickedness and idiocy of the dance-halls, where female innocence is nightly slaughtered, of the secret salacities of "flat parties" and of the illicit guzzling of worse than villainous liquors.

Using initials only, and condensing copiously—for the present—we feel it would be a service to morality to line up some of the facts presented in our correspondent's indictment.

Let's start with the Childs faggot factory. As we have viewed the midnight scene ourselves—and been approached on several occasions—it is no news to us except as to details furnished. In Childs, it seems, there is "the other side of the subject." The *sailors!* For if the painted men and boys who go there in swarms to "get" them are partly to blame, what about the "enlisted" men, in or out of uniform, who park there expressly to meet the perverts. Every night there are from twenty to fifty visitors in uniform, occasionally as many as a hundred. Many let it be known that they are "gobs" in civvies and ostentatiously display their

Figure 2.1 *Broadway Brevities*, November 1923.

within the restaurant. Before turning to the testimony of this mysterious source, *Brevities'* own, unidentified editorialist (almost certainly Clow) offered some background. "We have known Broadway, man and boy, for 27 years," the article claimed; "we knew Columbia Hall, on Cooper Square, in the 1800's and after, the Black Cat on Bleecker Street about the same period, with its 'Boston May,' its 'Chicago Pearl' and the rest, we knew, too, that little rathskeller just off Broadway, east, on 21st Street, probably the most brazen emporium of homosexual depravity that ever disgraced New York."[46]

After this quick tour of *fin de siècle* queer life, the author of the introduction is quick to add that "Broadway is, today, steeped in sexual perversion to a degree unparalleled in its history."[47] Here, the typeface changes and shrinks, and we supposedly enter the text of the anonymous communication provided to the magazine:

> Let's start with the Childs faggot factory. As we have viewed the midnight scene ourselves – and been approached on several occasions – it is no news to us except as to details furnished. In Childs, it seems, there is "the other side of the subject." The sailors! For if the painted men and boys who go there in swarms to "get" them are partly to blame, what about the "enlisted" men, in or out of uniform, who park there expressly to meet the perverts. Every night there are from twenty to fifty visitors in uniform, occasionally as many as a hundred. Many let it be known that they are "gobs" in civvies and ostentatiously display their tattoed [*sic*] hands and arms, using "salty" and "seagoing" lingo for the benefit of the pitiful youths – chorus boys, men-milliners, interior decorators et al.

The account continues for another page and a half, and while names are offered only in skeleton form, the accompanying descriptive bits would not make identification difficult:

> During daytime – for there is no pause in this carnival of lechery – many of the gang hang out in Bryant Park, where, for instance, Jean St– has been seen when in town from his California estate, he being the former Jack T–, a plain Wanamaker salesman, who married into the smart set. Another

> "habitchue" of Bryant Park and the hoofery aforenamed is a certain little fat man, manager of a well-known ladies' shop in 57th Street, who is one of the best known of the "queens" and used to park at a famous Club on the Avnoo during the war.[48]

An unusually official editorial in the next issue of *Brevities* (December 1923) announced that the previous issue, with its damning exposé of Childs, had sold out on over three hundred newsstands. This was proof, it seemed, of public interest in the magazine's coverage of the degeneracy allegedly running rampant in the city. And so, in its January 1924 issue, *Broadway Brevities* launched the detailed, monthly "Nights in Fairyland" series. Several factors might explain the expansion of *Brevities*' exposés of queer Manhattan in its final year of publication. It is likely that the claimed growth in readership following its first steps in this direction proved too much of a boon to the magazine's circulation to be cut short. We might also see the rush to continue these exposés all through 1924 as a way of retreating from the sorts of celebrity-focused attacks on reputation that had marked the magazine's history until then. In early 1924, *Broadway Brevities* was just weeks away from a series of far-ranging indictments by a federal grand jury for mail fraud, the charge used by prosecutors to address the magazine's extortion of money from well-known New York figures in return for silence about their private lives. Investigations of the magazine by federal prosecutors, *Variety* reported in April 1924, had been going on for a long time.[49]

Clow's later memoirs suggest that, during the later stages of the magazine's history, he avoided appearing on New York's streets for fear of retribution from those he had wronged.[50] It is possible that a new focus on spaces of queer sociability – in articles that described places and behaviours but offered few recognizable names – offered one way of calming the legal and personal threats now focused on Clow. This, in any case, seemed to be Clow's expectation, and when critics of the magazine failed to find, in this new crusade, evidence that the magazine and its editor had somehow reformed and attained virtue, Clow's bitterness and anger became all the more pronounced.

THREE

NIGHTS IN FAIRYLAND
Investigating Queer Nightlife

Are You Reading the Series of Sensational Articles, "NIGHTS IN FAIRYLAND" Exposing the Notorious Haunts of Perversion in New York City?

NOW RUNNING IN BROADWAY BREVITIES

As a Result of These Exposures, at Least Three Dens of Outlawed Love Have Been Closed by the Police.

JULY ISSUE ALL NEWSSTANDS

Display advertisement, *Daily Mirror*, 26 June 1924, 16.

Brevities' "Nights in Fairyland" series joined a rich corpus of narratives detailing investigative journeys through nocturnal Manhattan in the years before and after 1900. These included stories of the "sin tours" undertaken by the Reverend Charles H. Parkhurst in the 1890s, the moral crusader Anthony Comstock's account of his visit to the queer Greenwich Village meeting place the Black Rabbit in 1900, and the more prosaic reports of moral reform groups such as the Committee of Fourteen, whose "case studies" often took the form of short narratives with mildly melodramatic flourishes.[1] The thirteen instalments of "Nights in Fairyland," like most of *Broadway Brevities*' content, went unsigned, but they were largely (and probably exclusively) written by Stephen G. Clow. Three years after the series ended – and after he had been convicted for mail fraud, served time in prison, and then been released – Clow reflected on his nightly routines during the months he spent exploring queer New York:

> The series on New York's degenerates had confirmed in my mind the advisability of a bodyguard, and so an old Broadway pal of mine, "Gentleman" Jack O'Brien, a former noted pugilist of both brawn and brain, was glad to mingle business and pleasure by accompanying me wheresoever I journeyed after nightfall. Jack and I would play pool from 7 to 10 P.M., with the editor handicapped, and beaten, invariably, at fifty points, and then we would set out in Greenwich Village to spend long hours in cafés guesting the pitiful creatures we were attacking in "Brevities." Jack was a good cartoonist, and drew numberless profiles of weird subjects, later to be interpolated in my articles. This body-guard arrangement was a pleasant and profitable one.[2]

In a gallery of the eccentric personalities who surrounded Stephen G. Clow and *Broadway Brevities*, the boxer "Gentleman" Jack O'Brien would warrant a central place. Named John Rostacher at birth, Jack O'Brien would use the name "New York Jack" O'Brien throughout much of his boxing career, in part to distinguish himself from the "Philadelphia Jack" O'Brien whose time in the ring roughly coincided with his own.[3] By the late 1910s, Jack, now presenting himself as "Gentleman" Jack, was, like many ex-boxers, earning money through appearances in exhibition matches with other old-timers of the ring, but his various other activities brought him into the worlds of journalism and show business in which Clow moved. O'Brien pursued a career as a vaudeville performer, touring as a monologist and performing on occasion in New York venues.[4] In many respects, his double stature as athletic figure and Broadway personality was typical of New York's "sporting culture," whose history can be traced from the "Flash" papers of the 1840s through the later writings of one-time sports journalist Damon Runyon (author of the short stories on which the musical *Guys and Dolls* was based).[5] The weekly *Police Gazette*, endlessly reinventing itself, filled its covers with Broadway stars and its back pages with boxing news during the years in which the first incarnation of *Broadway Brevities* was published.

Beginning with its August 1924 issue, Jack O'Brien quickly became a significant presence in the pages of *Broadway Brevities*. An item in that issue, with the title "Gentleman Jack O'Brien Will Divulge His Secrets of Beauty," invited women readers to consult him on the secrets of preserving their "youthful beauty and charm" and to contact him through the magazine's own offices.[6] Later in the same issue, four pages were given over to a feature titled "Gentleman Jack O'Brien Chats on Many Different Subjects," certainly one of the first and only periodical columns devoted in roughly equal proportion to beauty tips and news from the boxing world.[7] It was with Gentleman Jack O'Brien that Stephen G. Clow set out on his series of visits to many of the locations of Manhattan's queer night life. (In these articles, the narrator refers to his companion as "Lou.")

Fairyland in Midtown

In "Night No. 1 in Fairyland" (January 1924), Clow and his partner visit a queer dance hall near Columbus Circle. Like most of the early episodes of the series, this one begins as a straightforward account of a journey into the Manhattan night. While the first place visited goes unnamed, its location is identified: "A stone's throw from where the raucous 'L' shrills around the curve at Sixty-sixth Street and Columbus Avenue is the reputed headquarters of the notorius [*sic*] 'Battleship' Kate 'Diamond Tooth' May and her brothers and sisters in perversion."[8] The article spends some time setting the scene outside the club. "The time was about nine-thirty. A sort of zero hour for Broadway on a Saturday night. At that time the theatres have almost two hours before vomiting their denizens that soon after cover the pave like migrating ants on the march. We decided that we would not enter the place just then. First we would note the lay of the land."[9]

When Clow and his companions eventually enter the establishment, they follow a group of uniformed sailors to a gallery above the dance floor. This first episode of "Nights in Fairyland" sets in place many of the key narrative tropes to be found in later instalments. Just as an "arrival scene" became an expected feature in classical reports of anthropological fieldwork,[10] journalistic investigations of nightlife often began with a reporter's arrival at a nightclub, submission to the scrutinizing gaze of a doorman, and entry into a space of lively sociability.[11] The narrator of "Nights in Fairyland," faithful to this tradition, would then seek out one or more customers who served as informants:

> We approached one young man, whose absolutely beardless face, delicate features and flamboyant jewelry proclaimed his avocation. We weren't wrong, for after we had offered him cigarettes and called for three splits of ginger ale, he succumbed to the new sympathetic environment. He told us that he had experienced unusual instincts as early in his childhood as he could remember. He was very clever at sketching and he worked as a commercial artist. He said his name was Paul V— but that among his "intimates" he preferred to be called "Polly." Lou and I called him Polly thereafter and he seemed very pleased.
>
> He told us bluntly why he came to the dance hall. The sailors foregathered there, and although he preferred normal associates to the "Jackies" centred there to seek such as he, his "conquests" were consequently both numerous and remunerative.[12]

The sexual economy described here is one involving sailors, presumably on leave, and a local queer population typically connected to the arts or show business. In a convention deeply rooted in stereotypes about sad queer lives, this episode, like others that follow, ends with the successfully coupled going off to their pleasures, while the neglected linger, forlorn, then slip away. "At about twelve bells, which is the 'weeding out' hour, the maudlin and motley crowd began to disperse. It became easier to recognize the foppish young men who remained until then without 'making' anybody. But after a few languorous glances toward the remaining male visitors, the Nancies slowly filed out, their wimperings of disappointment easily audible."[13]

Episode two of "Nights in Fairyland" (February 1924) remains in the territory of Columbus Circle. Its opening paragraphs set queer life amidst other varieties of lawlessness and marginality in the area, before turning to the episode's main destination: the Childs restaurant on 59th Street. "Columbus Circle," Clow begins, "is a curious place peopled by curious, nay, queer denizens who seethe round its serried edges. They are a herd-people and they gather in small groups, causing the polizei of the neighborhood to be doubly wary. Queues composed of sailors, effeminates, crooks and narcotic addicts are ominous. When the witching hour strikes, just as if an invisible bell wether were leading them, the habitues of Columbus Circle march into Childs' Restaurant, on its fringe."[14]

It was Childs of course, that had prompted the prequels to "Nights in Fairyland," in late 1923, and it was in Childs, it seems, that queer Manhattan was at its most conspicuous and rowdy. In *Gay New York*, George Chancey confirms Clow's claim that Childs's 59th Street branch – known as "Mother Childs" – was the best-known queer meeting place among the chain's various outlets. This second episode describes a series of encounters in Childs's 59th Street branch, between navy men and local, effeminate gay men, "sailors and their frilly young friends." The former gobble down plates of pancakes and eggs while the latter "peck idly at club sandwiches" and gossip among themselves. Here, too, the fate of large numbers of this effeminate second group is to end their evenings abandoned and exploited: "They rise, many to find their overcoats and hats missing from the hooks along the walls, filched by sneak thieves. If they complain, they get little comfort, because a policeman will not listen long when it is an effeminate who addresses him. They slink away to their mysterious hovels, to arise the next day and go about their work, millinery, interior decorating and such kindred crafts. The more fortunate ones stay a while longer. They are Shubert chorus men, and often don't have to rise earlier than 10:30 for rehearsal."[15] The image of Childs offered here is that of a meeting place for young, working-class gay men – sailors on leave and those working at the lower levels of Manhattan's theatrical and textile industries. Later episodes of the series find Clow and his companions visiting more upscale midtown queer gathering places, like the Double R, where an older, more elite queer clientele could be observed interacting with little of the raucousness or sense of personal risk that so clearly characterized Childs.

Downtown: Paul and Joe's

With its third episode, the "Nights in Fairyland" series begins its exploration of establishments further downtown. The subtitle of "Night No. 3 in Fairyland" (March 1924) identifies its destination as "'Paul and Joe's,' a Nest of Carousing Androgynes" and is preoccupied with cross-dressing and other assaults on the boundaries of gender. That Paul and Joe's was an Italian restaurant prompts Clow's indulgence in a display of erudition in which he follows an epigraph from Pliny into a historical parallel: "Some classicist or other, essayed that all roads lead to Rome. This statement is still as peculiarly applicable today, in the Carnal 20th Century as it was when first uttered; for the footloose pilgrim in this Vale of Viciousness will find – all roads lead to Paul and Joe's – the Rome of the vast, uncharted Fief of Fairydom."[16]

Paul and Joe's is described at some length in George Chauncey's *Gay New York*. Chauncey notes that it had been "one of the best-known gay personality clubs in the Village in the 1920s,"[17] when it began featuring drag performances. At the time of Clow's visit, it was located in Chelsea, on 19th Street between Fifth and Sixth avenues, having moved there in 1924 from 62 West 9th Street. At that earlier location, it had been the target of a well-publicized raid by Prohibition enforcement agents,[18] and Chauncey suggests its relocation was an attempt to avoid the crackdown on gay establishments affecting the Village.[19] Clow paints Chelsea as a wilderness full of menace, with "dark factory hallways, havens of groups of wastrels, loafers and libertines."[20]

Apparently alone on his visit to Paul and Joe's, Clow is seated beside a large empty table, which is quickly taken over by a group of some eighteen cross-dressing customers. Clow seems fascinated by the conversation of the group sitting alongside him, noting their distinctive manner of speaking. "A few samples of the androgynic vernacular will be interesting to those readers unfamiliar with this hybrid tribe: 'If I knew you were coming I'd have baked a cake.' 'Laugh, dearie, and show your bridgework.' 'Hold the baby and I'll stir up a pan of biscuits.' 'Be your age, dearie?' 'I'm saying nothing – my lips are sealed.'"[21] The behaviour of customers at Paul and Joe's, we are told, differed in at least two ways from that observed in the spots already visited, like Childs. In the first place, members of the effeminate dining party are described as eating without "masculine" escorts, revelling in a sociability of their own – perhaps, Clow suggests, because this removed any fear of having their lovers stolen away. Paul and Joe's was also distinct from places already visited in that it was a significant meeting ground for lesbians. After noting their presence, *Brevities*' reporter explains that "I refer to the 'Horsewomen' who make this table d'hote palace their rendezvous every Saturday and Sunday evening. Their depredations against the morality of the land are far more virulent than those of the male androgynes. The male is at least, amusing. But the Lesbian is not even that. She is gross. Immoral to almost unbelievable depths, morose and designing."[22]

These comments, and the third episode overall, introduce the structure of judgment that presides over much of the series: sad but endearing effeminate gay men are set in contrast to coteries of hardened and manipulative lesbians out to spoil their evening's prey. *Brevities'* reporter is particularly fascinated by "a Horsewoman with two extremely pretty women at her table," who plies her victims with drink before pushing them into a cab.[23] The episode ends with an extended paragraph that resurrects the earlier analogy with ancient Rome. Of Paul and Joe's, he concludes, "there it stands, a monument to bizzarrerie, a very vault of outlawed love – a Rome under Nero. And like Rome, the wrath of the gods will inevitably vent itself upon it and scatter its evil denizens in oblivion."[24] Apocalyptic visions like these would become a common means of ending the episodes of "Nights in Fairyland," as if to short circuit any pleasure readers might take from the tantalizing details of queer appearance and behaviour that made up most of each report.

Midtown and the Double R

For the fourth instalment of the series (April 1924), *Brevities'* reporters return to midtown, to the Double R on 44th Street. The episode begins by setting that institution within a topography of queer spaces:

> While they mention the notorious Mother Childs at 59th with raucous merriment, while they speak of Paul and Joe's with a simpering smile, while they crack coarse jibes about Trilby's and Terrace Garden, the "Double R" has a clientele so 'elite' that it is spoken of only in whispered endearments. Fairydom has its own code and its own caste. Old Mother Childs – the sailors; Paul and Joe's the flotsam and jetsam of the Village and its purlieus, in an atmosphere of simpatico: but the "Double R" – a haunt of refined and taciturn segregation, a place set apart for the sensitive and the meticulous. It is the home of Fairyland's nobility.[25]

This instalment as a whole seems propelled by in interest in sociological differentiation, further distinguishing between places according to the professions of those who frequent them:

> Fairyland's denizens, please remember, display the same lines of demarkation [*sic*] that distinguish normal society. Money is a principal factor, occupation an important cleavage. Achievement in some phase of the arts or sciences cuts a big figure. Hence, among dance hall perverts you will find day-laborers, clerks, department store salespersons; in Paul and Joe's man-milliners, dressmakers and clerks in banks and counting houses. At the "Double R" gathers the creme de la creme – artists, writers, actors, a physician or two, and of course – naturally – the well-known sister Horse-women.[26]

The Double R coffee house had opened in November 1919, at 108 West 44th Street, then moved to 112 on the same street by the time *Brevities* published this account. It was run by Monroe Douglas Robinson, who, like several of the establishment's directors, was related to former President Theodore Roosevelt. (A second version of the Double R, with a more explicitly artistic atmosphere, was known as the "Argentine Branch," and opened at 726 Lexington Avenue in 1921.[27]) *Brevities*' reporter tells us that the sexual inclinations of patrons at the Double R were not apparent during the day, when the place attracted a predictable flow of Broadway customers and taxi drivers seeking coffee. Then, around 6 P.M. – suppertime – there was an overlay of customers both conventional and deviant, "[an] amalgam of chorus-boys, stenographers and a chorister or two, one or more Lesbians, regulars of both sexes employed in nearby film offices." A more exclusively queer clientele, of elevated social and professional standing, would take over the café after 8 P.M.[28] Lesbians, the narrator suggests, are a minority among the café's customers, and of low social standing, since those of any status remained "within the guarded gates of Sutton Place" (the well-known home of the aforementioned Elisabeth Marbury and her coterie).

Clearly impressed by the world of the Double R, *Brevities*' reporter concludes the episode with one of the most gentle and liberal of all passages in the "Nights in Fairyland" series:

> The "Double R" has, forsooth, more than a good excuse for existence. It is not an incubator of effeminacy, a hotbed of vulgarity and filth, like other androgynic nests. In fact it acts as a sort of check to this hideous social evil because it affords the more genteel perverts a refined place to see and be seen in. This stripe crave, as we normal beings do, a setting not suspeto. Here their weaknesses are not aired before a mob of gaping, grimacing, leering curiosity-seekers. They keep to themselves, and who shall begrudge them the pleasure they derive from the enjoyment experienced in a pseudo-normal environment. Not this writer, at any rate – and there's so much worse to come![29]

Among the features of the Double R fascinating *Brevities*' reporter is the richness of the conversation to be overheard there. It is not simply that, in an establishment frequented by people of refinement and professional status, exchanges are tasteful and rich in information. They are fascinating as well, the author suggests, because, even when both participants are men, conversation resembles the "usual colloquies between normal married couples."[30]

Trilby's and the Village

The following issue of *Broadway Brevities* (May 1924) is chock full of coverage of queer Manhattan, evidence of the extent to which the preoccupation with queer life was spilling out of the "Nights in Fairyland" series into other parts of the magazine in its final year. A feature titled "Splashing Around in the 'Turkish Baths'" tells of the "weekly orgies of the 'Saturday Afternoon Club,'" which met at a bathhouse in lower Manhattan, and of another bath, located in an uptown respectable hotel, "in which the more luxurious male sylphs frolic."[31] With "Night No. 5 in Fairyland," however, the series retreats, if only for a moment, from exposé and scandal, into the flights of trans-historical reflection and pontification that would mark later instalments. The first page of the episode offers up well-established lore concerning homosexual liaisons across the sweep of Italian history, noting that Julius Caesar engaged in "'homo' sprees" and that Leonardo da Vinci cavorted with peasant men. What puzzles the author is the fact that this tradition of same-sex love "is curiously without reference to androgynes, or those psychopathic hybrids we today are pleased to call fairies."[32] Clow – for it is certainly him – then moves to introduce the main focus of this fifth episode: a visit to Trilby's, "the natural successor of these ancient androgynous stomping grounds."[33]

Clow begins with what is almost a tribute to the place: "TRILBY'S! The mere mention of it brings a sigh of contentment, for happy, hectic "homo' hours spent there, to the pink face of practically every interior decorator, man-milliner and *tailleur pour dames* in New York. THRILL-BY'S!"[34] Trilby's was to be found in a basement at 13 Greenwich Avenue, in the Village. Clow calls its location a "dimly-lit cellar," just as, elsewhere in the series, he would speak of the Village club Dolly Judge's Flower Pot and its "dim lights."[35] In a distinction that is unsurprising but worth mentioning, the series typically describes midtown meeting places as brightly lit, with a constant circulation of people in and out, while venues in Greenwich Village are more likely to be found in semi-darkness at the bottom of stairs, hidden from the world outside.

As he enters Trilby's, Clow notes a quick hush, then hears one of the patrons whisper to a companion, "Keep quiet, there he is." The author explains: "I had been recognized as BREVITIES' investigator, and I feared that it would be a lean night for 'camp,' because of my identity apparently being known. At the moment I entered, the subject of Brevities' 'Nights in Fairyland' was being discussed by a group of aberrants."[36] Clow's cool initial reception aside, his visit to Trilby's is marked by moments of warm sociability. While a group of "Latin androgynes" scowl at Clow and his companion when they finally leave, their departure nevertheless elicits a flurry of "cheery good-byes" and invitations to come back from others. Clow is clearly fascinated by "Trilby" herself, whose reign over the customers and staff seems complete: "She conducts Trilby's after the fashion of a *maitre d'hotel* of the Parisian Hotel Metropole. She is keenly sympathetic with androgynes, who of course are by far her main custom. In her naive way she calls them 'temperamental boys.'"[37]

That Clow was recognized upon his entrance as the author of the "Nights in Fairyland" series is scarcely surprising, given his own claims about the series' effect on *Broadway Brevities*' circulation and the likely interest in it among those who frequented New York's queer spaces. Nevertheless, the reaction to his arrival at Trilby's is the first acknowledgment, in the series, that the articles were being read or having any effect. Clow's account provides us with one of the first examples of any kind of response to "Nights in Fairyland" from the worlds it claimed to document. If his new notoriety limited Clow's ability to move with ease through such worlds, it might serve, as well, to explain a shift in the tone and substance of the later episodes of "Nights in Fairyland." More and more, these are marked by a growing self-reflexivity, with Clow devoting paragraph after paragraph to musings on the history of homosexuality and its causes, symptoms, and possible treatments. As this kind of content expands within the series, the lengthy visits spent in clubs and cafés are fewer and typically of shorter duration. And, as members of the public began responding to the series, in letters sent to *Brevities* or commentaries published elsewhere, the remaining instalments spent much of their space responding to these, as we shall see.

An Uptown Party

The most peculiar and intriguing instalment of the "Nights in Fairyland" series is no. 6 (June 1924). It begins in pedantic fashion, with Clow enumerating the ways in which psychologists and criminologists, from Krafft-Ebing through Cesare Lombroso, had cast the homosexual as lawless and psychopathic. What is lacking in this treatment, Clow suggests, is any consideration of the social life of the "invert," or any acknowledgment of their place within the social fabric. In a lengthy paragraph worth quoting in its entirety, if only for the way it combines recognition of the ubiquity of homosexuality with an inevitable denunciation, Clow writes that

> with the possible exception of Oscar Wilde's "Dorian Grey," the social life of the invert has hitherto been untouched upon in modern times. It is a significant fact that there are estimated to be in New York City alone between 75,000 and 125,000 fairies or androgynes. They clutter and poison every calling and station of life. So it is evident that they are quite a substantial section of the warp and woof of our metropolitan social fabric. The time when this condition was discussed only in smoking rooms, behind

> fans and during medical meetings is no longer. One meets them everywhere. The male can single an androgyne out at his club; the woman can discover the Lesbian at her charity ball; the college man can find a solitary fairie on the campus, and the university girl may collide with a female psychopath in her dormitory.[38]

Then, as if the magazine was short of material for "Night No. 6," Clow quotes more than a page from Krafft-Ebing's *Psycopathia Sexualis* that describes "The Woman-Hater's Ball" held in 1884 in Berlin. (The text that *Brevities* reproduces was, in fact, a newspaper article reprinted in Krafft-Ebing's book.)

As it turns out, this lengthy display of erudition has little to do with the main purpose of episode 6 – that of recounting Clow's trip to a private apartment party at the home of someone he calls "Chloe." Clow tells of meeting the host and a group of associates "at an uptown restaurant," then being invited back for a party at Chloe's apartment further north, in the nineties. Chloe, we are told, is an "official in a large corporation," well-respected and of normal appearance by day, but given to wild extravagances at night. "His perverse anomalies," the article tells us, "seem to manifest themselves only after dark." As the group arrives at the apartment, the host retreats for several minutes into the bedroom, returning utterly transformed by an overlaying of Orientalist and French adornments: "He had evidently shaved, and laved his whole body. His cheeks were pink, not only with the lush that follows a warm bath, but with cosmetics: his lips were red, almost to purpling. Over his squat form he had thrown an elegant Japanese kimono, figured with herons and blossoming trees. His small feet were encased in scarlet mules, such as are found in the boudoirs of elegant ladies."[29]

The group assembled here, we are told, is a cross-section of queer Manhattan, but Clow's description also makes clear how close we are to one of that world's elite inner circles. "The guests were a motley crew of fairies," he writes, "Lesbians, two or three ordinary characters and one sailor. There was one very well known woman, the willing prey of half the Lesbians in New York; the notorious Elsie D ____; a fairy who is a ballet dancer in an internationally known ballet corps; another Lesbian, whose rather menial vocation kept her out of the regular aberrant social swim; a well known interior decorator also an androgyne; and the sailor, who was a desperate looking character with tremendous hands and fore-arms."[40]

Whether "Elsie D ____" was Elsie de Wolfe, the well-known decorator and, until 1926, domestic partner of Elisabeth Marbury, is unknown. In any event, as this evening moves on, it descends into an orgy of lovemaking, drunken dancing, and a coordinated assault by two lesbians upon their young prey. In a moment late in the night, and as the episode ends, our narrator sneaks away: "I tiptoed out of the apartment, noiselessly closing the door behind me, into the clean air, and as the fog searched the folds of my clothing it seemed to find my skin, and I felt purged from the foul, vicious air. in that cavern of viraginity and androgynism. Dawn had come."[41]

Summer Doldrums and Brief Visits

The spectacle of Chloe's party in episode no. 6 represents something of a dramatic high point in the series. In contrast, episodes 7 and 8 (July and August 1924), with their relative brevity and roaming focus, convey a sense of summer doldrums. In "Night No. 7 in Fairyland," the author writes as if he were alone on what he calls his "night-prowling," which leads him to visit a place in Greenwich Village called the Little Gray Hen. That establishment was run by a woman named Helen Dixon, who apparently had seen the success of Trilby's and decided to "make a bid for whatever fairy patronage there happened to be lying around loose."[42] The narrator's excursion to the Little Gray Hen follows the series' well-established flow, beginning with a description of its discrete location (which required that one go down steps and into a cellar) and its relative concealment at 3 Greenwich Avenue, in the shadow of the Jefferson Market court across the street.

As the sounds of the city outside give away to the high-pitched cacophony of "fairy voices," the narrator finds, to his surprise, an atmosphere of friendly sociability. He is soon seated with three people who turn out to be friends of his, and whose presence there he did not suspect before entering. Several paragraphs offer summaries of the conversations transpiring among customers, interwoven with descriptions of their dress and gestures. All of this builds to a description of the stage show, which was a regular and much-cherished feature of Saturday nights at the Little Gray Hen:

> Two of the fairies, one a slim Latin creature, and the other a handsome, well-set-up androgyne, detached themselves from the crowd and proceeded to the rear of the place, whence they emerged a few moments later. The taller one was in a red gown, a wig and a parasol, and the other had appropriated a stick and a slouch hat. They mincingly walked to the center of the room to the strains of "Margie" played on the piano. Their act was an imitation of that of Savoy and Brennan, and they negotiated it rather well for amateurs. The act, which is familiar wherever vaudeville is played or discussed, consists of rapid-fire "gagging," with the female character as a friend of the mythical Margie. The rollicking adventures of Margie form the points of the various jokes. Each pointed sentence was greeted with the same shrieks, without which no fairy gathering is complete.[43]

As this act concludes, it is announced that the "Ziegfeld Follies Number" will commence, and in our narrator's telling, "every fairy deserted the room to be properly rerouged and powdered for their parts as chorus girls." In the absence of scholarly or journalistic mentions of the Little Gray Hen, it is difficult to judge its place within the history of cross-dressing performance in Greenwich Village.

Episode no. 8 (August 1924) describes a summer in which queer life has slowed down or moved elsewhere. A return visit to Trilby's finds only two gay customers drinking coffee. Under the subheading "Where Are the Androgynes?" Clow describes the effects of summer on queer Manhattan life: "In brief, the Village is virtually fairy-less in summer. The 'girls' go to the shore for the most part. We learn that at the Rockaways, for instance, is a summer 'camp,' peopled by eight or ten of the more prosperous androgynes, where they frolic and pet to their hearts' content."[44] The meandering trajectory of this episode takes us then to the Blue Goose in the Village, described as one of the few places in that neighbourhood in which, despite the summer, an "intermittent fairy clientele" may be found. Clow and his companion are repelled by the door attendant's pressure upon them to enter, however, and they move on to Dolly Judge's Flower Pot at no. 5 Christopher Street, but here too, as at Trilby's, they encounter an "off" night: "Over the dim-lighted rooms seemed to brood a deadly ennui breathing of lost souls and hopes, and of illimitable, ghastly despair thinly veiled under crude camaraderie."[45]

The languorous boredom of summer, for Clow, seems to make even more obvious the emptiness of those frequenting places like Dolly Judge's Flower Pot. Judge herself, who is "dressed to the last extreme of mannishness," conveys "that indefinable malaise, that furtive hopelessness that no affected gayety can even temporarily disguise." Clow comments on Dolly's pet monkey, who roams the establishment at will, and in the simian's half-closed eyes, he claims to discern "a stifled passion to give articulation to its intense disgust with fairies in general and its current ownership in particular."[46] Clow concludes this episode by apologizing for its brevity.[47]

Episode no. 9, after several pages of editorial comment on a range of issues, returns to Dolly Judge's Flower Pot, the focus of the previous instalment. Shortly after his arrival there, Clow recognizes the distinctive voice of Florence Beery: "Good old Florence! She wandered here from Hollywood nine months ago and has had more than her share of palpitant vicissitude – with men, with women and with creatures who were neither."[48] We have seen, in the previous chapter, how Clow and *Brevities* seemed privy to an abundance of details concerning Beery's life and loves and had reported at length on the recent controversy over her book, *For Love of Women*. Here, at Dolly Judge's Flower Pot, Florence is found in the company of a younger woman who, in *Brevities*' account, labours to keep her from flirting with others in the room:

> The slim, dark, dignified creature who was squiring Florence Beery, and never losing site or bold [*sic*] of her for a single minute, was Jerry G____. "Jerry," obviously reared in an atmosphere of refinement, was a most curious Lesbian type. She did not have the distinctive Lesbian timbre in her voice, nor by her general demeanour, could one surmise that she was heiress to the congenital – and sometimes acquired – homogendrous vice. But I was informed on credible authority that "Jerry" was a past mistress at this sin of her own choosing.[49]

Clow is seated with two companions, who engage some of the younger women customers in conversation. It is then suggested that the group relocate to a speakeasy and Florence Beery and "Jerry" are convinced to come along. In the two pages that remain, this ninth episode develops the idea, already floated in the series, that the hold of lesbian predators over their prey far exceeded in intensity that which typified relationships between men. And yet, the article concludes by claiming that *Brevities*' own exposés of lesbian behaviour had succeeded in curtailing it: "But we believe that we are successful in throwing the vivid calcium on their dark doings, and as a result their profane activities in New York have NOTICEABLY LESSENED. At least they, the Lesbians, do not patrol the cafés and Village tea rooms in search of human prey, which was the case a year ago, prior to our now world-famous exposures."[50] How *Broadway Brevities*' "Nights in Fairyland" series could have curtailed such behaviour, other than by drawing police attention to the existence of certain establishments, is not specified, but we learn, in the last episode, that the police closed The Little Gray Hen in two locations.

Episode 10 finds the narrator leaving the Double R café on 44th Street to follow a couple of fairies who have announced they are heading to Childs. Clow is curious, inasmuch as recent rumours – what he calls "gypsys [*sic*] warnings" – have told of a police crackdown on the Columbus Circle branch of the Childs chain. "Tarrying a little in the rear," Clow learns that the two individuals are headed, in fact, to a new Childs, of which he was unaware, located in the Falkenhayn apartment building on 5th Avenue between 58 and 59 streets.[51] We are treated to descriptions of the fairies at this newly discovered venue "dishing the dirt," but what strikes Clow most is the absence of lesbians. These, a friend told him, were more likely to be found at a place called Louis', located at 17th West 49th Street. The following day, Clow goes to Louis' with Gentleman Jack O'Brien and another companion, identified only as "that brilliant bibliophile, Joseph R. F——." Chauncey's *Gay New York* notes the popularity of Louis' among queer populations, both in its 1924 location and, later, when it had moved to West 46th Street. Chauncey echoes, as well, *Brevities*' perception that the crowd at Louis', dominated by theatre people, was of "a better type" and more well-behaved than that to be found downtown. Still, the final page of this instalment, prompted by the appearance of a few lesbians in the restaurant, returns to the vicious condemnation of such women that was by now overrunning any other apparent purpose of the series. "Night No. 10 in Fairyland" concludes with the suggestion that, were psychotherapy to fail as a treatment for lesbians, "it were better for our generation that they be confined in asylums for the remainder of their lives."[52]

■■■

By this point in the "Nights in Fairyland" series, large portions of each episode were devoted to answering the series' critics, clarifying its purpose, and feuding with the editors of other magazines. The lengthy, even leisurely accounts of evenings on the town gave way to impassioned, sometimes convoluted attempts to put out fires. Of the various responses to the series acknowledged in the magazine, we may single out three for summary and analysis.

Queer Geographies

The first response involved the claim that "Nights in Fairyland" was too focused on queer life in midtown and Greenwich Village, and that its neglect of queer activity further uptown, among those of higher social standing, reflected the author's class prejudice or simple ignorance. A correspondent writing as "Mother Superior" had insinuated this neglect in a letter that *Brevities* had published. In "Night No. 10 in Fairyland" (October 1924) we find Clow scrambling to answer the charges.[53]

One rationale Clow offers for the series' neglect of queer life among social elites was that the places already visited in the series – Paul and Joe's, Trilby's, and the Gray Hen – were likely to attract the "high-class fairy" from uptown in search of companionship. In contrast, the "low-lived fag" would be unlikely to venture into the "gilded" environments of richer parts of the city. And so, we are asked to believe, a focus on these establishments of lower status was more likely to capture a broad sampling of Manhattan queer life.[54] Still, something in the accusation clearly offends Clow, who goes out of his way to convince the reader that few were better placed than he to provide an account of queer goings-on within the city's upper crust: "be you advised," he tells Mother Superior, "that I can charter a Yellow, and in fifteen minutes arrive at the place where aberrants, high in the seats of the Knickerbocker mighty, can be discerned disporting themselves after the well known fairy fashion."[55] In fact, the account of an evening spent in Chloe's uptown apartment, in episode 6, had already offered a glimpse into this variety of queer life.

In "Night No. 11 of Fairyland" (November 1924), we find the series' first and only reference to queer life among the Black populations of New York. The episode opens with a quick, panoramic view of the racialized order of queer Manhattan: "FAIRYDOM has its 'quarters.' In the Bowery poor and shabby fags of every breed may be seen; in the Bronx, fags of Jewish descent; in Mulberry street inverts Italiano; in Chinatown the comical oriental urning. Not less may be observed in the colored neighborhood of Lenox Avenue, on that long reach from 110th Street to 160th Street, hordes of 'big boys,' flamboyantly arrayed, plying the oldest and most noxious of all trades. And so on throughout the city – throughout the nation – throughout the world."[56]

In truth, *Broadway Brevities*' treatment of race, throughout the magazine's first incarnation, had more in common with the society magazines that preceded it, like *Town Topics*, than with the irreverent, vulgar digest magazines of the 1920s (like *Hot Dog* or *Capt. Billy's Whiz Bang*) with which it was sometimes lumped in later memory. While the society magazines were consistent in their exclusive focus on white populations, the folksy humour magazines that flourished in the 1920s were full of racist jokes and cartoons, or poems offering versions of Black American "dialect" speech. *Brevities* seemed mostly oblivious to the presence of African-Americans in the city, even when, in 1920, a Broadway show starring the Black performer Bert Williams borrowed the magazine's title for its own. More generally, we may see *Brevities*' geography of queer Manhattan as confined to a relatively narrow, albeit active, swath of the island: the regions below Columbus Circle and north of Houston Street. Harlem is missing from this cartography, as is the Bowery, so important to mappings of gay and lesbian life in earlier periods of the city's history.

Venomous Outrage

A second set of responses to the "Nights in Fairyland" series was less coherent. It involved the accusation that *Broadway Brevities*' attacks on queer life, rather than offering proof of a new and virtuous moral purpose for the magazine, represented nothing more than an amplification of the unscrupulous, destructive tendencies that had marked it since its launch. The July 1924 issue of *Broadway Brevities* carried an editorial, its title in all-caps, claiming "BREVITIES FEARLESS EXPOSES OF JOURNALISM JUSTIFIED." The frantic, defensive tone and denunciative anger of the piece suggest something of the climate at the magazine, which was now awaiting (and presumably preparing for) its trial for mail fraud. Pointing to forces that had reacted negatively to the "Nights in Fairyland" series, the article insists upon the necessity of its "crusade": "Now, the smug-faced moralists are beginning to crawl from their hypocritical cocoons, and are inclining to 'view with alarm' the appalling prevalence of homogendrous vice. Here in New York these same pharisaical fools have 'viewed with alarm' the exposures which BROADWAY BREVITIES has been brave enough to make."[57]

While it is unclear who else had expressed "alarm" at the "Nights in Fairyland" series, Clow uses this rant to denounce a publisher whose life and career had occasionally intersected with his: "Even the obscure pamphleteering panhandler of the Village 'Quill' – and pardon is begged for yanking him out of limbo for a moment – has raised his slobbered voice against our crusade."[58] While Clow and *Greenwich Village Quill* editor Bobby Edwards shared certain important friends, as we shall see in a later chapter, and moved in overlapping networks, their relationship was marked by what appeared to be ever-increasing levels of animosity. Clow's savaging of Edwards in his July 1924 editorial was likely in response to this attack, which appeared in the *Greenwich Village Quill*'s issue of June 1924 and made early reference to the judicial actions now underway against Clow and his magazine: "We heard that Broadway Brevities was pinched, but they still seem to be going. Our mephetic friend Klau, or whatever the opprobrious insect is who writes *Broadway Brevities,* seems to have some dirt on everybody. Certainly there is enough filth in one page of his 'Who's Who in Slime' to put him in Sing Sing for life." Edwards continues: "It is even intimated that he has something on Bro. Sumner himself. In case Mr Klau is not suppressed at his next opportune emergence we will assume as much, and that Bro. Sumner does not dare to do his obvious duty."[59]

Edwards's suggestion that Clow was in possession of personal information that deterred John Sumner (president of the New York Society for the Suppression of Vice) from going after *Brevities* is intriguing, but no further confirmation may be found. In any event, it is those plotting to close down *Broadway Brevities* who come in for the loudest anger in Clow's editorial, which concludes, again in all capitals, with this attack on his accusers:

> FIND A HATER OF BROADWAY BREVITIES – FIND THE CERTAIN NUMBER OF PRIVATE LADIES AND GENTS NOW CONSPIRING TO THROTTLE ITS BRAVE VOICE – AND YOU WILL FIND A GANG WITH "PAST PERFORMANCES" THAT REEK TO HIGH HEAVEN, AND THOSE "PAST PERFORMANCES" LINK THEM WITH JUST SUCH PERVERTS AND MORAL LEPERS AS ARE IMPLICATED IN THE EPIDEMIC OF PERVERSION NOW MAKING DECENCY A BY-WORD IN NEW YORK CITY![60]

The claim that "perverts" and "moral lepers" were behind attacks on *Brevities* would suggest that those going after him for blackmail were to be found among the queer communities described and denounced in the magazine's pages. In fact, as already noted, the charges and affidavits brought against *Brevities* and its staff, which had been publicly announced in May 1924, had little to do with the magazine's treatment of queer life and no apparent relevance to the moral crusade in which Clow and the magazine now claimed to be engaged. These charges were directed at Clow's other dirty work, his attempts to extort money from celebrities and business figures for indiscretions in their personal or professional lives.

Intimations of Queerness

The third response of readers to the "Nights in Fairyland" series involved the suggestion that those responsible for the articles might themselves be homosexual. Half of episode 12 was spent responding to a letter signed "Exzema – The Bowery Butterfly" and dated 24 November 1924. It claimed to have been sent from the "Home for Ancient Fags, Squeedunk on the Hudson," though whether this return address adorned the original letter or was an editorial invention on *Brevities*' part is unclear. The letter is reprinted in the magazine, presumably in full, and its main message is quite remarkably direct:

> Since you are so interested in the welfare of humanity in this respect and are so against the doings of homo-sexuals, how come that whoever it is who writes your afore mentioned articles is so familiar with all the fagot terms, places of meeting, etc., for you know the old saying, "birds of a feather," etc., and any one with a half a grain of sense can readily see that these articles are merely written by a "passe" [*sic*] b—— who, not being able to fly her queer form around without fear of being beaten by rough trade, is now trying her best to make things unpleasant for her younger and more campish sisters.[61]

The paragraph that follows urges *Brevities* to go after the "queer doings" to be found in so many current Broadway shows, but this seems inconsequential relative to the accusation that precedes it. The letter's "P.S. – I dare you to publish this missive" is clearly in reference to the suggestion that the "Nights in Fairyland" series was itself written by a gay man.

To readers of the series who might have wondered how Clow and his companions fit so easily into the coteries they met on their various outings, the question of whether Clow himself might have been gay was likely to occur to his readers. Likewise, the accusation that the series' author was "passe" and spiteful toward the members of a more youthful scene would have been especially hurtful to Clow, most of whose declared enemies – like the log-rolling literary critics and modernist writers he despised – were younger than him. Clow, who was obviously under no obligation to publish the letter, responds in a way that seems intended to settle for good the question of his own inclinations: "We do now attest before God that, to the best of our knowledge and belief, each and every attache of this home-loving sheet is morally and chemically pure. No one having a hand in these already world-famous exposures but is coldly aloof from this most infamous of all traffics in sex."[62]

Almost as if he has lost focus, the author moves from this response to an account of wanderings around Times Square and Murray Hill, then over to Riverside Drive, dropping a number of names of queer individuals living in these neighbourhoods in disguised form. Then, curiously, the tone grows nostalgic: "The present generation must not think that these waves of unbridled homo-sexuality have beaten upon the shores of only our own era." We are then given the outlines of an earlier queer geography of Manhattan, one that Clow had already sketched at least twice in the magazine: "Years ago, there were the Black Cat on Bleecker, Columbia Hall, near Cooper Union, and dozens of fairy nests with big trade in the side streets near Madison Square. Indeed, the Everard Baths were once raided, and – years before that – the Lafayette Baths (where Robt. L– K- used to go) and, still other years before, the Ariston Baths, where Lillian Russell lived upstairs. The latter more than twenty years ago."[63] Finally, in a curious admission of vulnerability, before moving on to the ritual condemnation that concludes this episode like most in the series, Clow describes the risk of encounters with the fairy: "One glance from those lustrous, doe-like eyes is enough without the voice. The fairy's gaze, when you encounter it, does not, like the normal person's, shift from you indifferently, but lingers with soulful coquetry."[64]

The Series Concludes

With episode no. 13, in the January 1925 issue of *Broadway Brevities*, the "Nights in Fairyland" series came to a close. This would be the last issue of the magazine in its first incarnation, and, by the end of January, Clow would be found guilty of mail fraud and held in the Manhattan Detention Complex (the Tombs) while he awaited sentencing. This final issue of the magazine offers few clues about the forces closing in on it. Compared to other recent issues, it is relatively free of tirades against *Brevities*' enemies or over-wrought defences of its mission. In one of the rare cases of a man featured on the cover, this issue is adorned with a photograph of the entertainer and club owner Harry Richman.

"Night No. 13 in Fairyland" begins with the announcement that this instalment will simply "drop in, informally, here and there," and indeed, there is a randomness to this final entry. The author offers news of the opening of a "Fairy Private Club" on Christopher Street, an institution made necessary, he suggests, by an intensification of police raids on public establishments. Claiming to have gained entrance to the club, the author promises to provide full details of ownership and membership in a later instalment. *Brevities*' reporters then revisit Paul

Figure 3.1 Final issue, *Broadway Brevities*, January 1925.

and Joe's restaurant in Chelsea, and while the description of queer goings-on there differs little from that in the third episode, the clientele now seems to include more people from the outer boroughs – a sign, the narrator claims, that the coverage appearing in *Broadway Brevities* had drawn new customers to the place.[65] (This new popularity of Paul and Joe's following coverage in *Broadway Brevities* was confirmed in the observation by car thief Jackie Rogers quoted in the Preface.) A noteworthy feature of this episode is a full page of drawings of "Fag Types" by Gentleman Jack O'Brien. as observed in the Village and at the 59th Street Childs.

The episode ends with the attempt to find Helen Dixon's Little Gray Hen club, first visited in "Night No. 7 in Fairyland" but subsequently forced out of the Village. It had reopened, the author claims, at 50 Lexington Avenue, but there, too, it had been closed by the police. The author and his companion find themselves on a street so empty and desolate that "we thought we were in Brooklyn." They grab a taxi: "'To Dolly Judge's in the Village,' we yelled frantically – 'and whip up the spare tires.'"[66] This is the last line of the thirteenth episode of "Nights in Fairyland." An editor's note promises that the next instalment will take readers to a Turkish bath. That episode was never published.

After-lives of "Nights in Fairyland"

To fully understand the impact of the "Nights in Fairyland" series would require that we know more about two sorts of possible effects. One was the role of *Brevities'* coverage in leading the New York police to close queer venues like the Little Gray Hen. In the advertising copy quoted at the beginning of this chapter, we find *Brevities* taking credit for the shuttering of three such places. Conversely, *Brevities'* coverage may have amplified the visibility and appeal of locations like Paul and Joe's or the venues of midtown, whose more broadly based popularity may have rendered them less vulnerable to police action directed specifically at their gay and lesbian clientele.

At the time of its publication, the "Nights in Fairyland" series seems to have received little or no comment in the New York press. One hostile response to the

Figure 3.2 "Fag Types." *Broadway Brevities*, January 1925.

series came from across the ocean. *Jazz: A Flippant Magazine* was an English-language periodical published in Paris from 1924 to 1927, edited during the time that concerns us by an Arthur de Grezan.[67] (Its tone, the masthead promised, was "*humoristique, théâtral, sportif.*") The "jazz" of the title referred more broadly to the spirit of an age than to a musical form, and the magazine was full of columns chronicling Parisian nightlife and advertisements offering pornographic books or "exotic relationships." In its 15 November 1924 issue, *Jazz* mounted the first of two attacks on *Broadway Brevities* and its exposés of queer life in New York. An unsigned column, "Between Ourselves," began its assault by noting that certain unspecified forces were attempting to import a puritanical "suppression of vice campaign" from the United States into Paris itself. The author pointed to *Brevities*' series on queer Manhattan as a model of what such a campaign might bring with it:

> Our concern is with a series of articles entitled "Nights in Fairy Land" which are advertised as an exposure of the Greenwich Village homosexual haunts. From the sociological and all sorts of other "ogical" points of view we suppose that the disciples of Catullus and Sappho are a little wanting, our feeling, however, is that as nearly all the cleverest people since the world began have been a little warped in their sexual activities, we would sooner have all the homosexuals in the world than the filthy minded garbage crawlers who turn out the monthly 35 cents worth of tripe mentioned above.[68]

The *Jazz* columnist saw the "Nights in Fairyland" series as an expression (if not an instrument) of the ascendant climate of intolerance in the United States. "If the New York police were to turn their attention to the dung heap wallowers of *Broadway Brevities*," the column concluded, "they would be better employed." That *Jazz* followed *Brevities* closely is clear from the French magazine's "borrowing" of a tiny drawing of an effeminate man – which had illustrated "Night No. 9 in Fairyland" – to adorn the title of an article on "Berlin's Fairy-Land."[69] It is unclear whether Clow ever saw *Jazz*'s attack on him; it goes unmentioned in the last two issues of *Broadway Brevities* published after the *Jazz* article appeared.

In its 15 February 1925 issue, *Jazz* returned to *Brevities* with a lengthier treatment. It made clear that its (unnamed) author, writing as "The Lounger," had been following the just-concluded *Brevities* trial with interest and no small degree of satisfaction:

> No, it's not the blackmail business that we've got up against Mr G. S. Clow [*sic*], the gentleman who is standing trial, it's the canting snivelling hypocrisy of his dirty rag that, under the cloak of exposing social evils, supplies a regular aphrodisiac, in the shape of doses of Sex talk, the prime object of which is to tintilate [*sic*] the mucky desires of an Onanic public who publicly supporting the Purity leagues, privately appease their miserable sexual appetites by delving into the muck raking tripe of "Broadway Brevities" and a host of other putrescent rags of a similar nature.[70]

Later in his career, Clow quite obviously recognized the titillating, voyeuristic appeal of his exposés of queer life. As later chapters show, Clow recycled material from the "Nights in Fairyland" until the end of his life – first in those New York–based periodicals for which he wrote in the early 1930s and then, a decade later, in magazines he helped to launch in Toronto. If the gossipy timeliness of these "Nights" would fade with time, Clow could still dredge up old anecdotes from the series to conjure the image of a Golden Age of Manhattan nightlife, one in which queerness came to function more as a sexy effervescence that had faded with time than a scourge to be condemned.

Deciphering Stephen G. Clow

Given the intensity of Clow's commitment to exposing queer life in the 1920s (and again in the 1930s), we cannot help but speculate as to his motives. Was Clow simply exploiting, for commercial reasons, that well-documented shift in attitudes that, by the 1920s, had made the "homosexual" both a distinct target of legal action and an object of public fascination? At different moments in his career (in 1924 and again in the 1930s), we find Clow calling loudly for legal action (or violence) against queer people even as he proudly brandished his insider's knowledge of the scenes in which they moved. The easiest explanation of Clow's preoccupation with queer lives is that he himself was a closeted gay man and that his tirades against queer life functioned at multiple levels: as strategic efforts to deflect the suspicions (or even accusations) that might gather around him; as resentful attacks on circles and scenes that, for reasons and in ways unknown, might have failed to accept him; and as the acting out in public of internal struggles of which he was scarcely aware. If each of these explanations gathers up well-worn psychological tropes, long used to "understand" the behaviours of the closeted queer man, each would also, in particular moments, find support in Clow's words or actions.

FOUR

THE DIRTY WORK OF BLACKMAIL

While Stephen G. Clow appeared to suffer no consequences for *Broadway Brevities*' treatment of queer New York in its "Nights in Fairyland" series, the other dirty work in which he engaged, that of blackmail and extortion, brought him imprisonment and disgrace. This chapter begins our account of this dirty work by delving into three of the most elaborate scandals in which *Broadway Brevities* was implicated and from which it sought to profit. Two of these were show business scandals and involved the tragic deaths of women working in the film industry – scenario writer Zelda Crosby and actress Claire Seymour. The third centred on promoters of the relatively new "science" of chiropractic, which Clow believed might generate lucrative advertising possibilities for his magazine within New York's theatrical communities. These three scandals affected Clow and *Broadway Brevities* in very different ways. Clow's involvement in the Zelda Crosby case was the possible cause of a hushed-up change in *Broadway Brevities*' ownership and an influx of money to the magazine. *Brevities*' exploitation of rumours surrounding the death of Claire Seymour resulted in the purchase of advertising by one of Hollywood's most high-profile filmmakers, D.W. Griffith. And while the attempted extortion of money from chiropractic educator B.J. Palmer was hardly a high-profile show business scandal, it left a paper trail on which prosecutors in New York based their first criminal charges against Clow and his magazine.

The Arts of Blackmail

Of the unanswered questions surrounding Stephen G. Clow's life and career, one of the most intriguing has to do with where, and from whom, he might have learned the arts of extortion and blackmail. The practice of collecting secrets about people's intimate lives, then threatening to publish these if payment of some kind was not made, had a long history in the worlds of sensational publishing, in New York and elsewhere. Cohen, Gilfoyle, and Horowitz have shown how the editor/publishers of New York's weekly "flash" papers of the 1840s supplemented revenues from newsstand sales and advertising with money from potential targets of malicious reporting, who paid editors to keep silent about their misdeeds.[1] The blackmail racket exposed by the *Brevities* trial of 1925 was one for which magazines and newspapers might have been invented. It was easy for unscrupulous publishers or editors to disguise their gathering of embarrassing information about individuals as part of the normal routines of reporting. Likewise, the threat to make public such information could assume concrete form as the intention to publish it (rather than simply "reveal" it to interested parties, as other forms of blackmail might threaten). And, perhaps most importantly, any money paid by victims to people wielding the threat could be disguised as part of a periodical's cash flow – as payment for advertising or purchase of shares in the magazine. *Broadway Brevities* made the demand for advertising the central feature of its blackmailing strategy. There is reason to believe that on at least one occasion, the sale of ownership of the magazine brought other benefits from one of its targets.

If Stephen G. Clow had served an apprenticeship in the art of blackmail, one possible teacher was Colonel William d'Alton Mann, publisher of the society and gossip magazine *Town Topics* from 1891 until his death in 1920. In 1906, Mann was the focus of a highly publicized criminal trial after he brought suit against Norman Hapgood, editor of *Collier's Weekly*, for libel. Hapgood had published an editorial accusing Mann of running *Town Topics* as a blackmail racket – of drafting items that might embarrass members of New York society and then offering to "pull" the stories in return for payment. Mann's libel suit against Hapgood, it quickly became apparent, was ill-advised. *Collier's* had conceived the offending editorial deliberately to push Mann to sue in order that a trial might expose his operations.[2] The testimony of witnesses at the trial confirmed Mann's sleazy practices and described them in detail. His techniques included warning people that the magazine had news harmful to their reputation, then offering to pull the news in return for payment. This payment was usually disguised as a purchase of stock in the magazine or as a fee for inclusion of one's name in a forthcoming book-length directory of important people. The trial made public a long list of names of well-to-do people who had paid Mann for his silence. A jury acquitted *Collier's* of the charge of libel brought by Mann, and indeed, the court procedure unfolded as if Mann and *Town Topics* were the defendants. Mann died in 1920, but *Town Topics* lingered until the early 1930s, when it was shut down after the New York Bureau of Securities revealed that its later owners had continued selling stock to those of social standing in return for the magazine's silence about their private lives.[3]

Clow may well have followed the 1906 *Town Topics* trial with interest, though the larger question is whether at any point he had been involved in the magazine's operations. A search of digitized copies of the complete run of *Town Topics* turns up no mention of his name, and while articles in the magazine were normally unsigned, there are none whose focus or style are clearly Clow's. Nevertheless, a 1939 biography of American artist Louis M. Eilshemius includes an undated photo of Eilshemius sitting with a man described as "the bland Stephen G. Clow, then connected with the spicy society gossip sheet, Town Topics, and who was to become notorious as the publisher of the blackmailing Broadway Brevities."[4] In the 1925 *Broadway Brevities* trial, a witness testifying in support of blackmail charges against Clow and his collaborators on the magazine noted that one of the latter, A.S. Brown, had been known to her earlier through his associations with *Town Topics*.[5] In the memoirs Clow published in 1928 following his release from prison, he traced his own transformation into hard-core blackmailer to his hiring of Brown in 1922 (the year, he claimed, that marked the beginning of his descent into dirty work).[6]

The Film Industry Morality Panic

The two-year period from 1920 to 1922 was marked by a steady series of scandals within and around the American film industry. Olive Thomas, the lead actress in the film *The Flapper* (1920) and a key figure in the emergence of a Hollywood star system, died of a drug overdose in Paris in 1920. While the death was ruled "accidental," press reports claimed it had followed a "wild party" in Montmartre. In July 1921, the attorney general of Massachusetts rekindled public interest in a scandal involving a party for film industry executives and personnel that had been held in a Massachusetts roadhouse, the Mishawum Manor, in 1917. That event, it was alleged, had involved an orgy of wine and sex, with the participation of prostitutes. Among those present at the Manor were Jesse Lasky and Adolph Zukor, top executives of the Famous Players-Lasky Corporation, who allegedly paid large sums of money to local public officials in return for their silence about the party. Then, on 5 September 1921, actress Virginia Rappe took ill in San Francisco at a party in the hotel suite of film star Roscoe "Fatty" Arbuckle. Rappe died of internal injuries on 9 September, and Arbuckle was charged with manslaughter. In 1922, in an effort to placate public outrage and hold off governmental regulation amidst this thicket of scandals, the industry established the self-regulating Motion Picture Producers and Distributors of America, Inc. (MPDDA), hiring former US postmaster William Hays as its first president.[7]

While the controversies surrounding the deaths of Olive Thomas and Virginia Rappe are well known to historians of Hollywood, less has been said about another death, which would lead to Stephen G. Clow's most elaborate and mysterious involvement in a film industry scandal. Zelda Crosby (née Anna Shuster) was born in New York City in 1898. She entered the film industry as an adolescent, with small acting roles in at least two films, then moved into employment off-screen, first typing scenarios and soon writing continuity treatments and scripts. Press coverage of Crosby's life repeated the industry's judgment that she was "too beautiful" to appear onscreen, but it was clear that she showed genuine talent as a writer.[8] While much of Crosby's continuity work went uncredited, she is confirmed as a scenario writer for the films *Wedding Bells* (1921), *The Desperate Hero* (1920), and *Everybody's Sweetheart* (1920).

On 16 June 1921, Crosby was discovered unconscious in her apartment on East 55th Street in New York. Diagnosed as having taken an overdose of the drug Veronal (one of the names under which the barbiturate barbital was marketed), she was taken to Bellevue Hospital, where she died on 19 June. The medical examiner who first reported on Crosby's death ruled that it was the result of an accidental case of poisoning. The case might well have ended there had it not been for the involvement of Stephen G. Clow and the larger context of heightened public scrutiny of film industry morality. Over the summer of 1921, rumours about Crosby's life and the circumstances of her death circulated with mounting intensity in New York City and within film industry circles. Friends of Crosby had apparently been surprised to learn that she died destitute, and that her funeral expenses had been covered by the Welfare Association of the Famous Players-Lasky Corporation.[9] At the same time, other details began to emerge regarding the immediate aftermath of her death. *Variety* was among the publications that speculated, soon after the announcement of Crosby's death, that she had died by suicide after being spurned by her lover, a film industry executive.[10]

By the end of the summer, newspaper reports were claiming that Stephen G. Clow had been seen entering Zelda Crosby's apartment shortly after her death,[11] and he would soon become a high-profile player in the affair. He told newspaper journalists that he had, in his possession, new information about Crosby's death and intended to present these to New York County District Attorney Edward Swann. This information, Clow boasted, would force a reopening of the medical examiner's original investigation and would rival, in sensationalism, news of the aforementioned 1917 Massachusetts orgy at the Mishawum Manor, now the focus of new judicial interest.[12] Newspapers began hinting, without mentioning his name, that Zelda Crosby's lover had been one of those chief executives of Famous Players-Lasky who had also been a key participant in the 1917 Mishawum Manor party.[13] The executive had allegedly thrown over Crosby for a new romantic interest, described in a wire service news report as a theatrical star "whose name in shimmering electric lights helps swell the nocturnal borealis of Broadway's tenderloin district."[14] Other reports claimed that a "woman friend of the dead girl was given $25,000 to suppress the facts of the sordid romance and is now being kept a virtual prisoner in a private hospital at a cost of $50 per day."[15] This unidentified friend was said to have prepared two affidavits containing the details surrounding these events. These, Clow told reporters, were in his hands and would be given to the assistant attorney general.[16]

By late August, sensationalizing newspaper reports were noting that, despite Clow's claims to have important facts about the case in his possession, he was not bringing them forward.[17] On 21 September 1921, the chief medical examiner for New York held secret hearings for the purpose of reconsidering the cause of Zelda Crosby's death. Clow had apparently already spoken to the examiner prior to the hearings, in another closed session. Among those who came to testify were Anna Schuster (Zelda's mother), a Mrs Gross (Crosby's housekeeper), and a woman identified as Mrs Hollywood, of the scenario department at Famous Players.[18] These hearings established that Crosby's mother was in possession of a letter from Zelda in which the now-deceased woman claimed that she was despondent because of a failed love affair and wished to take her own life. A second letter, with detailed instructions for the distribution of Zelda's possessions, had been left for those who found the body. These letters were presumably distinct from the affidavits allegedly prepared by Zelda Crosby's unnamed close friend.

As a result of the September hearing, Chief Medical Examiner Charles Norris revised the original ruling on Zelda Crosby's death, finding that she had died by suicide. While this brought legal closure to the case, it only intensified the waves of gossip that surrounded it, fuelling the tale that tied Crosby's death to rejection by a highly placed film industry lover. Housekeeper Gross would claim in later newspaper accounts that her first telephone call, on discovering Crosby's unconscious body, had been to the Famous Players studio, and that individuals from the studio had come immediately to the apartment.[19] In other reports, Gross was said to have told the coroner of multiple visits to the apartment by private detectives interested in the sorts of social gatherings Crosby had held there.[20] As for Clow, he now claimed to have seen neither of the letters left by Zelda Crosby,[21] and press coverage of the September hearing made no mention of the affidavits that he had earlier claimed to be holding in his possession.

In its September 1921 issue, as the mystery of Zelda Crosby's death continued to hang over New York, *Brevities* looked back at the Massachusetts scandal:

> Referring to that now extremely chestnutting affair at Mishawan [*sic*], where the movie maggots got caught with their (dress) goods, of course the dear papers couldn't go into the exact details. As a matter of fact BREVITIES had the complete story a few days after the affair was pulled off – in 1917 wasn't it? – but hesitated to publish for lack of complete verification … By the way, can anyone explain the mysterious elimination, from all recent lists of guests, of the name of a famous picture-theatre man of Broadway who, in the earlier reports, was stated to have been present?[22]

It is unclear who this "famous picture-theatre man of Broadway" was, but *Brevities* was almost certainly invoking the Mishawum events in order to make them a backdrop for the death of Zelda Crosby.

The Sale of *Broadway Brevities*

The story of Zelda Crosby's death assumes larger proportion in light of claims that a magazine threatening to publish affidavits linked to the event had been purchased by people connected to "a large film concern." The show business paper *Variety* advanced this story in its issue of 8 July 1921, adding that the sum paid to buy this unnamed magazine was said to be $25,000.[23] As Clow was the likely agent for these affidavits (selling them, if not arranging for them to have been produced in the first place), it is possible to conclude that *Broadway Brevities* itself was the magazine purchased by a Famous Players executive in order to buy its silence. Undermining this theory are references, in one newspaper account, to unnamed interests buying up "an entire edition of a weekly periodical" in order to guarantee its silence about the Zelda Crosby affair. *Brevities*, at this point, was a monthly.[24] As well, given that Clow's public hints about information in his possession were made most loudly in August 1921, it is difficult to understand why he would be pressuring his targets if the magazine had already been sold in June or July for money intended to buy his silence. It is also possible, as another historian has suggested, that the magazine purchased by people acting on behalf of Famous Players was the scandal-ridden *Film Truth* – a "small, and obscure, little magazine" as historian Anthony Slide described it[25] – whose last issue appears to have been that of July 1921.[26] (Still, that periodical, like *Brevities*, was published monthly.)

In fact, *Broadway Brevities* was sold in 1921, to an unnamed buyer who seemed to want little more than to make sure that the magazine temporarily ceased to exist. At the magazine's trial for mail fraud, in 1925, Assistant District Attorney Maxwell B. Mattuck revealed the sale without naming the purchaser, and Clow, in his testimony, confirmed it. More specifically, Mattuck suggested in his questioning that Clow had been paid money in 1921 to abandon the magazine.[27] Mattuck further noted that the magazine had been immediately relaunched following its "demise," with Clow's name no longer appearing on the new masthead, despite the fact that he retained editorial control. The only significant change, the prosecutor suggested, was a reorganization of *Broadway Brevities*' ownership and a renaming of the proprietary company from "Broadway Brevities, Inc." to "Brevities, Inc."

This mystery is compounded by contradiction and duplication in the numbering of issues of *Broadway Brevities* in the first half of 1921. One issue of the magazine bears a cover date of June 1921 yet indicates "May 1921" in its interior masthead. Another issue, with entirely different content, is dated "May 1921" both on the cover and inside. Both publications carry the same issue number (No. XV). The signs of a periodical in disarray are clear, but to connect them to the Crosby affair we would require two assumptions: that Clow was privy to information concerning the woman's private life prior to her death in June and that attempts to extort money from a Famous-Players executive on the basis of his liaisons with Zelda Crosby had begun before she died.

The July 1921 issue of *Brevities* was identified as vol. 1, no. 1, suggesting a new beginning, and the officers listed on the magazine's masthead changed. None of those listed in the June 1921 issue remained. George A. McCormick was now president; Thomas O'Connell vice-president; and Janice Clow (Stephen's wife as of 20 November 1920) secretary and treasurer. Nowhere in this first issue of the rebooted *Brevities* do we find an explanation of the reorganization of the magazine's management structure or renumbering of issues. If the shift in *Brevities*' masthead indicated a new ownership structure for the magazine, we may wonder whether Clow's silence was bought by a Famous Players executive, or people acting on his behalf. If payment to Clow for withholding accusations against that executive in the Crosby case was disguised as a purchase of the magazine, this would explain a number of things: the failure of the affidavits made by Zelda Crosby's friend being made public, the otherwise astonishing absence (given Clow's connections to the event and the high volumes of attention it received elsewhere) of any coverage of Crosby's death in *Broadway Brevities* itself, and the sudden re-incorporation of the magazine with new officers. That the magazine continued to publish suggests that any payment was not really intended to shut down the magazine but to purchase its silence on a specific matter.

By the fall of 1921, newspapers were running full-page feature stories linking Zelda Crosby's story to the death of Olive Thomas and other Hollywood scandals.[28] Readers were told that Crosby and Thomas had been friends and were reminded that Crosby had written (and sold to the Selznick corporation) the scenario for Thomas's last film, *Everybody's Sweetheart.* In a wide-ranging interview with journalists, Stephen G. Clow, identified in this instance as an expert on the "night life" of American cities, blamed the recent Arbuckle tragedy on the ubiquity of "illicit booze" and called for the enforcement of "real prohibition." Summoning a sense of outrage, he went on to bemoan the degraded moral character of the New York theatre world: "Broadway today is 16,000 times as bad morally as it was a few years ago. Frightful tales of pillage, attack and white slavery come to me from every quarter." Clow set Crosby's death against this backdrop of moral decline, claiming that she had "killed herself over an affair with a millionaire movie producer."[29]

Stephen Clow's involvement in the Zelda Crosby case over the summer of 1921 stands as one of the most remarkable sequences of events in his life and career. The profiles of the people involved, the amounts of money allegedly changing hands, and the ties to a transformative national panic over film industry morality endowed the Zelda Crosby affair with dimensions far beyond those of the other scandals on which Clow reported or from which he sought to profit.

Targeting D.W. Griffith

On 2 September 1921, a telegram signed "Broadway Brecites" (*sic*) was sent to the office of filmmaker David W. Griffith at Griffiths Studios in Mamaroneck, New York:

> WOULD LIKE TO RUN FULL PAGE PHOTOGRAPH YOURSELF ALSO EXTRA PAGE ADVERTISING IF POSSIBLE IN CONNECTION WITH YOUR PUBLICITY FOR TWO ORPHANS ON WHICH YOU ARE USING SUCH EXTENSIVE SPACE IN XXXX [STRIKE-OUT] OTHER PUBLICATIONS
>
> DO YOU THINK IT RIGHT TO IGNORE OUR MAGAZINE TERMS HAVE ALREADY BEEN DISCUSSED WITH MR. GRAY MAY WE HAVE THE PLEASURE OF YOUR IMMEDIATE ORGANIZATION THROUGH MR. GRAY TO CATCH OUR OCTOBER ISSUE CLOSING IN A FEW DAYS[30]

The telegram mentioned a man named "Gray" – D.W. Griffith's brother Albert Gray, general manager of the Griffith organization – and was intended to solicit advertising in *Broadway Brevities* for the film *Two Orphans*. This was the original title of Griffith's *Orphans of the Storm*, scheduled to open in the United States on 28 December 1921. *Brevities*' contacts with the Griffith organization apparently reached back to the previous year, during the production of the film *Way Down East*, and it was in connection with an alleged scandal involving this earlier title that the telegram was sent.

On 25 April 1920, Clarine Seymour, an actress in Griffith's stock company, died during the making of *Way Down East*, under circumstances that remain disputed. Seymour had been hired to play the relatively minor character Kate Brewster, a role eventually taken over by the actress Mary Hay. A widely circulated account claimed Seymour's death was the result of an operation for "strangulation of the intestines,"[31] but competing explanations would persist. Biographies of Griffith refer to the death as being by "mysterious affection" or "during emergency surgery."[32] Still another explanation, on a blog devoted to "The Dark Age of Hollywood," blames the cold weather in which *Way Down East* was filmed, and repeats a claim made by the film's star, Lillian Gish, that several of those involved in the film had fallen ill with pneumonia.[33]

Broadway Brevities set out to exploit public uncertainty over the cause of death of Clarine Seymour by threatening to print some of the rumours circulating in film circles about D.W. Griffith's treatment of the woman. The magazine's 1921 telegram to the Griffith organization made no mention of that death but mobilized several of the techniques used by the magazine's staff in their initial approaches to possible victims. A favourite among these was the expression of injured pride, the complaint that their magazine was not being taken seriously. ("Do you think it right to ignore our magazine?") Garrett Lloyd, an executive in the Griffith organization, scrawled a curt response on the back of the 2 September telegram, stating simply that "our adv. Council finds itself unable to avail itself of the opportunity to take 2 pages in your Oct. issue."[34] In a petulant telegram sent a week later, which suggested he had not seen Lloyd's response (or that, in fact, it had not been sent), Clow complained of not receiving any reply. "I cannot understand why your advertising is placed elsewhere and Brevities ignored."[35]

Brevities then moved to insinuate that the magazine was in possession of information harmful to the Griffith company. A note mailed to D.W. Griffith, dated 13 October 1921, warned the director that *Brevities* had been seeking dirt on Seymour's death and raised the spectre of other scandals, both sexual and financial. While the communication was unsigned and written as if it were a warning from a third party, it is reasonable to suspect that *Brevities* itself was its source:

> A friendly tip, Broadway Brevities has detectives digging up the death of Miss Seymour who worked for you say they are going to make a Fatty Arbuckle case in New York. Believe they sell their stories to a newspaper news service said they are to rip case wide open followed her life from day you asked to be introduced to her in a hotel in Los Angeles to her death Miss Gish to be involved also say they will show not using true name and hear they have data on flotation of stock.[36]

The issue of *Brevities* from the same month ran a peculiarly ominous paragraph-long item on Griffith that intensified the menacing tone. It began by noting that the set for Griffith's new film, *Two Orphans*, contained a guillotine and that, in one scene, actors in the film were grouped about "this deadly contraption." The item continued: "It is estimated that in less than an hour everyone in the set could be successfully accommodated with decapitation … Now if we could be there for about an hour … But really, it isn't right to talk this way."[37]

The Griffith archives contain no further correspondence involving Clow and *Broadway Brevities*. However, the testimony of Garrett Lloyd, identified variously as Griffith's scenarist and advertising manager, would be a key event in the magazine's later trial. On 20 January 1925, as he told the court about his dealings with *Brevities*, Lloyd described visits to the Griffith company offices by Nat Kunnes, who had presented himself as an "advertising solicitor" for the magazine. From the witness stand, Lloyd pointed to Kunnes, sitting in the court as a defendant, and said "He's the man." Kunne's visits, Lloyd claimed, had happened in late 1920 or early 1921. The witness described Kunnes, in these meetings, as having been "so nervous that his lips trembled."[38] Lloyd admitted in his testimony that he had signed contracts on behalf of the Griffith organization for advertising in *Brevities*. He continued: "Broadway Brevities had already printed an article about the death of a young girl during a motion picture's making, so I went to Mr Gray, our general manager, and suggested we give Broadway Brevities some advertising. We had $1,000,000 invested in the picture and we didn't want any mud thrown at it. Boosts don't hurt you, but knocks do, so I recommended two pages of advertising – $300 a page – $600 in all." By the time of the magazine's closure, Lloyd testified, total payments to *Brevities* for advertising had reached $2,000.[39]

All through 1922 and 1923, we find *Brevities* delivering on its promises to reward the Griffith organization with positive coverage in return for this advertising money. A full-page publicity shot of actress Betty Jewel in the August 1922 issue referred to "her debut in the great Griffith feature, 'Orphans of the Storm,'"[40] and a long review of that film in the October 1922 issue hailed Griffith's "tremendous artistic effort."[41] Then, in its January 1923 issue, *Brevities* seemed to pull out all the stops. A two-page review, with the title "David W. Griffith's Epochal Picture Creation 'One Exciting Night,'" was almost parodic in its gushing praise: "It is hard to imagine a film with higher possibilities for 'attendance records' than 'One Exciting Night' … And it shows that the master of screen-craft is at home in any métier, so vast and resourceful is his genius for the screen."[42] The July 1923 issue of *Broadway Brevities* featured a full-page advertisement for

Griffith's latest film, *The White Rose*.[43] In October, a mini-feature with the title "Another Masterpiece from Griffith" wrote glowingly of the contest to name Griffith's forthcoming film on the American Revolutionary War.[44]

The surviving correspondence between *Broadway Brevities* and the Griffith organization leaves us some of the clearest hints available of the magazine's success in extorting money in return for advertising. Other attempts, with different targets, were sometimes rebuffed, and many of those who paid the magazine for its silence did not bother disguising this as payment for advertising. The Griffith case makes clear the extent to which payment to the magazine might result in not only the suppression of harmful reporting but also lavish praise and promotional attention.

The Chiropractic Wars

On 10 April 1924, newspapers across the United States carried the news that Stephen G. Clow and two of his collaborators had been arrested the previous day on charges of using the mails to defraud. The charges were brought by a federal grand jury following several months of investigation. The specific crimes invoked were those of using the postal system to extort money and undertaking a conspiracy for that purpose. These charges made it a federal case rather than a municipal or state action against "immoral" or obscene publications, which were common in the 1920s and 1930s. Charges of mail fraud were often used by the US federal government to go after people against whom other charges might be difficult to prove, or to bring a federal dimension to crimes that might otherwise be appropriate for lower jurisdictions.[45]

The initial charges against *Brevities* were based on a single complaint concerning behaviour that might be construed as blackmail. This had come from B.J. Palmer, head of the Palmer Chiropractic School, which was based in Davenport, Iowa. Palmer claimed that *Brevities* had threatened to expose his school and its methods if he refused to purchase advertising in the magazine.[46] The accusations against *Brevities*, laid out in a document signed by US Postal Inspector William M. Pierson, described the strategy allegedly employed by the magazine:

> It was ... part of the said scheme and artifice, for the said defendants to attempt and cause to be attempted the procuring of the insertion of advertisements in the said magazine by the aforesaid Palmer upon threats made to the said Palmer that in the event of his failure to insert in the aforesaid periodical the said advertisements, attacks would thereafter be made upon the said Palmer and his business, occupation and profession in the said journal. It was further part of the said scheme and artifice for the said defendants to insert and cause to be inserted in the aforesaid periodical certain unscrupulous and indecent matter concerning the said Palmer by reason of the failure of the said Palmer to yield to the threats of the defendants as aforesaid.[47]

Gordon Kahn, identified as the assistant editor of *Brevities*, responded to the accusations made by the Palmer Chiropractic School with a public statement before the trial began: "There is no truth in the charges against this publication," Kahn said. "The attack is made on us by a chiropractor named Palmer, whose methods we exposed. What we did was a public service. The exposure took place three years ago and the indictment today is brought about through vengeance."[48]

Brevities' infatuation with the chiropractic profession might be dismissed as one of the magazine's idiosyncratic sideshows were it not for the role the Palmer Chiropractic School came to play in Clow's arrest and trial in 1925. A remarkably well-researched study, published in the journal *Chiropractic History* in 2013, offers details about the extent of Clow's obsession with the chiropractic profession and the firmness of his belief that it might provide a regular source of advertising revenue for *Broadway Brevities*. The article tells the story of a chiropractor named Francesco X. Sauchelli who, looking for ways to rescue his failing practice, discovered that patients could be found within New York's theatrical set through advertisements in magazines covering the Broadway scene. Sauchelli met Clow in late 1918 or early 1919 and began feeding him articles that touted the benefits of chiropractic treatment. Clow jumped on the opportunity to offer favourable coverage of such treatment in the hope of attracting advertisements from those who practised it. In fact, the *Chiropractic History* article tells us, this advertising did not materialize to the extent that Clow had hoped and Sauchelli had promised.[49] Clow's anger at the Palmer Chiropractic School for refusing to purchase advertising in *Broadway Brevities* led to a series of published denunciations of the school that claimed to expose its fraudulent practices.

Brevities' attacks on B.J. Palmer and his chiropractic school were some of the most vicious to be found in the magazine. They were directed less at the medical status of chiropractic itself than at Palmer's alleged attempts to dominate the profession and destroy the careers of other chiropractors who did not follow his methods. The three-part article "Bartlett Joshua Palmer, the Shylock of Chiropractic," in the September, October, and November 1922 issues of *Broadway Brevities*, was one of the few series in *Brevities*' history actually signed by Stephen G. Clow himself. The tone of the articles is remarkably unhinged, even by Clow's standards:

> Swinehounds, bellyachers, reptiles, renegades, cheaters, parasites, loafers, liars – these are among the sweetest of the epithets he [Palmer] has lavished on the helpless "mixers" [practitioners of a brand of chiropracty different from Palmer's]. Helpless, because on his Davenport Towers are implaced batteries of machine guns ready to spray a deadly hail of bullets upon any practitioner who dares to emit a word, or carry out an act that he, the mightly [*sic*] Oracle, the blood-thirsty Fooh-Bah of Palmerism has not set with his seal and superscription. In his basement an embattled affray of Hoe and Kelly groan and shriek through the long day and fearful night, vomiting the "Foolish House News" and carloads of posters, tracts and pamphlets through whose pages he is able to visit the terrors of his vengeance upon those he hates.[50]

Elsewhere in this series, Clow accuses B.J. Palmer of ethnic insults (of calling Italian practitioners of chiropractic, most probably Sauchelli himself, "wops") and of cavorting with young women in a New York apartment as they "patted Palmer's hair and kidded the old man silly."[51] The length and tone of Clow's three-part tirade against Palmer clearly had motives that went beyond the refusal of the Palmer Chiropractic School to purchase advertising in *Broadway Brevities*. Clow was incensed by what he saw as Palmer's efforts to control the profession by denouncing practitioners who showed no allegiance to his school but might nevertheless be interested in helping Clow and Sauchelli promote the profession in New York.

Had the case against *Brevities* been based solely on Palmer's complaint, events might have unfolded very differently. Certainly, the director of a chiropractic school in Davenport, Iowa, had little of the political clout or social profile likely to generate journalistic interest in New York or to provoke a widespread judicial investigation into blackmail. The prosecutor's original decision to base the arrest of Clow and his associates on Palmer's complaint alone appeared to be motivated by two factors. In the first place, Palmer was able to produce, as evidence, detailed letters in which Clow clearly pressured him to advertise in *Brevities*, threatening him with increasingly negative coverage of his school should he refuse. These were among the sturdiest proofs of *Brevities*' tactics to be made public, and among the very few that made use of the mails exclusively. At the same time, the public announcement that at least one victim was willing to sign a complaint against *Brevities* showed the government's commitment to taking action against this kind of extortion. This encouraged other injured parties, who would not have wished to be first, to now come forward as part of a broader move against *Brevities* and its practices.

The Brevities Indictment

The *Brevities* trial, in January 1925, would make the front pages of newspapers in New York and across the United States. It would bring Clow national notoriety and public humiliation and, for the rest of his life and career (and in his obituaries), would stand as the event for which he was best known. During the trial, a series of well-known theatrical stars, sporting personalities, and industry executives would tell a courtroom full of spectators and journalists how they had been pressured into paying money to *Brevities* and its staff to avoid negative publicity about their private lives or the enterprises with which they were associated. In a decade full of high-profile, sensational criminal trials in the United States, the claim by the *New York Sunday News* that the *Brevities*' proceedings were "the greatest show on earth"[52] was an overstatement, but it captured the circus-like atmosphere in which the trial unfolded. Press coverage of the *Brevities* proceedings was abundant and rolled out across the country in syndicated articles and photographic spreads.

Coming to Trial

The prosecution of Stephen G. Clow and *Broadway Brevities* unfolded in three phases. The first involved the initial arrest of Clow and two of his staff members on 9 April 1924 in response to a single complaint involving the use of the mails for the purposes of blackmail. This complaint had been made by the Palmer Chiropractic School and was investigated by the office of US Postal Inspector William M. Pierson.[53] The second came on 5 May 1924 when a federal grand jury brought down an indictment containing twelve counts of mail fraud, significantly expanding the number (and public profile) of people claiming to have been victims of *Brevities*' practices. Finally, on 19 January 1925, the *Brevities* trial began in United States District Court in Manhattan. It lasted until 29 January, when verdicts were handed down by a jury.

No newspaper appeared better prepared for Clow's initial arrest, on 9 April 1924, than the *Atlanta Constitution.* Its front-page lead, the following day, was a model of information-rich compactness: "Steve Clow, the 'Wolf of Broadway,' whose mind is an encyclopedia of old and new scandal in the theatre, the movies and Park avenue society, was arrested Wednesday for the first time in his long and daring career as a publisher of 'Broadway Brevities,' a small magazine known in the night life of New York as the 'Gold Diggers' Textbook.'"[54] The *Constitution* article described Clow as a "a pudgy-middle-aged man in no physical shape for a fight." It noted that he had been arrested, along with A.S. Brown and Charles J. Greene, at the *Brevities* premises in the Knickerbocker Building at 39th Street and Broadway.

Andrew S. Brown, later identified by Clow as his "chief-of-staff," had joined the magazine after ten years working on other society and scandal magazines (including *Town Topics*). Charles J. Greene was described in press coverage of the trial as an "advertising solicitor" for *Brevities*, and much would be made of his English accent, matinee idol looks, and the sympathies he curried with jury and audience. In the trial, Greene recounted having made his way to New York via Canada after his discharge from the British army.[55] Clow, Greene, and Brown were held on bail ($3,000, $1,500, and $3,000 respectively) pending a hearing scheduled for the end of April.[56] No charges were laid against Ella Hoyt, president of Brevities, Inc., the company publishing the magazine, nor its vice-president, Thomas O'Connell. (Ella Hoyt was Clow's niece – the daughter of his sister Mary – and living in Boston by this time; the extent of her active involvement in *Broadway Brevities* is unclear.)

In announcing the arrest of Clow, Greene, and Brown, William Hayward, US district attorney for the Southern District of New York, told the press that the move against *Brevities* was part of a broader cleanup of publications that were basically functioning as instruments of blackmail.[57] In a statement of his own, Assistant District Attorney Maxwell B. Mattuck, who would prosecute the case, likewise referred to other periodicals being targeted, noting that most of them had some connection to Broadway and the theatrical world.[58] The show business newspaper *Variety* linked the *Brevities* arrest to judicial action against another gossip magazine called *Cat's Meow*, whose editor, Henry Stucker, was accused, like Clow, of running his magazine as a blackmail racket.[59] However, no matter how much the trial of Clow and his magazine was initially framed as part of a broader move against Broadway magazines engaged in blackmail, the *Brevities* case was the only judicial action involving such crimes to garner widespread press coverage during this period.

Prosecuting attorney Mattuck would complain, on several occasions, about the difficulty he had convincing people to testify in the *Brevities* case.[60] Nevertheless, when a federal grand jury handed down its indictment on 5 May 1924, it was clear that, following the original complaint by the Palmer Chiropractic School, several more people had co-operated with prosecutors in their investigation. In a twenty-one-page document, the grand jury listed extortion attempts directed at a range of Broadway personalities, corporation owners, and entrepreneurs. B.J. Palmer's name was there, to be sure, but so were those of Lee Shubert; Frank B. Masten; Evelyn Neville; Texas Guinan; Scott's Preparations, Inc.; Dainty Form Corporation; and Childs, Inc. For each case, the indictment provided details as to the postal communication used to extract money. To conform to statute of limitations restrictions concerning mail fraud, the infractions listed in the indictment had all occurred after 5 May 1921, three years to the day before the charges were handed down. The general charges were that the magazine and its staff were engaged in "obtaining from the victims their money and property by means of false and fraudulent premises … [and that they] did for the purpose of executing such scheme and artifice and attempting so to do, use and cause to be used the mails and Post Office establishment of the United States for the transmission of letters, magazines and other writings."[61]

On 14 May 1924, Clow and his colleagues entered a formal plea of "Not Guilty." In response, Assistant Federal District Attorney Maxwell S. Mattuck claimed publicly that a great many people had overcome their reticence and offered to come forward as witnesses. One week later, the attorney acting for the defendants during this preliminary phase, Broadway-based lawyer Herman Joseph, filed a pro forma motion to dismiss the charges against Clow and the others. This was denied, and the trial was scheduled for December 1924.[280] It would not begin until late January 1925.

FIVE

BREVITIES ON TRIAL

Eight months passed between the *Brevities* indictment and the opening of the trial. During this period, the magazine was apparently benefitting from its new notoriety. In its November 1924 issue, an "Announcement" claimed that the magazine had reached new levels of success: "Broadway Brevities is now on sale in the principal cities of the United States. It is at present a top seller in New York, Chicago and Detroit. Wherever introduced Brevities soon takes a newsstand lead over all competitors."[1] In its final four issues, *Broadway Brevities* had added unsigned gossip columns on Chicago ("Chicago Chatter") and Detroit ("Detroit Dribbles"), clearly with an eye to expanding its appeal. In June 1924, perhaps to counter any such expansion, interests with no apparent connection to the New York periodical had launched a weekly magazine called *Chicago Night Life and Society Gossip*, which borrowed *Broadway Brevities*' size, part of its title, interior layout, and front-cover typefaces.

During the second half of 1924, Clow set about organizing his defence. In a later account of his years with *Broadway Brevities*, Clow would claim that he had grossed $150,000 from the magazine and spent most of it on his "boulevardier lifestyle," leaving him only $10,000 at the time of the trial.[2] That amount, he said, had gone to his lawyers. As his chief defence attorney, Clow engaged William J. Fallon of the firm of Fallon and McGee. Fallon was already, and would

Figure 5.1 *Chicago Night Life and Society Gossip*, 1 December 1924.

remain, one of the most mythologized lawyers in American history, though not because of any association with *Broadway Brevities*. He was best known for having defended gangsters Arnold Rothstein and Nicky Arnstein in cases related to the fixing of the 1919 World Series. Fallon's talents, lifestyle, and personality would be the focus of Gene Fowler's *The Great Mouthpiece*, a posthumous biography, published in 1933, in which the *Brevities* trial is not mentioned.[3] In 1925, Fallon was only two years away from a death attributed to alcohol, and in 1924 he had been publicly humiliated (though acquitted) on charges of jury tampering. Nevertheless, as journalist Westbrook Pegler noted in his coverage of the *Brevities* trial, Fallon's lingering reputation as a trial attorney might well have dissuaded potential prosecution witnesses or complainants from taking part in the court action. "Fallon's cross-examination," Pegler wrote, "is enough to make a witness with anything to hide, shrivel in the chair."[4]

The jury trial of "United States versus Stephen G. Clow and the Broadway Brevities," originally scheduled to begin in mid-December 1924, finally opened on 20 January 1925, with Judge Julian Mack of the United States District Court presiding. In its coverage of the trial's opening, the *Daily News* speculated that "witnesses will be composed of three types of New York society: the business man, the theatrical celebrity, and the man about town," a list that obscured the large number of women testifying but effectively captured the variety of personality types to be heard from. The same article also repeated the prosecution's promise to the jury that they would hear testimony from prominent theatrical producer Florenz Ziegfeld and film director D.W. Griffith, though neither of these would appear in court.[5] Between the original indictment (in May 1924) and the opening of the trial, a fourth defendant had been charged: "advertising solicitor" Nat Kunnes, whom Garrett Lloyd of the Griffith organization had named as a significant figure in *Brevities*' extortion of advertising money. Kunnes's presence at the trial became a source of comic relief for journalists covering the proceedings. Reporters described him, variously, as an "erratic little man" and "a tiny man almost hidden behind an enormous pair of horn rim glasses."[6]

The Trial Begins

The jury in the *Brevities* trial was sworn in on the morning of Tuesday, 20 January 1925. In the afternoon, the prosecuting attorney laid out the government's case, reading excerpts from issues of *Broadway Brevities* and warning the jury and audience that "mud would fly."[7] The prosecution's first witness was Gordon Kahn, who, in the interim between the first arrests of *Brevities* personnel and the opening of the trial, had apparently left his position as assistant editor of *Broadway Brevities* and now testified against the magazine. Kahn would quickly follow a career path like that of many who passed through the Broadway-focused press on their way to more prestigious venues. After working for *Broadway Brevities*, Kahnt would write for *Zit's Theatrical Weekly* before moving on to the *New York Herald* and the *New York Mirror*. Like Mark Hellinger, who had also worked for *Zit's*, Kahn went from newspaper journalism to a career in Hollywood. His first produced screenplay, for the 1931 film *X Marks the Spot*, was set in the worlds of New York tabloid journalism, though it contains no explicit references to Clow or to *Broadway Brevities*. Gordan Kahn is remembered today as one of the screenwriters fired by the Hollywood studios in the 1940s for alleged involvement in communist activities. He would later write the book *Hollywood on Trial* (1948), about the anti-communist witch hunts in the film industry.

In his testimony at the *Brevities* trial, Kahn claimed that most of the information used by the magazine to attack people came from anonymous telephone calls and letters.[8] Mattuck's questioning of Kahn centred on *Brevities*' attempts to extract money from John Bowman, owner of the Biltmore and Commodore hotels. Kahn testified that when Robert J. Kennedy, advertising manager for the hotels, had rebuffed the magazine's initial attempts at extortion, *Brevities* had published items suggesting the hotels tolerated prostitution on their premises. Indeed, the Bowman hotels had been one of the most frequent targets of *Brevities*' attacks over several months. In its August 1922 issue, *Brevities* had called on Bowman to undertake a cleanup of his Biltmore Hotel, describing it as a "Mecca of the demimondaine."[9] Kahn told the court that an unsigned letter sent to John Bowman had read "Jack, they're getting after you. A Friend," and Kahn identified the handwriting as Clow's. Eventually, the hotel chain purchased advertising in the magazine.

On 21 January, the court heard from Garrett Lloyd, advertising manager for D.W. Griffith. The details of Clow's extortion from Griffith have already been discussed, but two further revelations illuminate the murky relationships on which the events in question rested. Under cross-examination by defence attorney William J. Fallon, Lloyd admitted that he was a friend of *Brevities* advertising solicitor Andrew S. Brown, one of the accused, and conceded that this friendship probably played a role in his ultimate decision to purchase advertising in the magazine. Lloyd further revealed that Nat Kunnes, the *Brevities* employee who had first pressured him to buy ads, had returned to visit him on future occasions, offering to testify against Clow in any action that the Griffith organization might initiate against the editor.[10]

Miracle Cures and Beauty Treatments

Several of the prosecution witnesses who testified in the *Brevities* trial were associated with health and beautify products, and their cases were similar enough that they may be briefly summarized together. Witness Arthur J. Karr was treasurer of the company Scott's Preparations, which manufactured a "beauty treatment" called Mineralava. Karr described an initial visit to his office by Charles Greene, who offered advertising space in *Brevities* and threatened negative coverage of Mineralava in the magazine's pages if this were not purchased. When Karr refused, *Brevities* claimed the product was "hokum," "Outrageous Humbug," and "Ordinary Mud" in passages from the magazine read aloud to the court.[11] In similar testimony, Evelyn Neville, treasurer of the Dainty Form corporation, which produced a "fat-reducing compound," described how, when she refused to purchase advertising, *Brevities* had cast doubt on the scientific basis of its product. It ran a full-page take-down of the product with subheadings like "'Dainty-Form Chemist' as hard to find as Usher's Green Stripe."[12] George F. Kerr, advertising manager and partner of Masten and Co., manufacturers of a product called Vitamin, told the court of being approached in 1922 by a man calling himself McKenna. The visitor, who was really *Brevities* advertising solicitor Andrew S. Brown, bragged that *Brevities* had all the dirt on goings-on in New York, including information harmful to the personal reputation of the company's president, Frank B. Masten. Kerr testified that when he had refused the pressure to advertise, the magazine published descriptions of Vitamin as a "terrifying product."[13]

Businesses like these were a recurrent target of *Brevities*' schemes, and central to the defence's later claims that the magazine wanted nothing more than to perform a public service by exposing fraud and quackery. This strategy floundered in the face of evidence that the magazine had promoted most of these products in their editorial content until the moment when their manufacturers refused to purchase advertising.

Thrilling Broadway Tales

Near the end of the trial's second day, the prosecution called Helen Lee Worthing to the stand. Her turn as witness heightened journalistic interest in the case and confirmed its status as a genuine Broadway story. Worthing was a well-known performer in the Ziegfeld Follies who would achieve some success onscreen in the late silent film period. In her tragic and relatively short life (she died in 1948), she was the victim of physical assaults, drug addictions, forced institutionalization, and the scandal of a secret marriage, eventually revealed, to an African-American doctor. In 1922, Worthing had attempted suicide by ingesting bichloride of mercury, apparently in despair over press coverage of a dressing-room fight between herself and another chorus girl.

Brevities had revelled in the off-stage tragedies of female Broadway performers, taking particular delight in the signs of their decline: their failed marriages, drug addictions, and any recourse to practices intended to hide the signs of aging. In 1922 and 1923, *Brevities* published a number of items containing derogatory references to Worthing. Its February 1923 issue included, as part of a two-page feature full of Broadway gossip, an item with the title "'Helen of the 'Follies' Heads Defence League," which began as follows: "BROADWAYITES in the know are tied in knots at the biggest laugh of the season! This laugh is the organization of the Ziegfeld Chorus Defence League with – who do you think as manageress? – Helen Lee Worthing? Helen's been known as the 'bichloride kid' since her reported attempt last fall to boost trade for old man Campbell."[14] The "old man Campbell" referenced here was undoubtedly Frank E. Campbell, owner since

1898 of a Manhattan mortuary that hosted the funerals of several generations of Hollywood stars (including, eventually, Fatty Arbuckle).[15] Calling Worthing the "bichloride kid" was one of several cruel references *Brevities* made to her attempted suicide, which the magazine hinted had been little more than a publicity stunt. At the *Brevities* trial, prosecutor Mattuck read into evidence an October 1922 *Brevities* item describing Worthing as having "hit the bichloride route."[16]

Worthing's picture appeared on the front page of the *Daily News* on the day following her testimony, with a caption stating that she had paid "to have her pretty face printed on the cover of Broadway Brevities."[17] On the stand, Worthing described how *Brevities* first approached her in 1922, offering to keep her name out of the publication in return for a cash payment. When she refused to respond, derogatory references to her, like those cited above, appeared in the magazine. Worthing further testified that in May 1923 she had received a visit from Charles Greene, who offered to print Worthing's picture in *Brevities* if she paid $150 to the magazine. At Worthing's request, Greene telephoned Clow from her apartment and received the promise that, if Worthing were to make the payment, she would appear on the cover and all unfavourable coverage would stop.[18] Worthing accepted the offer. Her picture filled the cover of *Brevities*' July 1923 issue.

At day's end on Friday, 23 January, as the *Brevities* trial adjourned for the weekend, the judge alerted everyone in attendance to the possibility that nighttime sittings might be necessary the following week. When the trial resumed on the morning of Monday, 26 January, those present were treated to testimony widely viewed as sensational.[19] This day's proceedings included accounts of relatively minor blackmailing approaches by the *Brevities* staff to the Vivaudou perfume company (which paid $500 for an end to negative coverage) and the H.R. Mallinson silk company (who refused payment). However, the greatest public interest was directed at what the *Daily News* called the "'Thrilling Broadway Tales' of 'modiste' Edith Bobe, boxing promoter Tex Rickard and show business personality Peggy Hopkins Joyce."[20]

Edith Bobe, described in one account as "the best-informed individual on Broadway next to Steve Clow,"[21] was a milliner and costume designer. In 1924, she had been robbed of $25,000 worth of jewels from her apartment. The interest of *Brevities*' staff in her predicament rested on their knowledge of the fact that, at the time of the robbery, she was in the company of a married man, Robert

Figure 5.2 *Broadway Brevities*, July 1923.

Hague, an executive of the Standard Oil Company. (Hague would later divorce his wife and marry Bobe.) In her testimony, Edith Bobe said *Brevities* had asked for $350 to guarantee its silence about the liaison, but that she had initially refused. Mattuck read into the record apparent references in *Brevities'* January 1924 issue to "Mlle Bobe and her married gent" and "Miss Bobe's mysterious career."[22] The following issue carried a long paragraph on Bobe and her liaison with "Haig," which noted that "Bobby's got a perfectly good little wife and a couple of kiddies attached to his domestic menage."[23] Seemingly defeated, Bobe had sent the magazine $75, asking that it be used to pay for an advertisement promoting the recent book by journalist Nellie Revell, *Right Off the Chest.* A separate approach by the magazine to Robert Hague was rebuffed.

Peggy Hopkins Joyce, who at the time of the trial (and as a result of her marriage to a Swedish count) was now known as Countess Costa Morner, would become one of the trial's most important witnesses. She was certainly among the most illustrious. Joyce was widely believed to be the model for the character Lorelei in Anita Loos's 1925 novel *Gentlemen Prefer Blondes* and was viewed as a personality almost perfectly emblematic of her era. She appeared in films and Broadway shows throughout the 1920s and was known for a series of marriages and affairs with wealthy men, about which she spoke and wrote publicly with little restraint. *Town Topics*, the long-lived gossip weekly, regularly carried items on Joyce, and her name ran through a long series of features in the daily press of the 1920s, either in the columns of others or in confessional pieces she wrote herself.[24] Joyce had been approached by *Brevities* in late 1923, after derogatory references to her had appeared in the magazine. These included the claim that she was one of those financing the latest version of Earl Carroll's *Vanities* show, and that the theatrical producer Oliver Morosco "had a pair of forceps put on her bank roll."[25] Joyce was appearing in *Vanities*, she testified, when she was visited by Clow in the company of a man named D.J. Thomas, who identified himself as *Brevities'* secretary. Clow and Thomas promised that degrading references to Joyce in the magazine would cease if she purchased advertising. Joyce paid Thomas $200 to have her picture reproduced in *Brevities* and for an end to the magazine's insulting coverage.

Joyce's testimony was pivotal in the trail because she had asked Thomas for a receipt for the $200 and been given one. When he had learned of this, Clow, conscious of the danger it posed, had sent *Brevities'* staff member Andrew S. Brown to Joyce's dressing room to ask for return of the receipt, but Joyce refused. Thomas himself then visited her, in despair, claiming that Clow had fired him for providing the receipt and begging her to give it to him. Again, Joyce refused. In his book on the culture of the 1920s, novelist and journalist Donald Henderson Clarke claims that Peggy Hopkins Joyce's possession of a receipt for payment to *Brevities* made her the most important witness in the trial.[26] Thomas's naive honesty meant that prosecuting attorney Mattuck was able to show the court the only existing proof of payments made to *Brevities* by someone claiming to have been a victim of extortion.

As it happened, Joyce's payment did improve the tone of the magazine's coverage of her, albeit briefly. In its October 1923 issue, before payment was made, the magazine had commented viciously on her appearance: "Peg looked like the headline of the Empire State Express with her 40-carat solitaire diamond, but unfortunately her looks have said goodbye. She's as thin as a fence rail and rather pitifully faded and forlorn."[27] In its December 1923 issue, however, under a flattering photographic portrait of Joyce, the magazine offered up excessive praise: "Dazzling the 'Vanities' S.R.O. each night. A peculiar thing is the general idea of Peggy as a heartless vamp. As a matter of fact this beautiful girl's personality is of a most unaffected simplicity, with sweet, wholesome ideas about life and living and brimming with an almost childish charm that wins all hearts."[28]

Joyce's life was interwoven with that of other participants in the trial in ways that underscored the tightly knit character of the Manhattan circles in which *Broadway Brevities* circulated. Joyce had dated Clow's attorney William Fallon, a fact used to explain Fallon's absence from the courtroom on the day of her testimony. He was replaced as defence attorney by his partner, Edward F. Reynolds.[29] In his cross-examination of Joyce, Reynolds laboured to show that Joyce had mixed with Clow socially at nightclubs, as if to suggest that her courtroom rancour toward him was invented for the trial. Reynolds asked the witness whether, while touring in Indianapolis in 1924, she had not sent Clow a telegram containing the salutation "love and kisses," suggesting a warm rather than adversarial relationship between the two.[30] Joyce denied the existence of any such telegram, though Fallon, when he returned to arguing the defence's case, threatened to introduce it as evidence.

The last of the high-profile witnesses in the prosecution's case against *Brevities* was sports promoter George Lewis "Tex" Rickard. The place of Rickard in US sports history rests on several accomplishments: he founded the New York Rangers and built the first version of Madison Square Garden. That said, Rickard's testimony against *Brevities* had little effect on the outcome of the trial. He claimed that he had paid *Brevities* $250 after the magazine ran "uncomplimentary references" about him. After the payment, the magazine named him "Richard the Great" and described him as "an asset to charities and the friend of clean sport."[31] Rickard's presence on the witness stand, however brief, was widely noted in press coverage of the event.

The Defence Begins

The prosecution unexpectedly closed its case at the end of testimony on Monday, 26 January. By this point, as newspapers noted, the trial had become a circus, with large numbers of would-be spectators storming the courtroom as the doors opened. A lengthy news-wire article described a large crowd at the courtroom on the morning of 27 January and claimed that the prosecution's decision to rest had left many witnesses (most of them women) frustrated. With its colourful evocation of the atmosphere surrounding the trial, the article is worth quoting at length:

> Disappointment reigned today in the ranks of the little army of sensation hounds who crowded the courtroom of Federal Judge Julian A. Mack, hoping to get the "low down" on the private lives of some of Broadway's glittering figures.
>
> They had returned, these habitués of the great white way, eager to take the stand for a second time and deny the truth of stories which the scandal sheet, "Broadway Brevities," had printed against them – allegedly in an effort to extort money for "advertising."
>
> But – the United States, so Judge Mack told the White Way women, is not at all interested in, whether, for instance, Peggy Hopkins Joyce (the Countess Costa Morner), has been married five or twenty times, and what

> she did in between marriages, nor is it interested in the question of whether Edith Bobe, the modiste, who recently starred in a front page jewellery robbery here, is a "cradle snatcher."
>
> Money Only Questions
>
> The only question before the court, Judge Mack told them sympathetically, is whether or not they were made to pay money to avoid having these "unkind words" printed about them.[32]

The disappointment of those who might have thought they would be called to testify rested on the fact that the trial would not offer a platform in which they might refute claims made about them in the magazines. As Fallon began to make the defence's case on the morning of Tuesday, 27 January, his room to manoeuvre had already been narrowed by a ruling from Judge Julian Mack (alluded to in the news report quoted above) establishing that the government, in order to establish the magazine's culpability, need not determine the truth or falsity of articles appearing in *Broadway Brevities*. The prosecution merely needed to show that any information possessed (or claimed) by *Brevities* was used in an effort to extort money from victims.[33]

As Fallon made his opening remarks to introduce the defence's case, the multiple lines of his strategy became clear. One was to paint Clow as a crusader for truth, who exposed quack remedies (like Vitamin) for various kinds of ailments and the use of businesses (like the Bowman hotel chain) as fronts for vice operations. A second was to show that those claiming to be victims of *Brevities* and its staff were, in many cases, on friendly terms with their accusers – an unlikely state of affairs, he suggested, if *Brevities* had been blackmailing them. Finally, Fallon hoped to show that the so-called victims of *Brevities*' blackmail were often the ones initiating any discussion of payment for silence, and that they did not make these payments under pressure.

The first day of defence testimony was taken up with examination of three members of the Brevities staff: Andrew S. Brown, Charles Greene, and Nat Kunnes. Brown, sometimes described as Clow's "chief of staff," testified that *Brevities* simply approached the rich and famous to encourage them to promote their ideas or favourite causes by advertising in *Brevities*. The magazine made no threats, he insisted; it was simply the case that "big men advertised their hobbies, as big men often do."[34] Much of the drama provided by Brown came during his cross-examination by Mattuck, when the *Brevities* staffer provided a list of well-known financial, industrial, and cultural elites who had all paid money to the magazine. Numerous newspapers covering the trial printed the list of names alongside the amounts that they had paid according to Brown: "Otto H. Kahn, $150; Julius Fleischmann of Fleischmann's Yeast Co., $500; Jesse Lasky, head of the Famous Players-Lasky Corporation, $2,500; Averell Harriman, president of the United American Lines, $250; Arthur S. Friend, president of Inspiration Pictures, $250; Archie Selwyn, $250; Mr Bonwit of Bonwit, Teller, $150; Jake Ruppert, owner of the Yankees, $250; Rosina Galli of the Metropolitan Opera Company, $250; Percival Hill of the American Tobacco Company, $100; F. J. Godsol of the Goldwyn Pictures Company, $150; and Joseph Seaman, head of the Seaman Paper Company of Chicago, $1,000."[35]

The intent of these payments, Brown insisted, was to purchase space in the magazine in which these prominent figures might promote their ideas or passions. Thus, he suggested, the banker and railroad magnate Otto H. Kahn paid for the publication of one of his speeches simply as a way of disseminating his ideas. In cross-examination, the prosecution countered that many of these payments had resulted in no actual advertising, a fact that Brown found difficult to explain. Jules Fleischmann had advanced money for advertising space that he never used, though Brown pointed out that the magazine had published vague mentions of the health benefits of yeast, the product that made Fleischmann his fortune. Joseph B. Seaman, vice-president of the Seaman Paper company, was another of those who paid money to the magazine's advertising solicitors with no subsequent submission of advertising content. That *Brevities* might have been in possession of compromising information about these people (typically involving marital infidelity) was irrelevant, Brown claimed.[36]

Brown's testimony was rich in insights into *Brevities* operations. In contrast, Charles Greene and Nat Kunnes, who followed him on the stand, were described in newspaper accounts as doing little more than amuse the courtroom audience and irritate the judge. Kunnes had settled into his role as the trial's buffoon and insisted to Prosecutor Mattuck and Judge Mack that he was ignorant of any illegal goings-on: "'I don't know anything,' he told Mack; 'no one knows anything.'"[37] The testimony of Charles Greene, who told the court that he had learnt a great deal about the workings of *Brevities* in the course of the trial, consisted largely of a narrative of his move to the United States from Canada and inability to find secure employment in his adopted country.[38]

Stephen G. Clow on the Stand

On 28 January 1925 – at long last – Stephen G. Clow was called to testify in his own defence. The *New York Sun* described him as "a well dressed man of polished appearance," while other reports commented on his grey, ashen face.[39] Asked to define his position with *Brevities*, Clow said he was "chief executive and business manager" of the magazine.[40] Clow's main line of defence was to simply deny any accusations of having intimidated the people who had been approached about advertising in *Brevities*. He admitted to employing up to twenty-five advertising solicitors but added that "I told them to exercise great caution and to avoid anything off color."[41] Later, Clow claimed to have known of only one case in which a *Brevities* staff member had tried to intimidate a potential advertiser, and he insisted that the advertising solicitor in question (who went unnamed) had been dismissed from the magazine as a result.[42]

Straining credulity, Clow insisted all through his testimony that he had never been privy to the rumours and gossip circulating around those, like Otto Kahn or Colonel Jacob Ruppert, from whom he was known to have received money. Fallon sought to build evidence of friendly ties between Clow and those who had testified against him, eliciting from Clow the fact that he had been a friend of Evelyn Neville (of Dainty Form fame) for eight years. Fallon returned to the claim, made earlier in the trial, that Clow and Peggy Joyce had been seen going to nightclubs together, suggesting they were friends, and he reintroduced the story of the telegraph from Joyce to Clow, in which the former offered "love and kisses." Clow's attorney still held out the promise that Joyce would return to the court under a new subpoena to confirm sending the communication, whose friendly tone could weaken the prosecution's claim that the relationship had been adversarial.

Mattuck's cross-examination led to two admissions that added sparkle to what was otherwise predictable testimony on the part of Clow. Those in attendance had noted Stephen Clow's listlessness throughout the trial, and Mattuck asked him directly if he had been using the soporific drug paraldehyde. Clow admitted he had, then quickly added that he was no "dope fiend."[43] In *Hollywood without Make-Up*, his 1948 book of show business reminiscences, journalist Pete Martin describes Clow as "a gentleman distinguished among other things for habitually drinking a mixture of ether and paraldehyde as a sedative," a practice that contributed to the image of decadence that had settled on him by the mid-1920s.[44] Clow's other admission came when Mattuck questioned him about the breakup of his marriage to Janice Carson. "You separated from your wife in 1922?" Mattuck asked. Clow answered "Yes," then told the court that, on her departure, Carson had taken one of the account books containing information on monies paid to *Brevities* for advertising. "Did you not threaten to stop paying her alimony unless she returned your book?" Mattuck asked, but an objection by Mr Fallon was sustained.[45]

While the full story of Clow's financial entanglements with Janice Carson and the circumstances of her departure may never be known, Mattuck circled around them as if they were central to his case. The prosecutor hinted that Clow had abandoned publication of *Brevities* in return for payment in 1921 and then brought his wife in as treasurer as a way of keeping his own name off the magazine's masthead. As the questioning continued, Clow displayed quite astonishing confusion over the date of his wife's departure: "'In November, 1921, or November, 1923. I'm quite sure it was November, 1923,' he answered."[46] Mattuck went no further in pursuing the circumstances of the 1921 abandonment and immediate revival of the magazine, leaving unasked any questions that might have linked this to the Zelda Crosby case or the blackmail of highly placed film business personnel. If Janice Carson had really taken with her key documents about *Brevities*' business dealings, and if her whereabouts were now unknown, this was obviously convenient for Clow.

The defence then took an unexpected turn. William Fallon called prosecuting attorney Matthew Mattuck to the stand as a witness. Fallon asked him why key individuals who had been named as sources of payments to *Brevities* had not, in fact, been made to testify. Fallon named Otto Kahn, Averill Herriman,

Jules Fleischmann, and Jesse Lasky as among those whose names had been drawn out of witnesses' mouths without themselves having to testify and face cross-examination. This tactic, Fallon suggested, had served to "becloud the issue through suggestion and innuendo.[47] Fallon concluded his questioning by inviting Mr Mattuck to cross-examine himself. In the words of one reporter, "the Assistant District Attorney then told the court that the government had not called all its witnesses but had put on the stand only those whose testimonies would be 'typical' and 'indicative of the methods employed by the defendants."[48] No one spoke of possible pressure on the prosecutor from these prominent figures, who clearly wished to avoid testimony (and the cross-examination that would certainly follow).

Final Arguments

On the morning of Thursday, 29 January, the prosecution and defence proceeded to make their final arguments, with Fallon going first. The defence attorney began by entering a motion to have the proceedings dismissed on the grounds that the prosecution, in its arguments, had not confined itself to matters having to do with the use of the mails to defraud.[49] Indeed, a close reading of press reports of the trial finds little discussion of the use of postal communications to carry out Clow's various schemes, but the motion to dismiss was denied. Fallon then began his summation.

Early in Fallon's remarks, the basis of his defence of Clow and *Brevities* was made clear: "'The most despised man in the world is the man who starts a moral crusade." Clow was engaged in such a moral crusade, his lawyer argued, and his aim was "nothing less than the moral cleansing of New York City, for the people's protection."[50] It was the lot of such crusaders to be despised, Fallon continued, and for their detractors to seek to uncover ulterior motives. The defence attorney suggested, with no evidence, that *Brevities* had frequently refused to take advertisements from companies engaged in medical quackery and argued that, had the magazine only been interested in payment, fraudulent companies of all sorts would have rushed to purchase advertising in its pages. Fallon hailed Clow as "a public benefactor who has exposed people who preyed upon a gullible public."[51]

As he continued, Fallon raised the stakes. Under attack in the *Brevities* trial, he charged, in ascending rhetorical flourishes, were "honest journalism," "the American jury system," and "public health."[52]

Mattuck's summation of the prosecution's case began with his rejection of Fallon's moral high ground and a promise to stick to the facts. The assistant district attorney went through the testimony of each of the witnesses in the trial, claiming to show how, in each case, payments had been demanded and usually received in the face of threats of derogatory coverage in *Brevities*' pages. Mattuck's arguments were carefully constructed. With respect to Helen Lee Worthing's suicide attempt, for example, the attorney acknowledged that the first two mentions in *Brevities* might qualify as legitimate news coverage but that repetition of the items until such time as Worthing purchased advertising constituted extortion. Mattuck departed from prosaic detail only near the end of this summation, as the *New York Sun* reported: "'There is no meaner type of crook,' added Mattuck pointing to Clow, 'than the man who tries to extort money for silence. People are afraid of Clow. What chance has anyone got? Put yourself, jurors, in the place of any of my witnesses. What would you do if you were objects of attack? Gentlemen, I ask you for consideration for those who have been attacked by Brevities.'"[53]

Verdicts and Sentences

The jury members began their deliberations late in the afternoon of Thursday, 29 January 1925. A little over two hours later, at 6:35 p.m., they returned to offer a verdict. Stephen G. Clow and Andrew S. Brown were found guilty on all nine counts with which they had been charged – eight for using the mails to defraud, plus an additional count of conspiracy. Nat Kunnes escaped the conspiracy charge but was guilty on the eight other counts. Charles Greene was acquitted. Clow, Brown, and Kunnes apparently sat silently when the verdict was read, while Greene was seen to collapse under the emotional strain. The judge announced that sentencing would be handed down two days later, on 31 January.[54]

At the sentencing hearing, Fallon begged the judge for mercy toward Clow, whom he described as a "mental and physical wreck." "I have a feeling of mercy," the judge said in his response, "for those burglars who yield to the sudden temptation to take money. I have a feeling of mercy even for those who commit murder in the second degree. But men who intentionally plan and design to destroy publicly reputations by such attacks as these are beyond the pale of any decent man's conception of the demands of mercy."[55]

Clow was sentenced to six years and one day in the United States Penitentiary in Atlanta.[56] While imprisonment for the eight counts of mail fraud was to last five years, Judge Mack made it clear that he wished for Clow to serve separate time for conspiracy. This explained the additional year and a day.[57] Clow was also fined $6,000 and the magazine itself an additional $11,000. Further publication of *Broadway Brevities* was halted through a ban on its circulation through the mails. Brown was sentenced to two years in prison and fined $7,500, while Nat Kunnes was remanded first to the US Marshal's office and then to Bellevue Hospital for examination as to his mental state. (*Billboard* reported this under the heading "'Brevities' Solicitor Insane."[58])

In the memoirs he published as a syndicated newspaper series in 1928, Clow regretted having engaged a high-profile lawyer to fight the charges that had led to this harsh sentence. Of William Fallon, he wrote that "instead of subjecting him to a glaring defeat, I'd much better have taken the plea available to me and spent a short term in the Essex, N. J. bastille." Clow added that, "instead of that, egged on by 'friends,' I went to battle in as hopeless a cause as ever occupied a judge or a jury."[59]

The *Brevities* trial, along with successful convictions of Pan-Africanist Marcus Garvey and anti-fascist Italian-American newspaper publisher Carlo Tresca, would solidify Assistant District Attorney Mattuck's reputation for skill in wielding the "mail fraud" charge as a way of carrying out other prosecutorial objectives. In a trial presided over by the same judge as the *Brevities* proceedings, Mattuck won a guilty verdict against Garvey for using the mails to sell "worthless" stock in the Black Star Line shipping company, which had been established to provide transport for Blacks wishing to settle in Africa. Mattuck could find only one instance in which the sale of shares in the Black Star Line involved the use of the mails, but this was enough to convince a jury and for Judge Mack to sentence Garvey to five years in the Atlanta penitentiary.[60] Carlo Tresca, who was targeted by fascist organizations in the United States (and would be assassinated in 1943, allegedly by mafia figure Carmine Galante), was convicted in 1924 of offering information on birth control through the mails. He was sentenced to one year in the Atlanta penitentiary, a sentence considered wildly excessive for a crime that normally resulted in a small fine.[61] The Atlanta terms for Garvey, Tresca, and Clow overlapped, though it is unclear whether they met in prison. Curiously, Mattuck was among the handful of people who attended Clow's funeral in 1941.

Following his sentence, Stephen G. Clow lingered in the Manhattan Detention Complex (the notorious Tombs) until March, trying without success to raise the $15,000 he needed to be released on bail pending an appeal. When neither the money nor the prospect of an appeal presented themselves, and aware that time in the Tombs would not count toward fulfilment of his sentence, Clow ceased further actions. He was sent to Atlanta penitentiary in late March 1925.[62]

SIX

THE *NEW BROADWAY BREVITIES*

Steve Clow is now in the Atlanta penitentiary. He will be out soon. They tell me that he is going deep into New Jersey in order to raise dogs. He is through, he says, with Broadway.
Mark Hellinger, "About Broadway," *Sunday News* (New York), 23 January 1927, 2F.

As the *Brevities* trial ended, with most of its defendants convicted and sentenced, journalistic attention lingered for a time. Across the United States, newspapers published editorials cheering the verdict and denouncing the blackmailers as "blood suckers" and "parasites" who were corrupting the practice of journalism.[1] An eccentric opinion piece in the *St Louis Post-Dispatch* somehow took the *Brevities* case as proof of the imminent introduction of government publications "that will scrutinize the lives of citizens and parade their indiscretions and peccadilloes, not for profit, indeed, but in the name of universal righteousness."[2]

Prison and Release

Stephen Clow had entered the Atlanta prison in March 1925 after lingering in Manhattan's Tombs jail while attempts to raise bail and launch appeals ran out of steam.[3] In April, *Variety* reported that he had been given work duties in the prison doctor's office.[4] By September, Clow was writing under the byline "SGC" for *Good Words*, the prison newspaper. Although his name never appeared on the paper's masthead, Clow contributed signed bits to a regular column of news from the prison hospital and, as time went by, wrote full articles and editorials.[5] In early pieces for *Good Words*, with titles like "Making the Most of It," Clow waxed sentimentally and moralistically, reminding prisoners of the loyal women waiting patiently for their release, or urging them to follow prison rules and make the most of their incarceration.[6] Clow's "A Day in the Hospital," in the same issue, follows prison hospital doctors through a day of rounds, from 6 a.m. until 11 p.m. – the hour, he notes, in which "footsteps grow more infrequent in the corridors."[7] Another article by Clow, "What Makes Men Criminals," was published in the April 1927 issue of *Good Words*, just as his time in jail was ending. It summarized contemporary debates over the causes of criminality, and while Clow avoided taking a stand on the question, he concluded with a look toward a "happy humanistic era when the experts come to realize that only a hairsbreadth in most cases distinguishes the mind, soul and body of the man behind prison bars from the man outside them."[8]

In the same month, the *New York Times* reported that Clow was being considered for parole – he had been eligible since 22 March – and he was released from prison shortly thereafter. He had served a little more than two years of the original six-year-plus-a-day sentence.[9] Clow reflected on his prison experience in an article, "What Kind of Men Go to Prison?," published in the current affairs magazine *Plain Talk* the following year.[10] The Atlanta federal penitentiary had long been known as the "rich man's prison," and Clow estimated that at least ten millionaires had passed through its doors during his own confinement. He took delight in listing the former governor, congressman, secret service agent, authors, and theatrical personnel who had been his prison companions, calling the Atlanta institution the most intellectually brilliant community in the world.[11]

Upon his release, Clow returned to New York, presumably with little money left from his original *Broadway Brevities* exploits. Among those who appeared to remain loyal to Clow throughout his ordeal was Sime Silverman, editor of *Variety*. Silverman apparently sent Clow money while he was in prison and hired him for bits of editing work after his release.[12] *Variety* also went some distance in

How I Blackmailed

By the Convicted Chief of Broadway's Deadli[e]
for Six Years Clutched White Way and "4
Bleeding His Victims of Huge "
Uncle Sam Finally Broke Hi[m]
Reveals in His First Confess[ion]
Tricks of His Infamous G[a]
Innocent and Guilty an[d]
Protection to the Publ[ic]
He Once Terrorized

WHEN UNCLE SAM "GOT" HIM.
"Oh those weeks in the Tombs!" Writes Clow. "The suffocating misery and hopelessness which accompanies a first taste of bolts and bars!" A Photo of Clow in Faultless Evening Dress in Contrast to the Famous Prison with Its Bridge of Sighs

LOYAL TO CLOW.
Texas Guinan, Night Club Hostess, Who Refused to Testify Against the "Brevities" Editor Because, She Said, He Had Always Been a Good Friend to Her.

By STEPHEN G. CLOW

CHAPTER V.

EARSDROPPINGS

The Thrilling Story of Teddy Gerard and George Bronson Howard

TWO SIDES TO EVERY STORY

REG'LAR FELLERS

STEVE
KEEP YOUR EYE ON THIS DON'T !!
Under no circumstances ever print, even complimentary, any item relating to [redacted]
You are advised that a new and complete ventilating system is likely to be installed in your corpus if you ignore this suggestion

Figure 6.1 *Above and overleaf*
Stephen G. Clow, "How I Blackmailed the Stars of Society and the Stage," *Times* (Shreveport, Louisiana), 1 January 1928.

the Stars of Society and the Stage

t Scandal Ring, Who
'O" by the Throat,
ush Money" Until
and Who Now
on All the Innermost
ne as a Warning to
a

"I MADE THEM DANCE!"
A Unique Snapshot of Stephen G. Clow, Author of Three Confessions, at His Piano, with the Artist's Interpretation of Clow's Grim Remark: "No cowboy shooting up a western dance-hall made his victims writhe in such fear as did 'Brevities' with its 'innocent' little paragraphs."

HIS SECRET TOLD.
Barrie Baxter, Whose Tragic Romance with Teddy Gerard, the Actress (Ended by His Death), Was Revealed in "Brevities."

MADE GOOD "COPY" FOR CLOW.
Teddy Gerard, the Actress Who Had a Series of Sensational Romances with Men Which, Clow Relates, He Described in "Brevities" Not to Blackmail Her But to Enthrall Readers and Boost His Circulation. "But subsequent to that time, however," He Confesses, "almost every item grew to have a blackmail side."

Let me first explain that for some months I had been "riding" a certain famous movie actor, since gone into his last Fade-out. I had heard he was planning fistic retaliation on me, and although he did not know me by sight, he had got some sort of description of my enticing personality, and had happened to be sitting two tables from mine on this horrific occasion. BUT—one of the chaps in my own party happened to bear a striking resemblance to me, and, while I was visiting in the rear, the picture star had sicked a pugilistic pal of his on my double. As my double was talking in the 'phone booth, the pug had crept up behind him with an inkstand from the cashier's desk and banged him good and plenty. "Take that! you dirty blackmailing ——," he exclaimed as the glassy weapon descended. "Now, you'll leave my friend —— alone!"

Despite such dangers, however, there was not a 6 A. M. time that did not find me, with two or more pals, in some more or less hoodlum resort. In the shank of the evening, of course, I found it pleasant and profitable to patronise the swanky night places, such as the Parody Club or Texas Guinan's inimitable rendezvous on Forty-fifth. One of my favorite spots was Jimmy Kelley's in the Village. At all of these was continual "dishing of dirt" by visitors at my table; often a few little details would burgeon into a two-page scandal yarn in the next issue. I knew almost all the actual and near celebs at sight; but few of them knew me from Adam, and it often must have come as a thunderclap when they read in "Brevities" the following month a lurid story of some particular evening when, as they thought, unobserved, they were babbling and petting in a shady corner with a notorious libertine or the husband of their "dearest" intimate.

Occasionally, as was Ted Lewis' habit at the Parody, I would be accosted loudly by name and editorship, or N. T. G. would slip the news of my presence into the tell-tale ether. The best booster I had in this way was Tommy Lyman at Kelley's, who devoted most of his comic interpolations to "Brevities" and its there-present editor.

"Watch your step, little boys and girls," Tommy would wheeze, "Steve Clow's here tonight and you'll be in the next issue!"

This got a general laugh, with here and there a low, hissing sound. But Tommy meant it for the best.

I have spoken of Texas Guinan above, and it is well within the province of these revelations to mention her phenomenal loyalty to me when the dark days came and my old "friends" deserted en masse. Texas had been among the hundreds subpoenaed to the Grand Jury sittings. There she testified that all her relations with "Brevities" had been of a nature pure as snow; for some reason or other, however, she was threatened with contempt proceedings if she refused to appear as a witness. I later heard—though not from her—that she had told the prosecution they would have to take her down handcuffed, for she would go no other way. This news reached me about the third week of the seven I spent in the Tombs, and seemed to carry with it a flavor of ancient, heroic friendships. As a matter of pure fact "Brevities" had never used the faintest intimidation with Texas Guinan. The witness stand never saw her.

Oh, those weeks in the Tombs! I had filed an immediate appeal from my conviction, but was held in durance under $15,000 bail. For over six weeks I made frantic endeavors, mainly through pathetic appeals to former intimates by wire, letter and emissary, for contributions sufficient to cover this bail. Of the many solicited only two or three offered assistance.

Finally I realized that even were I able to produce such amount of bail, the U. S. Attorney would undoubtedly ask to have my bail increased; moreover, I could then perceive plainly the fatuity of any appeal in a Federal case so unsavory. So I made application to Maxwell Mattuck, the prosecutor, for immediate transfer to Atlanta, and he skipped me off the very next day.

Brown must have had more moneyed contacts than I did, for he made bail and left without the formality of a farewell to his old confrere —after a two days' stay. He had also entered an appeal, which was heard about nine months later. In confirmation of my own good judgment—the first I had used in six years—his conviction was affirmed, and he joined me at the southern bastile in January, 1926, when I had served almost a year of my sentence.

Some day I shall devote an entire article to the Tombs experience, and its thrills will instantly outmode the latest "horror" of lurid fiction. The reader can limn in his own mind the suffocating misery and hopelessness which accompanies a first taste of bolts and bars; did he know the Tombs as it was in February, 1925, the picture would be terror-perfect. Locked in a bug-infested cell for 22 hours of the 24 unless five dollars or more per week were forthcoming! The food was no treat to a man accustomed to Broadway's best. Thievish "trusties" who grabbed everything you had loose, in addition to the heavy sums extorted for cleaning your bunk. A chorus of blood-curdling yells, vile ditties and viler conversation going on steadily each afternoon from four to eight—sounds which, it seemed to me for seven awful weeks, must be coming from Dante's damned.

Of Solomon-like sapience are those unfortunates who accept their Federal sentences and go quickly as they can to Atlanta. In that vast, humane, hygienic institution comes back some measure of self-respect, of hope, of rehabilitation. "Go on and get it over!"—that's the slogan for almost all men decreed to serve under Federal process.

In the great southern fortress I found a continuing drama in meeting, as the days went by, acquaintances I had made in the Tombs. "Hello, old man! When did you get here?" "Oh, a coupla days ago!" "How's the old place? Do the boys still have to pay 40c apiece for tallows?"

That meant tallow candles, and for me they had proven the best available substitute, after ten, for the winking lost and gone incandescents of the night clubs.

My memories of the Atlanta pen will remain with me all my life, I both hope and fear. It is not an experience I want to forget, for I met many strange and stimulating people in that walled city and I lived with a healthy, clear-headed intensity that had been denied me in the artificial, hectic, soul-sapping environment of Broadway night life. Yet if I could, I suppose I would erase every second of prison from memory.

At first I was bewildered, just as a child is with a new home. I saw men in blue and white uniforms—there are 3000 of them in that community—living in an orderly, sane way. They were not beaten, cringing creatures, they held their heads up and went about their work without being driven. It was the first chance many of them had had to live well-regulated lives.

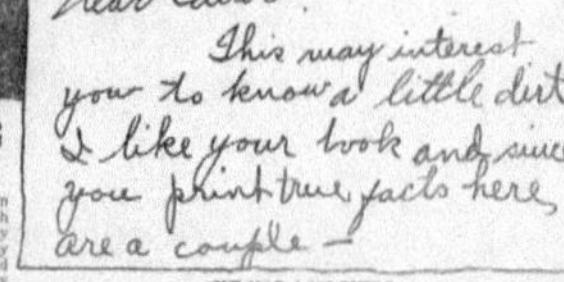

Dear Editor:
This may interest you to know a little dirt I like your book and since you print true facts here are a couple—

"WE HAD 1,000 EYES."
One of the Thousands of Letters "Brevities" Received from Anonymous Correspondents, "Tipping" the Editors to Scandal. Clow Explains That He Had Little Need to Look for Material Himself, So Vast Was His Army of Unknown, Voluntary Spies.

I don't mean to suggest that the life was a holiday, it wasn't. When a man is deprived of his liberty and locked inside a cell every night, that in itself gives him a secret sense of shame. He knows he is being punished, he is certainly not glad to be there. The life is rigorously Spartan, but no attempt is made to deprive him of his spirit of manhood, which in my own case had been badly cracked before entering. I needed to find that spirit anew and I did—in prison.

As I became more used to the life I actually did not regret being deprived of some of the things that had been so necessary to me before.

(To Be Continued.)

defending his reputation. Noting that Clow was a "brilliant writer," the unsigned author of the paper's "Literati" column argued that Clow had been brought down by the people around him and had stood up for them when the going got tough. "Anyway," the column concluded, "Clow is entitled to the break he's now getting."[13] In 1930, *Variety* complained of the ongoing lowering of journalistic standards in New York tabloid publishing, suggesting that the "'Broadway Brevities' of those days never commenced to print one-half of the scandal matter that daily columnists now publish without hesitation or blush."[14]

Clow Freelancing

The most outlandish feat of Clow's return to print was the twelve-part newspaper feature series "How I Blackmailed the Stars of Society and the Stage," distributed by the International Feature Service (part of the Hearst company's King Features Syndicate) between December 1927 and March 1928.[15] A blurb introducing the series' first instalment promised "the untainted disclosures of [Clow's] malodorous though adventurous reign as Manhattan's "Blackmail King."[16] Each chapter of the series, a memoir of Clow's life at *Broadway Brevities*, was spread across two full pages, with the article's text set amidst jumbled collages of photographs, expressive graphics, and inserts that included signed commentaries by people involved in the *Brevities* trial, like prosecutor Maxwell Mattuck. Throughout the series, Clow's posture moved between that of petulant victim (of people determined to bring him down), proud criminal genius (who had reinvented the art of blackmail), and wistful survivor (now able to look back on his misadventures with bemusement and a hint of nostalgia). The memoirs are of interest principally for the detail they provide about Clow's routines during the period he edited *Broadway Brevities* – his nights on the town, his management of *Brevities*' team of blackmail confederates, and, as time went on, his concerns about his own safety. Chapter VII tells a particularly horrific tale of Clow attending a society soirée, then being lured by the hostess into a private room where a boxer, incensed at Clow for a slight in the magazine, beat him senseless, injuring him enough that he required medical treatment and four days of convalescence in the hostess' apartment.[17]

After the publication of these memoirs, Clow rarely wrote of his life as a blackmailer or of his trial. While he would, from time to time, refer to his imprisonment, he did so mostly to bolster his new claims to expertise in matters of criminal behaviour and penal policy. In 1928, Clow announced that he was preparing a series of articles on "Famous Escapes from Atlanta" for the *New York World*. This, and his contributions to the magazine *Plain Talk* on such topics as "Broadway Angels" (investors in theatrical productions), pointed to a possible path into mainstream journalism and commentary, but this did not last long.[18] It was as eulogist of an earlier Broadway, however, that Clow found the voice that would become a key strand of his writing in what remained of his life and career. Shortly after his release, Clow began contributing columns of Broadway gossip and reminiscences to the digest-sized magazine *Smokehouse Monthly*, edited in Minneapolis (and later in New York) by Wilford "Capt. Billy" Fawcett. *Smokehouse Monthly* had been launched by Fawcett in 1926 as a spinoff of his highly popular magazine *Capt. Billy's Whiz Bang* (in which mildly vulgar "smokehouse poetry" was a regular feature). In the 1930s, Fawcett would become one of the leading publishers of popular magazines in the United States, with a genre-spanning array of titles that ran from the highly popular *Mechanix Illustrated* through confession, true crime, and fiction magazines (and, later, comic books and paperback novels).

Whiz Bang and *Smokehouse Monthly* were part of a wave of pocket-sized magazines of the 1920s, like *TNT*, *Whoopee!*, *Hot Dog*, *The Quirt*, *Fun*, and *Glynn's Jamboree*, in which folksy commentary, ribald poetry, cartoons, and brief, humorous stories sat alongside each other. From its launch in 1928 until 1933, *Smokehouse Monthly* carried regular columns that were unsigned but almost certainly written by Stephen G. Clow. Some of these bore the title "A Rounder on Broadway," but the most long-lasting was "Abroad on Broadway," which lasted until 1932 and was sometimes accompanied by another feature, "Sweeping up Broadway." In issue after issue, these pieces circle around Clow's one-time friends and occasional collaborators, and regularly revisit the period 1917–25, the years of Clow's greatest cultural power and ubiquity within New York show business circles.[19]

A version of Clow appears in thinly disguised form in *Bowery Murder*, a novel by Willard K. Smith published in 1929 in Doubleday's popular Crime Club book series. *Bowery Murder* belongs to a handful of tabloid novels published on either side of 1930 and set in the lower depths of New York newspaper publishing. Books in this wave moved their stories along with tabloid-like headlines dividing chapters or sections and were often full of passages mimicking fictional newspaper stories.[20] A recurring character in *Bowery Murder* is Albert F. Compagna, editor of "the somewhat scurrilous sheet known as *Broadway Briefs*," which was at least partially inspired by Clow's magazine. The book describes the elaborate procedures by which Compagna would present potential victims with information on their private lives, then offer his silence in return for financial contributions to the magazine. At the time of the crime that gave the book its title, the fictional Compagna was in prison on charges of blackmail.[21]

The Nightlife Columnists

By the late 1920s, it seemed clear that Stephen G. Clow would not join the list of high-profile Broadway columnists who were now writing under their own names for New York's daily newspapers. In the mid-1920s, as Neal Gabler has written, "columnists were everywhere" in the New York City press.[22] The columns that proliferated in that decade were of several sorts – some offered humorous observations of city life; others carried news of high society or regular commentary on specialized interests such as slang. The nightlife column, however, was the genre deemed to be most emblematic of the age. In the first two decades of the twentieth century, New York periodicals covering the theatrical field had begun featuring columns that mixed information useful to professionals with other bits of reporting explicitly offered as gossip. In 1910, the entertainment trade magazine *Billboard* introduced the short-lived feature "Broadway Brevities," with the subtitle "News and Gossip of Professional People and Events Gleaned Along the Great White Way." The weekly show business journal *Variety* (founded in 1905) would likewise mix news and gossip in recurrent features like "At the Cabarets" and "Personalities," both of which were introduced in the years between 1910 and 1920. While all these columns contained useful information – announcements of new shows or changes in the ownership of entertainment venues – they might also hint in gossipy fashion at romances, both public and secret, and reversals of social or financial standing.

In 1920, a struggling vaudeville performer named Walter Winchell began writing short paragraphs of back-stage gossip for the entertainment industry newspaper *The Vaudeville News*. Their success led to Winchell being hired in 1924 to write a column on New York nightlife ("Your Broadway and Mine") for the newly launched *Evening Graphic* newspaper.[23] The "nightlife column" took the journalist out of the confines of theatrical backstages and into the world of nightclubs and speakeasies, spaces of nighttime entertainment that had proliferated following the introduction of Prohibition in 1920. Part of this shift involved a migration of show business columnists away from the specialized entertainment industry press and into New York's mainstream daily newspapers.

Walter Winchell had contributed brief items to *Broadway Brevities* in its early days, but by the time of Clow's release from prison Winchell had far outpaced him and was on his way to becoming the most important American newspaper columnist of the twentieth century. This clearly rankled Clow, who, as we shall see, initiated a mostly one-sided feud with Winchell in the early 1930s. Mark Hellinger, whose column "About Town" began its run in the *Daily News* in 1925, likewise moved past Clow, though Clow had rescued Hellinger from *Zit's Theatrical Weekly* and recommended him to *Daily News* editor Philip Payne for the columnist position that launched his career.[24] Gordon Kahn, as we have seen, moved from *Broadway Brevities* to *Zit*'s and then, after various writing jobs on New York newspapers and magazines, found success in Hollywood as a screenwriter.[25] By 1927, Clow was quite clearly too old (at fifty-four) and probably too widely despised or mistrusted to join the wave of columnists covering the city's nightlife for New York's daily newspapers. Almost all those who did ascend to this status – people Clow knew, like Winchell, Hellinger, and Kahn, and others he probably didn't, like Ed Sullivan, Broadway columnist for the *Evening Graphic* (and, later, the *Daily News*) – would follow careers that eventually took them into the lucrative worlds of radio, film, and (for those who survived) television. Clow, in contrast, would remain in the world of magazines for the rest of his career, moving down the ladder of respectability as the years went by.

Broadway Brevities Reborn

In 1930, Clow attempted to launch a magazine with the stature and air of quality he seemed to be craving. In his memoirs, as if to retroactively redeem himself, he wrote of having planned such a magazine in late 1924, when he clearly felt things closing in on *Broadway Brevities*:

> I began making plans to disinfect "Brevities" and eventually suspend it in favor of a new weekly magazine I contemplated, to be called "The New Yorker" – not in any way to be confused with the present highly successful weekly of the same title. I had the cover-drawing made, and all preparations afoot for the switch to such a new publication. Better than anyone else I realized that "Brevities" had long since – and especially with the prosecution facing it – become so malodorous as to be "through" … So I conceived the idea of a weekly paper that would eliminate scandal entirely, go after ads on the dead "legit," and build up high walls of good will for a national distribution. Alackaday! It was a laggard resolve.[26]

In fact, the *New Yorker* that survives today launched its first issue with a cover date of February 1925, one month after the last issue of Clow's original *Broadway Brevities*. If his own "New Yorker" was not possible, Clow could still find his redemption in a new, "disinfected" revival of *Broadway Brevities*. On 18 June 1930, three years after his release from prison, *Variety* announced that "Steve Clow" was launching a magazine called the *New Broadway Brevities*, to be published by a firm called New-Broad Pub. Co., located at 116 Broad Street in New York's financial district.[27] A certificate of incorporation deposited with New York State's Corporation Bureau on 29 May 1930 named the directors of the new corporation as Alvin H. Minkoff of Brooklyn, Murray A. Schechtman of the Bronx, and Helen M. Hart of New Jersey.[28] Clow's name does not appear on the certificate, suggesting he had no financial interest in the publication, and *Time* magazine, reporting on the launch, clarified that the new magazine was being financed by "Wall Streeters."[29] When the first issue of the *New Broadway Brevities* appeared, bearing the date August 1930, its officers were listed as Robert W.

Patrick, president; Milton J. Anderson, vice-president; Alvin Wies, treasurer; and Stephen G. Clow, editor.

Clow's involvement in the *New Broadway Brevities* would last little more than a year, and the title would then continue without him, after being transformed from a monthly magazine to a weekly tabloid newspaper. In the brief period during which he exercised editorial control, Clow seemed determined to convince the world that this resurrected version was not the basis of a blackmail racket. He told *Variety* that he was only its editor, and that of "about eight pages of Broadway Gossip, nothing is scandal." The advertising rate card for the revived *Brevities* made clear that "there is no room in this publication for misrepresentation, intimidation or coercion."[30] *Time* reminded readers that Clow had once styled himself "the most famous and wicked blackmailer in world history," but observed that the new incarnation of *Brevities* made no mention of its predecessor.[31]

Women's Wear Daily devoted a paragraph to the arrival of the new magazine's first issue. It noted that the *New Broadway Brevities* was "bound in leather-tex and gold."[32] Whether this cover, bereft of any imagery, was meant to signal the new magazine's classiness or hint at illicit pleasures concealed inside is not clear, but this introductory issue, like the first few following it in this incarnation, was packaged between thick covers and on study paper stock that suggested luxury.

The inaugural issue of the *New Broadway Brevities* ran to 108 pages, more than twice the length of any issue of the magazine in its earlier incarnation. Filling these pages required a large roster of contributors, and Clow seemed to have assembled a group of Broadway professionals or personalities for the magazine, none of them left over from its predecessor. Announcing the launch, *Variety* reported that Mildred Luber, formerly of the *New York Journal*, "was with him on the advertising"; she would be one of the magazine's columnists as well.[33] Luber was typical of a new generation of collaborators who circled around some of the projects to which Clow was attached in the early 1930s – multi-skilled young people whose careers moved between radio, advertising, public relations, and journalism. In addition to handling the advertising for Clow's magazine, Mildred Luber contributed a column, "Coming Out of the Ether," full of short, light-hearted items about the world of radio. Devoid of any sensational innuendo, Luber's bits suggested that the magazine was playing it safe.

Figure 6.2 First issue, *New Broadway Brevities*, August 1930.

Other contributors to this first issue include Renee Carroll, who for several years was the hat-check girl at the popular New York restaurant Sardi's and, in 1933, would publish a book of nightlife reminiscences, *In Your Hat*. In the first instalment of her column in *Brevities*, "Checking Up on Broadway," Carroll describes her early career as a ballet dancer at Roseland, her subsequent move to Sardi's, and some of the famous people she met along the way. She concludes her column with more than a dozen short items of gossipy observation, written from a star-struck perspective that contributes to their innocent, unsensational tone: "Maxie Rosenbloom, the light-heavyweight champ, aside from his ring antics goes heavy for blondes, brunettes and redheads in a big way ... Now, listen: Katherine Cornell refused to sign her caricature until the ciggie was removed from her lips."[34] This first issue also includes "Seeing Stars," an astrology column credited to Laurel Miller, best known for her books *Astro-Psychology* (1921) and *Kabalistic Numerology* (1922). Miller's two-page feature is devoted in its entirety to reading the astrological charts of Broadway entrepreneur Texas Guinan, concluding that Guinan is possessed of a "religious urge, which will take her to a cloister eventually."[35] Elsewhere in this issue, we find a column on footwear and hair dye, "Beauty and the Beach," by Billie Gould, a public relations professional who worked in radio. A feature on cosmetics and beauty accessories by Constance Groves-Roberts is for the most part a string of promotional mentions, and the adjacent fashion column, "When As in Silks My Julie Goes," by Michael Wortzman, sits alongside a large display advertisement for the author's clothing shop.

This roster of contributors was hardly an A-list, but it showed Clow's ability to attract contributions from people who held positions and pursued careers elsewhere. Scattered among pieces in the first issue signed by others are one- or two-page features, bereft of any author's name, which are not unlike the clusters of gossip that filled the pages of the original *Brevities*. These, we may assume, were written mostly, or in their entirety, by Stephen G. Clow. One of these, "Peeps at Pineapple Parkway," hints at the domestic troubles and personal foibles of New York personalities but in an elusive and stripped-down fashion: "Solly Lang was rather embarrassed. Happening to buy a seat at a recent fight, next to one in which sat a cute little stranger trick, his friends kidded him pink about it. Betty Randolph, if you don't object, the millionaire kid of Pawk Avenue, has repaired to her Saratoga villa to watch the equines."[36] These items do let slip some secrets, but in the context of 1930, with gossip columns available all across the New York press, they would no longer seem as brazen as they might have in 1922. We may see their tightly crafted elusiveness as evidence of Clow's wish to avoid legal troubles, but we may also guess that he was trying to imitate the telegraphic rhythms of those, like Walter Winchell, who were now regarded as masters of the form.

The Clivettes of Greenwich Village

The most intriguing contributors to the revived *Brevities* were two members of the Clivette family, one of whom would remain a friend (and sometimes collaborator) of Clow for much of what remained of his career. The first issue of the *New Broadway Brevities* carried a one-page piece of political commentary, "The Cruel 'Single Moral Standard'" by Catherine Parker Clivette. The event that sparked the column was the arrest on moral charges of Emma Hammerstein, widow of businessman and cultural impresario Oscar Hammerstein. Clivette's brief article was a plea for equal treatment of men and women in those cases involving accusations of immoral behaviour. Its author was identified as "President, Society for the Prevention of Unjust Convictions."

Catherine Parker Clivette was one member of a family of some legend within Greenwich Village in the 1920s but scarcely known outside its boundaries. She was usually identified as founder or president of the Greenwich Village Historical Society, though she also attached herself to a number of eccentric and occasionally unsavoury political causes, such as the "Immigration Restriction League."[37] Catherine's husband, Merton Clivette, known as the "Man in Black,"[38] was a magician who achieved considerable fame before and after 1900 as a travelling vaudeville artist and author of books on conjuring. Since moving to the Village, Merton had turned much of his attention to painting and, in the last two decades of his life, apparently produced hundreds of canvases. After his death in 1931, he seems to have been quickly forgotten, until a very recent revival of interest, which includes a biography published in May 2023 and based partly on materials surviving in the Clivette family archives.[39]

In 1907, Catherine and Merton had a daughter, Juanyta (sometimes spelled "Juanita") Clivette. In her twenties, Juanyta would write regularly for the revived *Brevities* and she spent the 1920s and 1930s engaged in activities that traced lines of connection between literary circles in the Village and the worlds of sensational tabloid publishing based further uptown. Her apparent closeness to Stephen G. Clow helps us to better understand the links between these worlds, and to reconstruct some of the circles in which Clow moved following his release from prison in 1927. Juanyta Clivette first achieved national attention in 1920, when she was the focus of an unsigned full-page article syndicated to newspapers across the United States by the International Feature Service. Under the title "Mystery of 'Little Sappho' of Greenwich Village," the article develops the claim that, beginning at a very young age, Juanyta had begun writing poems whose style and themes bore a remarkable resemblance to those of the Greek poetess Sappho.[40] Rather than simply imitating Sappho, however, Juanyta claimed to be channelling her, as if inhabited by the Greek woman's soul. Eventually, Juanyta would drop the connection to Sappho and build a minor reputation in downtown Manhattan circles as a journalist and poet.[41]

In early 1923, when she was only sixteen years old, Juanyta Clivette was listed as one of the contributing editors of Bobby Edwards's little magazine, the *Quill*, which published her occasional poem and theatre review.[42] It is unclear when exactly Stephen G. Clow first became acquainted with Juanyta and her family, but their lives would cross his in the late 1920s and 1930s (and Juanyta Clivette would be one of the few people to attend Clow's funeral in 1941). By the fourth issue of the *New Broadway Brevities*, Juanyta was contributing a variety of features to the magazine. A one-pager titled "The Bad and Good Little Girls: A Study" was little more than a description of the fictional lives of the two types of women referred to in the title, the "bad" one ending up happy and well-supported while the "good" one suffered amidst a claustrophobic cluster of in-laws and domestic duties. Later in the same issue, "Ladies Choosing" pursued what was roughly the same theme: the dullness of marriage when compared with the pleasures of luxurious indulgence. Her third piece that month was a column about the neighbourhood in which she lived; with this Clivette found the format she would carry on with in future issues. Faithful to a long tradition of reporting on the

Mystery of "Little Sappho" of Greenwich Village

Psychology Explains the Interesting Case of a Child Who When Only Five Declared Herself the Ancient Poetess Born Again and Has Been Writing Poems Ever Since That Perplex Scholars

Sappho and Alcaeus, the Painting by Alma-Tadema Which Represents the "Violet-Tressed, Sweetly-Smiling" Poetess of Ancient Greece Listening to the Poems of the Poet Who Loved Her, But Whom She Did Not Love.

Little Juanita Clivette (in Two Poses), Who Believes She Is the "Reincarnated" Spirit of Sappho, the Poetess, and Whose Case Is Arousing Widespread Attention Among Psychologists.

A Famous, Very Touching Painting of the Unhappy Poetess Contemplating the Leap Into the Sea That Brought Her the Death She Sought.

Figure 6.3 Syndicated feature, "Mystery of 'Little Sappho' of Greenwich Village."

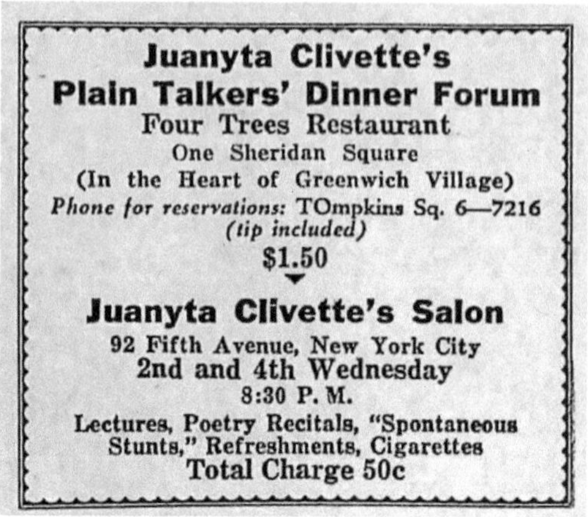

Figure 6.4 Advertisement, *Broadway Brevities*, 11 July 1931.

Village, "The Merry Villagers" was much less a compendium of current gossip than a myth-confirming rundown of colourful local characters and their lives.

During the months in which Juanyta Clivette's column appeared in the *New Broadway Brevities* (and in the weekly, tabloid version that followed), the publication ran regular advertisements for salons and other social and literary events that seemed to have been a key activity (and probable source of income) for her. These included "Juanyta Clivette's Plain Talkers' Dinners Forum" at the "Four Trees Restaurant," whose address was the same as the family home (1 Sheridan Place), and later "Juanyta Clivette's Salon," held twice monthly at 92 Fifth Avenue (to which the Clivette family had just moved). The latter promised "Lectures, Poetry Recitals, 'Spontaneous Stunts,' Refreshments, Cigarettes" for a charge of fifty cents. Juanyta Clivette slowly disappeared from the public record over the next two decades, turning up in brief notices of literary events happening in New York and publishing the occasional poem in newspapers.[43] Under the name Juanyta Clivette Aitkens, she died in San Francisco in 1980.[44]

Clow, Queerness, and New York's "Pansy Craze"

The first issue of the *New Broadway Brevities* is free of the preoccupation with queer lives that had marked the original *Broadway Brevities* in its last year, but this would not last long. In the second issue of the new magazine (September 1930), an unsigned feature, "Notes at Protest," whose placement and tone give it the air of an editorial, returns to Clow's long-standing fixation on gays and lesbians. The pretext for this resuscitated interest was the recent publication in the United States of Radclyffe Hall's lesbian-centred novel *The Well of Loneliness*. Comparing the present moment to that in which the original *Broadway Brevities* had cast its eye on queer life, the author writes that

> ten years ago it was considered vulgar and indecent to mention in print a certain social menace known as inversion. True, the unfortunate victims of this sexual aberration were all around us; active and impudent in all social circles, still more active and impudent in secret. The public, however, was not yet prepared for printed stigmatization of the evil. Today it is different – Allah be thanked! Along came a novel by an English author, entitled "The Well of Loneliness," picturing the doings and the pathetic frustration of "the woman of the species" – in short, a Lesbian …
>
> As has been pointed out again and again by psychiatrists and sociologists this "woman of the species" is far more dangerous to the community than her pseudo-male affinity. For a very plain and good reason: *The Lesbian is a professional seducer.*[45]

With this claim, Clow was tying his long-standing convictions to a more recent moral panic over lesbian predation that had led the New York State Legislature, in 1928, to pass the Wales Act, which prohibited any theatrical representation "dealing with the subject of sexual degeneracy, or sex perversion."[46] By the November 1930 issue of the *New Broadway Brevities* – sensing, perhaps, that the new magazine's reliance on tame gossip and miscellany was not producing the hoped-for attention – we find Clow announcing a new personal mission. A piece with the title "Is Your Own Daughter Safe? Safe from what? Safe from the Lesbian" returns to Clow's vision of lesbians as dangerous predators. He then reveals that he "has in contemplation a work dealing with the clinical and sociological side of inversion. Treating it, out of the knowledge of almost a lifetime's study, as it has not been treated before. Don't send in your orders yet. But you can keep posted, meantime, by an addiction to these sanctified monthly reveries."[47]

This fourth issue of the *New Broadway Brevities* brims with queerness. An unsigned two-page feature, "The Lisping Lipstickers," is close in tone and subject matter to some of the earlier 1924 episodes of "Nights in Fairyland." The piece begins by noting the widespread attention being paid by New York's daily tabloids to Jean Malin (born Victor Eugene James Malinovsky, and also known as "Gene Malin"), a female impersonator who was perhaps the best-known figure in the "pansy craze" that swept across nighttime entertainment in New York in 1930.[48] The apparent ubiquity of queerness in New York nightlife in the early 1930s clearly energized Clow's writing about the current moment, but also offered him the opportunity to wring new value from his long-standing interest in the topic. And so, in "The Lisping Lipstickers," he sets out to show himself much more versant with Malin's background and personal life than the uninformed columnists writing for other venues:

> To wit: Jean has been referred to as a "professional pansy," whatever that floricultural term actually means. [Other journalists have] also traced Jean back to the time when he presided at the subsequently blottoed "Rubaiyat" in the Village. Before that, all is silence. Ah, ha! But this gas-log companion remembers back farther'n that ... Mallin was once a cute little dancer in the chorus of "Mima" at the Belasco, along with two of his iridescent sisters, Gus Fontaine and Larry Hogan. And during the run of that obfuscation, as for many munz before, Jean was conspicuous, dearie, at drags, winning many first and second prizes – and, whoops! known as "Imogene Wilson."

As this 1930 article moves on, still pretending to instruct uninformed journalists, it begins sketching in a recent history of New York drag culture, detailing the ways in which Malin's original success at the Abbey club had prompted other venues to copy its focus on cross-dressing performers. With a dash of irony, Clow acknowledges that he is falling back into his old role as cartographer of queer New York: "seeing the suckercess of the sweet old Abbaye, rivals produced the Club Balais. (What is this – another Nights in Fairyland?)."[49] And then, as if this really were the newest instalment of "Nights in Fairyland," the feature concludes with a detailed mapping of queer nightlife in midtown:

> Now, seizing our megaphone again, how'd you enjoy knowing that Trinker's Tavern – here we are, fellows, in West 55 – displays a less pretentious fol-

lowing, while The Little Tavern – now we're in Vest [*sic*] 49 – is most "brilliant" on Sontag nights. But, honey, to see the temperamentals in their most "continental" phase just take your little feetsies along Fifth avenue from 42 to 59 any night from 9 to 12 to encounter them – in twos and fours, all made up and "camping." Quite in the matter, Lucille, of Paris and Berlin!

Probably within ten years we'll all be queer[50]

Twenty pages on, another piece, "We're Certainly to the Fag End! Have YOU a Little Fairy in Your Home?,"[51] scrambles to display even more of its author's grasp of the very latest fashions in gay-themed entertainment. With the pansy craze erupting around him, it seems clear that Clow, sensing a public interest in queer activity that exceeded any he had encountered in 1924, was rushing to reclaim a place as its best-informed chronicler: "The town has unquestionably gone invert-mad. Within the last few weeks at least five new night-clubs, flaunting fag entertainers, have opened and are going simply great. In a number of cases these enterprises have not only fag talent but fag backing. Is this the new thrill of a jaded city, or is it proof that androgynism, long mildly epidemic, has become acutely endemic."[52]

From here, the article moves back to years 1920–24 and to the Village, offering a summary rundown of the places visited in the original "Nights in Fairyland" series, naming Paul and Joe's, Trilby's, and Dolly Judge's. By 1930, we are told, the scene has drifted north, and it is with an update on the place of the midtown Childs restaurants in present-day queer life that the article concludes, not without speculating, once again, that "maybe we'll all be queer by 1940."[53] Curiously, Clow's tone throughout these 1930 articles is, above all, one of triumph, as if new worlds of queer nightlife have arisen around him in ways that recast the original "Nights in Fairyland" series as useful prehistory and him as the most seasoned observer of several generations of sexual nonconformity. Clow's twice-repeated prediction that, in a decade, all of New York would be queer, has shed the apocalyptic tone with which the original series concluded so many of its episodes. Rather, it seems intended to capture the giddy, unstoppable momentum that was taking New York nightlife in ever more inventive directions.

Feuding with Winchell

Like his obsession with queer Manhattan, Stephen G. Clow's resentment at the success of columnist Walter Winchell broke through the image of controlled dignity he apparently hoped to convey in the *New Broadway Brevities*. In 1922, the original *Brevities* had published a brief poem by Winchell, "In Memoriam," after the death of Broadway actor Frank Bacon.[54] In the same issue, Clow wrote with admiration of Winchell, who was still, at this point, writing for the trade publication *Vaudeville News*:

> How pleasant to turn the editorial eye from the "Log Rollers" and find, say, such a nice unobtrusive chap as Walter Winchell of the VAUDEVILLE NEWS quietly making his way into prominence by sheer force of his gifts! We've been complimented by several of his contributions – indeed, we carry one in this issue. Walter's poem on the death of Frank Bacon has been copied, we hear, throughout the country, and seems to leave no room in rhyme for any other epitaph of that great soul.[55]

In the following issue, in 1922, *Brevities* had published another of Winchell's poems, "Your Broadway and Mine," whose title would soon be that of the *Evening Graphic* column with which Winchell began his ascent to national fame.[56] In 1923, however, even as he was welcoming Winchell into *Brevities*, and while Broadway columns were proliferating across the New York press, Clow began lashing out at others he accused of purloining his style. In particular, he claimed to have invented what he called the "elliptical period," the use of three dots to separate items printed in long strings. "Now," he wrote in 1923, "everyone is using it."[57] Winchell – at this point a beginner whom Clow was happy to encourage – is not to be found in Clow's list of alleged plagiarists accused of stealing his elliptical period, but, in fact, Winchell had been using dots to separate gossipy items as early as 1920 – in a column, "Merciless Truths," published in the *Vaudeville News*.[58] When he began writing for daily newspapers, in 1924, the three-dot ellipsis quickly became Winchell's most famous and imitated stylistic signature, widely regarded as emblematic of the modern, telegraphic pace he brought to printed gossip. His biographer, Neil Gabler, wrote decades later that the dots gave Winchell's column "a jazzy, almost musical look; items now seemed to cascade down the page, each with its own urgency." Gabler quoted, as well, Ben Hecht's suggestion that Winchell wrote "like a man honking in a traffic jam."[59] Though the length of items in newspaper columns had been shrinking for some time – Dwight Macdonald later wrote of the "short punchy paragraphs," separated by asterisks, for which Hearst columnist Arthur Brisbane was already known[30] – the strings of words and dots in Winchell's writing seemed genuinely novel.

In the November 1930 issue of the *New Broadway Brevities*, Clow finally turned his anger on Walter Winchell, in a three-page feature with an all-caps title and wordy set of subtitles: "PARASITES WHO HAVE FATTENED OFF BREVITIES: Our Original and Unique Style of Banter Copied Everywhere – Columnist Winchell the Most Brazen and Contemptuous imitator – Boasted 'Winchellisms' But an Echo of Brevities (1916–1924)." In the article's most sweeping paragraph, Clow suggested that the original *Brevities* had been the source of all that was modern in sensational American journalism: "BREVITIES' first issue appeared in the saintly summer of 1916, and in the eight years following its peculiar literary and typographic inventions largely revolutionized the art of persiflage in America." Over a page and a half, Clow quotes passages from the original *Brevities*, claiming that they represent the first uses in American journalism of a wide variety of styles, article concepts, headings, and phrasings that would turn up as characteristic features of the gossip columns of daily newspapers in the 1920s. These include the headings "Famous Last Words," the phrasing of innuendo in the form of a question, the idea of "Broadway Monikers" (like "Gin Gulch," "Rum Ravine," and "The Main Stem"), and, most notably of all, the ellipsis. Clow reproduces a paragraph of his own from the August 1921 issue of *Broadway Brevities* in which short items trail down the page, divided by three-dot ellipses, reminding the reader, after it concludes, that "this is NOT an extract from Wallie Winchell's yessirday's column."[61] Given his earlier tirades against formal experimentation in literature and other art forms, it is hard not to see the irony in Chow's claims to have initiated a modernist revolution in journalism.

The final paragraph of this assault on Winchell proffers an olive branch of sorts, then concludes by revealing the real reason for the outburst: "Walter is an old pal, and it is with throat-choking grief that we are compelled to disclose where his so-called and, alas, absolutely uncredited 'originalities' took source from. However, it makes it easier to stifle our sobs in view of the fact that Walter has recently added insult and injury to barefaced plagiarism by announcing the demise of this fireside consort."[62] By "fireside consort," Clow meant his own magazine and, indeed, after recommending the revived *Brevities* in his column of 29 July 1930, Winchell had claimed, in an eight-word item on 20 October of the same year, that "'Broadway Brevities' folds up with the current issue."[63] Just a month earlier, perhaps conscious that predictions of the death of his *New Broadway Brevities* were on the horizon, Clow had spent a page offering statistics that claimed to confirm its success. It had sold out on over four hundred newsstands in New York and Chicago. Within New York alone, its sales were rivalling or even outpacing those of the magazines *Red Book* and *Cosmopolitan*, titles Clow identified as comparable in tone and readership. Winchell's announcement that the magazine was dying obviously cast doubt on those claims, and the reaction of Clow and his backers was swift. While the November 1930 issue of the *New Broadway Brevities* was on the stands, with its denunciation of Winchell for stealing Clow's stylistic innovations, the New-Broad Publishing Co. launched a $250,000 libel suit against Winchell and his newspaper, the *Daily Mirror*, for claiming that *New Broadway Brevities* was folding.[64] A summons directing Winchell and representatives of the *Daily Mirror* to appear in court was issued on 19 November.[65] (I have found no further reference to the lawsuit and can only assume it was dropped.)

Clow would continue editing the *New Broadway Brevities* well into 1931, though by March of that year, its page count was half that of six months earlier. The adoption of colourful, illustrated covers featuring show girls did not seem to be helping the magazine. Then, at some point in the summer of 1931, Clow left (or was made to leave) the publication. Reporting this news, *Variety* claimed that Clow had resigned and that he intended to launch another magazine, "covering both Broadway and Mayfair." Nothing apparently came of that. Clow would never again be offered the sorts of corporate backing and "Wall Street coin" that had made his *New Broadway Brevities* possible, and chapter 8 describes how the search for work drove him to projects of ever-diminishing esteem. Before returning to Clow's story, the next chapter follows a group of new editors and contributors who carried on with the *New Broadway Brevities*. Their legacy was the most brazen and long-lasting title in a wave of weekly tabloid newspapers that spread across the northeast of the United States in the years 1932–34.

SEVEN

TABLOID *BREVITIES*

The lower levels of periodical publishing in early 1930s New York brought forth a wide array of new or revamped magazine genres. These included gossipy weekly tabloids, pulp magazines carving out newly named niches (shudder pulps, risqué pulps, eccentric "character pulps"), prototypes of the comic book, and pocket-sized digests offering different combinations of ribald cartoons, smutty poetry, and pin-up photography. The circles that produced these publications were populated by a rich assortment of personality types both old and new. Among them were unscrupulous pornographers testing the boundaries of criminality, show business publicists with artistic aspirations and progressive politics, left-over Broadway personalities milking residual value from the scandals of their youth, and publishers from the Midwest transforming their folksy magazines of the 1920s into the foundations of New York–based publishing companies. As well, like any clusters of cultural activity, the sector of sensational publishing in early 1930s New York brought together people on the way up, working their way toward mainstream respectability, and others on the way down, reduced to the status of full-time pornographer or freelance seller of racetrack tips and gossip.

These worlds of sensational publishing in early 1930s New York are the focus of this chapter and the next. The life of Stephen G. Clow winds its way through our account but often moves to the sidelines as the careers of others come into focus. The short biographical sketches scattered through these chapters – of writers, editors, and illustrators – are intended to rescue from neglect a class of creators typically overlooked in histories of American publishing. They are also meant to show the threads of affinity and collaboration connecting different parts of this publishing world and tying them to broader contexts of cultural and political ferment. The tabloid version of the *New Broadway Brevities* was an important crossroads in the worlds described here.

A new incarnation of *Broadway Brevities*, free of any traces of Stephen G. Clow, was launched with a cover date of 17 August 1931. This was a very different publication from the leather-bound magazine printed on glossy paper that had been introduced under Clow's editorship the previous year. Selling for fifteen cents (Clow's had cost thirty-five), the new *Brevities* was a weekly, published on newsprint. Its masthead indicated that the New-Broad Publishing Co. was still behind the magazine and that L. (Lorain) Simpson, who had taken over as president of the firm halfway through Clow's tenure as editor, remained in charge. However, the publisher's offices were now in the Flatiron Building, at 175 Fifth Avenue, and as befit a publication now modelling itself on a newspaper, the list of officers included a circulation manager by the name of Theodore Epstein.

A banner running on the cover of each issue, just below the *New Broadway Brevities* title, claimed that the revamped publication was "America's First National Tabloid Weekly," invoking the loose definition of "tabloid" that had already settled into popular and professional understandings of journalism, in New York and elsewhere.[1] Originally, "tabloid" referred to any newspaper whose dimensions were half those of a broadsheet, as if the latter had been folded or cut in half.[2] The size of broadsheet newspapers had never been universally standardized, however, and the dimensions of so-called tabloids could vary from publication to publication. Measuring 10 × 13¾ inches, the weekly *Brevities* was slightly smaller than a typical 1930s New York daily tabloid, such as the *Daily News*.[3] In style and content, *Brevities* offered most of the features of the tabloid press identified by historians Adrian Bingham and Martin Conboy: "chatty, vernacular language, a visual style based on bold black headlines and eye-catching images, and content driven by the insistent pursuit of sensation and scandal."[4] While the tabloid *Brevities* borrowed the lurid headlines and sensational themes of the daily tabloid, its

New Broadway

15 cents a copy

BREVITIES

America's First National Tabloid Weekly

Vol. II, No. 3 New York, August 31, 1931 Price 15 cents

"BALLYHOO?" AW, BALONEY!

"Ballyhoo" Tries for Fame as Funster by Lifting Ad-Burlesques—BREVITIES *Exposes*

Ethridge's "Black Sheep" Paving Way for 10 Years Before Monthly Stole Gags

By Tom Davin
(Brevities *Special Snooper*)

"Ballyhoo," that faintly illegitimate brain-child of Mr. Norman Anthony, stirred up quite a hornet's nest of reproachful advertisers whose products that former editor of "Life" and "Judge" razzed crudely in his publication.

Just Saps

As every editor and advertising manager knows, the advertiser is a sap who pays for space in a much over-rated periodical and thus contributes to the support of its personnel. In the face of these facts, the advertiser is thus shown as a dull-witted fellow, easily bilked and with no perspective or sense of humor. But his stupidity and extravagance has some limits. There are some publications, believe it or not, into which he cannot be persuaded to place his notices. These are pseudo humorous magazines like "Ballyhoo."

With these facts in mind, Mr. Anthony started his periodical and, *faute de mieux*, socked John J. Advertiser right on the belly-button. Naturally, the space buyers yelled. But the tone of their caoin showed them to be in the wrong, as usual.

"Black Sheep" First

Instead of pointing out to all and sundry that the ad-burlesque idea had been used by The Ethridge Company, that distinguished advertising art service, in its uproarious house-organ "The Black Sheep" for over ten years, they shrieked and sued poor "Ballyhoo" to the tune of much publicity for that monthly.

See Pages 8 and 9 for
LOUDER and FUNNIER AD-BURLESQUES

Indeed, the slap-stick treatment of Mr. Anthony was a bit dull and humorless, so there may be some cause for their plaint. In this issue, however, Brevities wishes to show how such ad-burlesques may be made really funny without giving offense. (*Continued on page* 15)

This is an important ad. If it had not been conceived by The Ethridge Company, there might never have been any such magazine (?) as "Ballyhoo."

Caught in the Act!

Remember? Three weeks ago, on the front page of "Brevities'" first weekly issue, there appeared that drawing and joke about the man in the swanky bathroom yelling for the Mail Order Catalog. Well, if you want to see how that idea was lifted and ruined by "Ballyhoo" just look at the back cover of their current (October) issue. Tsk! Tsk! Read BREVITIES and laugh first, not last!

More "Ballyhoo" Baloney will be exposed in coming issues.

Figure 7.1 Cover, *New Broadway Brevities: America's First National Tabloid Weekly*, 31 August 1931.

lack of resources set it in a category of its own. With no salaried reporters assigned to journalistic beats and no photographers rushing to the locations of newsworthy events, *Brevities* could offer only headlines, stories, and cartoons that exploited sensational themes and little in the way of reportorial detail.

The first editor of the tabloid *Brevities* was Tom Davin, a young man rising steadily in New York media circles as a publicist and writer. Davin had previously written for off-centre magazines like *Beau* (published by the poet, bookseller, and soon-to-be-convicted pornographer Samuel Roth[5]), and, in 1927, he had been listed as "business manager" for *Creative Art*, a magazine founded that year by the artist Rockwell Kent. Davin appeared to move with ease between bohemian worlds downtown, midtown theatrical circles, and the mainstream publishing industry. As a publicist, he represented a variety of clients, among them Canadian prime minister William Lyon Mackenzie King and the pre–World War II government of Czechoslovakia.[6] We shall see later how his career eventually found him implicated in political struggles against fascism in Europe and its supporters in the United Sates.

Tabloid Tone and Style

In its guide to writers' markets for October 1931, *Writer's Digest* carried a long item on the new publication it called "Brevities Weekly," describing it as "a low-brow magazine for high-brows." This effectively captured the character of the publication, which indulged in vulgarities of all kinds but managed to convey a jaded, big-city smarts. *Writer's Digest*'s notice quoted a long message from the editor, presumably Davin, who explained what the magazine was looking for: "We need – Gossip items, such as Messrs. Winchell, Sobol, McIntyre, et al. are too timorous or indolent to reach out and print; 10 c per item; should be under 10 or 15 words; amusing anecdotes about real people and things. If slightly risqué, all the better – 1 cent a word; should be about 50 words each; decidedly novel short stories of 1,000 words – 1 cent a word; inside stories of newspaper or professional or national activities, of the type that papers cannot usually print because of many sacred cows … We buy rare action photos only with semi-risque angle."[7] Photographs are mentioned here, but they almost never appeared in the magazine, whose visuals were dominated by captioned cartoons and fanciful illustrations that wove their way around and through blocks of text.

This tabloid version of *Brevities* has become the most notorious of the title's various incarnations, in large part because of its provocatively titled front-page articles and the cartoons that appeared alongside them. Examples of both were displayed in the exhibition that opened New York's Museum of Sex in 2002, and others are regularly reproduced in online sites devoted to histories of queer life.[8] *Brevities*' lurid headlines, which appeared on the front and back covers of each issue, were the magazine's most striking feature. Like the headlines of late twentieth-century supermarket tabloids, they mimicked those of the daily newspaper, but their purpose was to titillate rather than report. The articles that followed normally contained few references to specific events or people and were often concluded quickly inside.

The most notable feature of *Brevities*' headlines was their tendency to push the limits of wordplay with the naughtiest of double entendres. In recent years, the best remembered and most frequently cited of *Brevities*' titles have been those promising stories of queer sexuality – symptoms of a preoccupation that had run through all versions of the magazine to date. These headlines played shamelessly with schoolyard terms or in-group slang for sexual acts, body parts, and queer people: "Chicago World's Fairies" (7 December 1931); "Fag Balls Exposed" (14 March 1932); "Pansies Blow U.S." (9 May 1932); "Queers Seek Succor" (4 July 1932); "Villagers Go Down" (1 August 1932); "Fags Ram Heinies" (19 September 1932); "Fagged Men Licked" (17 October 1932); "Sexy Sailors Blow" (12 October 1933). Likewise, the dozens of headlines referencing heterosexual behaviours drew on a broad lexicon of terms suggesting orifices, sexual positions, genitals, and acts of sexual exertion or violence. In a period of just over a year, these included the following: "Beach Babes Bared" (8 August 1932); "Nude Nuts Exposed" (15 August 1932); "Beauties Open Up" (5 September 1932); "Lovers Get Piece" (5 September 1932); "Suckers Go Deep" (12 September 1932); "Students Open Wide" (26 September 1932); "Stiff Vice Mounts" (3 October 1932); "Miners' Hot Holes" (10 October 1932); "Yanks Hop Abroad" (31 October 1932); "Peddlers Push Hard" (31 October 1932); "Mike Maids Jazz" (7 November 1932); "Movie Girls Muffed" (14 November 1932); "Nude Nuts Snapped" (14 November 1932);

Read: "Swinging Wide"—the Woman's Angle, by Juanyta Clivette

BREVITIES

America's First National Tabloid Weekly

Vol. III, No. 5 | New York, November 30, 1931 | Price 15 cents

DIRTY LINEN EXPOSED!!

Amazing Revelations by Your Laundryman Reveal That All Sins Come Out in the Wash

HOTCHACHA
See Page 2

Profound Analytical Research Shows How Key to Character Goes with Clothes "In the Bag"

YOU NEVER CAN TELL

FIRST IKEDAY: *"Let's be nice to him Billie; maybe he has a sister."*

By ANGUS DEY

(Who Washes Away the Sins of the World)

You may be the world to your heart, but you're only another pair of dirty drawers to your laundryman. Heeb, goy or boogey or descendant of a real man or of William the conqueror, you and your character are an open book to the man or woman who sorts your dirty clothes. French, English, German and Italian, all nationalities have their peculiarities from the washman's standpoint. Russians and Indians are fit subjects for weighty tomes, your dirty-clothes rusher will tell you.

All in the Wash

Not only nationalities and races but minor divisions of men such as Catholics and Hard Shell or Primitive Baptists have their little oddities, the wash bag reveals. As for the sexes, the experienced analist who is also a laundryman can tell the story of introversion, extraversion or perversion from one hasty glance at the undies and the shirt tails spread out before his all-seeing eye. Pansies, dikes, nymphomaniacs, (hot sisters, to you), and others all have their own quirks in the clothes line. And when lined up their garments tell the tale without apology and without reticence.

Aha! Those Napkins

Do you tuck a napkin in your pajama pocket? This is a serious question. If you do, it means something very definite to the clothes sorter. You may snicker at this, but as a man who ran a laundry while poring over the works of Steckel, Freud, Adler, Jung and a host of others, I can swear that many a fraternity man does just that. In the case of the normal collegian, the napkin means that he is riding his fraternity house for his bills, even stealing napkins to use for handkerchiefs.

(Continued on page 10)

Figure 7.2 Cover with illustration by Ken Browne, *Brevities*, 30 November 1931.

"Big Balls Popular" (12 December 1932); "Girls Nip Hard Nuts" (26 December 1932); "Hot Tools Grabbed" (26 December 1932); "Molls Take Screws" (9 January 1933); "Gem Beauties Mounted" (20 February 1933); and "Haulers Joints Oiled" (5 September 1933).

Captioned cartoons were the other prominent feature of *Brevities* in its new tabloid incarnation. These appeared all through the magazine and occupied key space on each issue's front and back covers. In the tabloid's first year, a large number of these were signed by Ken Browne, a Canadian who had moved to Greenwich Village in 1920 and worked first as a cartoonist for the *Sun* newspaper. Many of Browne's cartoons were focused on cross-dressing and transgender themes, and several of these continue to circulate today. They also played with heterosexual situations, wringing humour from the predicaments of aged men with younger women, sexually frustrated elderly females, or independent women on the make. In April 1932, Browne began a comic strip, "Bee Brevities," focused on the urban adventures of an independent young woman.

Ken Browne left the tabloid *Brevities* in May or June 1932. The online *Field Guide to Wild American Pulp Artists* suggests that he was hired at this time by Theodore Epstein, who, as of December 1931, was no longer listed as *Brevities*' circulation manager and was expanding his own publishing projects. Browne apparently worked with Epstein as art editor of various publications until the 1950s.[9]

The man who succeeded him as lead cartoonist for the tabloid *Brevities* was a curious figure named Henri Lamothe, who was identified as *Brevities*' "Arts Editor" (a newly created title) from October 1932 through mid-1933. The most offensive body of content in the entire legacy of *Brevities*' various incarnations is the string of racist cartoons Lamothe contributed to the magazine's covers and interior pages during this period. These traded in stereotypes referencing Black sexuality and laziness, revelled in caricatural images of Black women's anatomies, and recycled many of the notorious persona of American minstrelsy. Ken Browne's cartoons had been largely free of racial typing, and focused on disparities of class and age between characters who were almost exclusively white. These had helped to position *Brevities* at the outer edges of a universe of smart, urbane magazines of the time, like *Broadway Magazine* and *Manhattan*. In contrast, Lamothe's crude caricatures pulled *Brevities* closer to magazines like the

Figure 7.3 Ken Browne, "Bee Brevities," *Brevities*, 25 April 1932.

Calgary Eye Opener and *Capt. Billy's Whiz Bang* – titles that, by the early 1930s, circulated with lightly pornographic images inserted in their centres and racist jokes or cartoons scattered throughout.[10]

Lamothe, who liked to tell journalists that he had invented the Lindy Hop – focus of a well-known dance craze in the 1920s – would pop up in peculiar corners of American culture over the next half-century.[11] By the 1940s, he was art editor of the down-market *Bowery News* (subtitle: "The Voice of Society's Basement"), which trafficked in rude jokes, pin-up photographs, and ribald poetry and cartoons. Then, late in his life, Lamothe turned what had apparently been a fairground sideline – aquatic gymnastics – into a significant career as a geriatric high diver. In the 1970s, *The Mike Douglas Show*, *People* magazine, and *Sports Illustrated* all reported on his leaps from great heights into pools of water. These achievements led to an entry in the *Guinness Book of Records* and to his employment by General Motors, who used his aquatic feats to test the resilience of aging bodies.[12] In the early 1980s, the feminist environmental artist Jody Pinto painted a series of watercolours of Lamothe, whom she called "Saint Henri."[13] Lamothe died in 1987, aged eighty-three.

Read "In the Know" by Tony Wood

SEE PAGE 7

BREVITIES

America's First National Tabloid Weekly

Vol. III, No. 3 | New York, November 16, 1931 | Price 15 cents

SAPPHIC SISTERS SCRAM!

HOTCHACHA—See page 2

Depression Drives Ladies of Lesbos to Normalcy
Deserting Boat Boys for Jobs and Feminine Frills

JUST A PAL

RETIRING MOTHER: *"Don't sit up too late with that young man, Doris!"*
NOT SO RETIRING DAUGHTER: *"Ooooh! No! Mama, dear!"*

Village and Beeway Camps Left Lonely as Rich Dames Vanish. Only Old Guard Carries On

By CONNIE LINGLE
(No relation to the late Jake)

Depression has hit Lesbos. Along the lyric lanes of this half-light land of sex the lutes of the lesbians are muted in minors.

Eve Adams, once the queen of the third sex, has fled to Paris where her "Le Boudoir De L'amour" on Montmarte attracts the supple tongued sirens of the lesbian element.

Dashing Peter Carlyle, the terror of the old "Black Rabbit," that held sway at the corner of MacDougal and Minetta Lane in the Village, after her sensational swim from Welfare Island, has departed leaving behind her the wail of 1931.

Female A.K's. Out

The days of the Rich Dames with the wandering spouses are gone forever. The husbands can no longer dine the show-girls, and the wives can no longer dine and wine their mannishly attired soul-mates.

However, a few years ago there would have been a much different story to tell. Manhattan, once teemed with the third sex element. From Van Dam Street to the upper Fifties practically every speak was polluted with dikes and fags, anxious to seize upon the purse of the unwary and willing.

How many of you remember the late Dolly Judge, who first banded together the Third Sex at her notorious "Flower Apartment" that was situated on the corner of Gay and Christopher Streets in the Village? It was a gay and impromptu place where excitement reigned from nine in the evening until the wee hours of the morning. A seraglio of specialized sex. Its fame spread all over the country, and everyone of any importance whatsoever who ever dropped around the Village eventually ended up at Dolly's. Although the "Flower Pot" was not a clip joint in the actual sense of the word, it was financially backed by a group of cab drivers who lured their adventure-seeking customers to Dolly's and usually fixed them up for the night.

Gradually, however, the crowd started to drift uptown with Paul and Joe's, who moved from

(*Continued on page* 10)

Figure 7.4 *Brevities*, 16 November 1931.

Queer Cartographies

More than most publicly available New York periodicals of the 1930s, the tabloid *Brevities* showed an intense interest in the city's gay and lesbian life, especially in its first year. This interest, of course, had marked earlier versions of the magazine, but its treatment in the new weekly *Brevities* was magnified by the paper's tabloid format, with its cheeky headlines and illustrations. One of the earliest examples of this coverage, noted by historians such as George Chauncey, was "Sapphic Sisters Scram," the lead article in the issue dated 16 November 1931. Credited to a "Connie Lingle," the piece opens, like so many articles in *Brevities* during this period, with reflection on the ways in which the Depression has affected New York life: "Depression has hit Lesbos. Along the lyric lanes of this half-light land of sex the lutes of the lesbians are muted in minors."[14] In the paragraphs that follow, the departures of some of the scene's key people are taken as evidence of a lesbian culture in crisis: "Eve Adams, once the queen of the third sex, has fled to Paris where her 'Le Boudoir de l'Amour' on Montmartre attracts the supple tongued sirens of the lesbian element ... Dashing Peter Carlyle, the terror of the old 'Black Rabbit,' that held sway at the corner of MacDougal and Minetta Lane in the Village, after her sensational swim from Welfare Island, has departed leaving behind her the wail of 1931."[15]

Eve Adams, who would die in Auschwitz, was the author of *Lesbian Love*, a volume of life stories recently described as the "first ethnography of American lesbian life."[16] "Sapphic Sisters Scram" itself offers an impressively thorough account of the fate of lesbian meeting places in New York. The references here to Dolly Judge's "Flower Apartment" (Clow had called her establishment the Flower Pot) and to Paul and Joe's all echo descriptions from the "Nights in Fairyland" series of more than a half-decade earlier. This new treatment, however, describes these places in much greater detail, brings their histories up to date, and offers more names than Clow was willing or able to offer. Eventually, "Sapphic Sisters Scram" trails off into dubious lore about the pickup techniques used by lesbians – what the article calls their "method of procedure" – with particular emphasis on the approaches made to married women. It does so, however, without summoning (or feigning) the alarm at threatened innocence that ran all through

Clow's writing on the subject. Indeed, the most striking feature of this article is the reportorial clarity with which it describes an ongoing series of police actions against lesbian spaces. Noteworthy, as well, is the sympathy with which it describes a community struggling to survive in the face of well-coordinated repression. Scholar Anastasia Jones, in a comprehensive look at the vocabularies used in US tabloid papers of this period to talk about queer women, suggests that *Brevities*' treatment of such women – and this article in particular – displayed an unusual sensitivity to the range of ways in which female sexualities were performed and named.[17]

Three weeks after "Sapphic Sisters Scram," the cover story "Chicago World's Fairies," credited to a "Schwanda Schwbik," claimed that promoters of the 1933 Chicago World's Fair had plans to develop that city's "bohemian" north side, whose queer character *Brevities* described in detail: "To the initiate the near north side is known as Fairy's Paradise. In the furnished rooms and studios of the section that is separated from the heart of the city by the muddy waters of the Chicago River, the queers of the third sex seek refuge. Daisy chains and other complicated forms of group sex perversion are practiced in them. The haze of marijuana hangs like a deadly miasma over all. And literature and art are the screens behind which they hide while exercising their yen for sex gymnastics."[18]

Even as it mapped the boundaries of queer communities and enclaves, the tabloid *Brevities* did not refrain from imagining a world in which, as Clow had earlier predicted, queerness would be everywhere. A 1932 cover story on Harlem's legendary Masquerade and Civic Ball, perhaps the best-known event in the city's queer calendar, was credited to a "Buddy Browning" and given a rude title noting the large numbers of people present: "Fag Balls Exposed: 6,000 Crowd Huge Ball as Queer Men and Women Dance at 64th Annual Masquerade." The opening paragraph marvelled, in terms seemingly free of condemnation, at the spread of queer life: "The third sex is flooding America. It is no longer confined to side streets and obscure corners. Queer people, both men and women, who do not love or feel like ordinary men or women, are increasing. They have their own restaurants. Some bath houses cater to them. An intricate social system built up outside society is dominated by them."[19] The account of the ball that follows is unusually long and detailed, with lengthy descriptions of the refreshments served, the costumes worn, and the rituals performed. As it moves on, the article observes the "new level of audacity" in American queer life, then concludes by turning to an apocalyptic, denunciatory vision more typical of Clow's writing in earlier versions of *Brevities*: "And each year thousands of the curious come to look on. How many of them are sucked down into the whirlpool of perversion from which there is no escape? How many come as spectators and remain as members of that vast group which is neither male nor female as other people are male or female."[20]

Brevities' most detailed overview of queer life in Manhattan came early in its tabloid incarnation. An article bearing the lurid headline "Death Knell of Degeneracy? Police and Pansies No Longer Friends as Dirt Begins to Spread a Little Too Thick" in the 5 October 1931 issue begins with an account of New York police officers standing guard in the drag clubs that had proliferated during the previous year. The police, we learn, had quietly tolerated any dancing between men in conventional masculine attire and those wearing "feminine finery," but were moved to intervene when dance partners both wore pants. Early on, the article notes the popularity of drag clubs among the city's show business elite, and especially those around whom rumours of queerness had swirled: "Broadway celebrities made a fad of buying boxes to view the orgies, those in evidence in the parterre including Beatrice Lillie, Clifton Webb, Fannie Brice, Jay Brennan, Mabel Boll, Charlie Levine, Tallulah Bankhead and, of course, Carl Van Vechten, who never misses a drag."[21] Continuing with a word-filled page inside, the article offers what seems a well-informed, exhaustive history of the shifting places and events of New York's drag culture, from its "old haunts" (Rockland Palace, the Star Casino, Central Opera, and Alhambra) through "Frank's Place" in Brooklyn ("three blocks back of the Navy YMCA") and then to the more recently popular area surrounding Bryant Park in midtown Manhattan. The queer geography sketched here maps easily onto that drawn by Clow in his "Lisping Lipstickers" feature of a year earlier, but this new version is more finely grained and tightly packed with names and insider knowledge.

Front-page headlines referencing queer life became less common as the magazine moved into its second and subsequent years of publication. After "Queers Seek Succor!" (4 July 1932), which claimed that Boston was now the New Babylon – the global capital of queer life – *Brevities*' headline articles on sexual behaviour were more likely to focus on such phenomena as prostitution in trains and on cruise ships, the declining price of sexual services in New York, and the spread of brothels in out-of-town vacation resorts.[22] Reference to queer lives and behaviours continued to turn up as brief items in the gossip columns that filled the magazine's centre pages but were less and less common on the front pages with which the magazine announced itself to potential buyers.

Brevities' New Columnists

One of the early clients of Tom Davin, the publicist who served as first editor of the tabloid *Brevities*, was the performer Peggy Hopkins Joyce, whose testimony had helped to secure a guilty verdict for Stephen G. Clow in his 1924 trial. In the first few issues of the tabloid *Brevities*, under Davin's editorship, Joyce lent her name to the column "For Women Only," with a dateline of Paris, France, and a focus on fashion. Joyce disappeared from the magazine in October 1931, and Juanyta Clivette's column "Swinging Wide," the only feature carried over from Clow's version of the magazine, began carrying the subtitle "The Woman's Angle," as if Clivette had taken over that beat from Joyce. The first issue of the tabloid *Brevities* also contained a peculiar poem by Clivette, "Six Little Columnists," whose premise was that New York's top-flight nightlife columnists (including Walter Winchell, Louis Sobol, and Mark Hellinger) had all died and gone to heaven, then been sent back to earth when God found their company exhausting.[23] *Brevities*' tendency to snipe at high-profile columnists working for New York's daily newspapers had begun with Stephen G. Clow's resentful attacks on Walter Winchell and others. It would carry on, albeit in a more friendly, playful manner, throughout the life of the weekly tabloid.

The *Brevities* feature that came closest to matching the up-to-the-minute currency of the daily newspaper gossip column was "On the Bandwagon," credited during the publication's first two years to an R.J.D. and then to Charles Myron. Whether R.J.D. stood in for an individual or the magazine's collective resources, "On the Bandwagon" was a remarkably lengthy and wide-ranging collection of gossip. Typically, it filled at least one full page with tightly packed items separated by the three dots that were now an entrenched feature of the genre. In a periodical whose regular features often seemed like filler, as if their writers were at some distance from the centre of things, the items in "On the Bandwagon" seemed fresh and its author well-informed. The sample below includes news on the career shifts of high-profile film stars, sly innuendo concerning romantic relationships, and insider tips on urban rackets designed to fleece the innocent:

> Current rumors notwithstanding, La Garbo will make two, two more before sailing with the bankroll ... The stork has Joe Vanuti & his pretty frau beaming ... didn't Peggy Joyce follow bad boy Grant Withers westward? ... evidently Lily Pons publicity-divorce didn't take ... tho' June Knight is wowing the locals in Ziggy's Hot Cha! they didn't give her a tumble when she played the palace a year ago with Frances Williams ... creep Janes are working the taxi-lines ... if you find one in the cab you hire from in front of your favorite speakeasy, don't be amazed ... just a new racket, my lads ... laugh of the week is the fact that Ed Robinson, tough guy of the flickers, plays a harp ...[24]

While gossip like this filled the front pages of *Brevities*, its back pages were typically devoted to short columns and the conclusions of stories begun or announced on the front and back covers. *Brevities* was faithful to the tendency of tabloid papers to balance luridly singular headlines with a stable roster of recurring columns whose tone, focus, and level of credibility would become familiar over time. Indeed, what is striking about the tabloid *Brevities* is that, in a history apparently marked by financial crises, it remained remarkably consistent in tone and organization over its four-year existence. There were, to be sure, a few changes along the way. The issue dated 2 May 1932 introduced "Horse Sense," a page devoted to horse racing, and the magazine was soon offering to sell betting advice to readers through the mails. New columns devoted to the film industry ("Hollywood Lowdown" by "Alma Mater") or financial district gossip ("Wailing Wall Street" by "Jess Nevermore") were introduced at roughly the same time. These features would all continue until *Brevities*' demise, giving the magazine's inside pages a predictability that balanced the willfully sensationalizing novelty of each week's headlines.

Tom Davin and Hank Fuller

In its 11 January 1930 edition, the Baltimore *Afro-American* newspaper printed excepts from a column by *New York Graphic* columnist Louis Sobol, who described an evening spent at the "menage of the Messrs. Tom Davin and Hank Fuller." It was common for the *Afro-American* to pull news about social goings-on in Harlem from columns in the white-owned press, and the Sobol items recounted the columnist's various visits to uptown cultural circles. Whether Davin and Fuller were living in Harlem is unclear, but Sobol's description of the soirée mentions the presence, in their shared accommodation, of the important African-American writer, editor, and publisher Wallace Thurman.[25] Davin, it would seem, was sharing lodgings and hosting soirées at this point with the man who would soon replace him as editor of *Brevities*. Both Davin and Fuller, as we shall see, had close connections to cultural life in Harlem and to Black artists and journalists working in New York City. While the careers of many of those who passed through *Brevities*' roster of contributors are difficult to reconstruct (and often hidden behind pseudonyms), the first two editors of the tabloid *Brevities* left traces we may follow through the thickets of New York culture in the 1930s. The magazine's first editor, Tom Davin, and the man who succeeded him, Hank Fuller, both spent time editing *Brevities* on their way to other arenas of cultural activity. As well, each found his work inspired and transformed by the broadly based progressive politics that marked American cultural life between the early years of the Depression and those leading up to World War II.

Tom Davin would serve as editor of *Brevities* for fewer than four months, leaving after the issue dated 14 December 1931. Juanyta Clivette, plugging his appearance at Juanyta's Salon a week later, referred to him as "the removed editor of this family tabloid," suggesting he had been fired from the publication. In the issue following his departure, *Brevities*' page-two editorial, "Strictly Confidential," printed a lengthy "Memo from Mr Winchell" that began "Dear Davin" and complained about *Brevities*' apparently erroneous reporting on two lawsuits in which *Daily Mirror* columnist Walter Winchell was involved. "Get it right, Davin," Winchell's memo instructed, "and when you don't – try to correct a wrong assertion, which is what I am always doing."[26] Though Winchell's tone was paternalistic rather than spiteful, it is possible that Davin was sacrificed by *Brevities'* publishers in order to keep peace with the increasingly powerful columnist.

Whatever his reasons for leaving *Brevities*, Davin very soon turned up as associate editor of *Cosmopolitan*, a career change that syndicated columnist Gilbert Swan offered as proof of how "topsy-turvy" life could be in New York City.[27] He moved from there to a position as director of publications at the American Museum of Natural History and then to work in book publishing houses, as an editor with Robert M. McBride and Company and, shortly thereafter, at the newly launched Sheridan House.[28] Later in his career, Davin worked as a publicist for the pleasure boat industry. This outline of Davin's career, which suggests a movement into ever more respectable and middle-of-the-road professional situations, winds its way around another set of involvements that make him a much more interesting figure. These included an enduring interest in African-American culture. Early in his career, Davin had worked as a publicist for New York nightclubs, including the gangster-dominated Silver Slipper, in midtown Manhattan, and two Harlem music clubs, Connie's Inn and the Cotton Club.[29] He also had a life-long interest in jazz. A two-part interview he conducted with pianist James P. Johnson, published in 1959 in *The Jazz Review*, remains a much-cited contribution to jazz history.[30]

For several years, in the 1930s and early 1940s, Davin also moved within progressive political circles, leaving a record of activities and affinities that would hover over his name and reputation. In 1938, he stirred controversy when he spoke in Long Beach at an event organized by the American League for Peace and Democracy. Davin shared a bill with a Protestant minister and a Jewish rabbi and was himself introduced as a Catholic editor and publisher. After his Protestant co-panelist, the Reverend Vincent Brown, criticized Mussolini, Hitler, and Stalin for their persecution of religious groups, Davin rose to argue that, while it was appropriate to condemn Fascists for religious intolerance, the same charges did not apply to the Communist Soviet Union. Conservative Catholics at the event quickly approached Davin, demanding that he show his credentials as a Catholic and asking why he had not included Stalin in his roster of evildoers. Soon thereafter, the *Brooklyn Tablet*, the newspaper of the Catholic Diocese of Brooklyn, published a long text and several letters denouncing

Davin for allegedly misrepresenting the perspectives of the Catholic hierarchy, by making it seem as if they saw differences in the treatment of Christians under Fascism and Communism.[31]

The American League for Peace and Democracy, organizers of the Long Beach event, represented a broad coalition of progressive and anti-war voices, including those of the Communist Party. In a response published in the *Brooklyn Tablet*, Davin tried to downplay his remarks at the 1938 meeting, but it is clear that he was deeply involved at this point in left-leaning political work. In the "Readers Forum" of the magazine *New Masses*, a major voice for Communist opinion and analysis, Davin wrote in 1939 of the tragic failure of the American Catholic church to support the Republican cause in Spain.[32] Davin's name turns up on lists of those involved in raising money for the Spanish Republican forces, and he was a member of the Medical Bureau and North American Committee to Aid Spanish Democracy in 1938 and 1939.[33] In 1940, a full-page advertisement in the *New York Times* announced the launch of *PM*, the left-leaning New York newspaper that is remembered for its political commitments, high production values, and ability to attract talented writers, illustrators, and photographers. Among the *PM* personnel listed in the advertisement was "Tom Davin, formerly of Sheridan House, publishers," now apparently taking up a position as the newspaper's head of research. How long Davin stayed at *PM* is unclear, but his involvement in its launch was one more confirmation of the political affinities that marked his career until the early 1940s at least.

The left-wing political activities that brought Davin into the public record occurred several years after he had left the editorship of *Brevities*, and there are no traces of such commitments in his writings for the magazine during his brief stint as editor. In the masthead of its 4 January 1932 issue, following Davin's departure, *Brevities* identified its new editor, with no fanfare or introduction, as Hank Fuller. Like Davin, Fuller would remain with the magazine only a short time, leaving after the 28 March 1932 issue. Personally, it appears, he was closely connected to Davin, though as Fuller moved into more intense and clandestine forms of left-wing political militancy, there are no traces of a continuing link between the two men. Three of *Brevities*' most blatantly political headlines appeared during Fuller's brief editorship. "Capitalists Communists Beware" (25 January

1932) carried the subheading "Existing Classes Threatened with Destruction by U.S. Fascist Group." However, the article that followed, signed by a Don Cherry, carried no mention of fascism nor threatened "classes" and was an eccentric piece devoted to exalting the political savvy of Depression-era vagabonds or hobos. Another headline, "Italy Fights Here! Mail Bombs Exposed" (18 January 1932), led into an article, signed by Fuller himself, claiming that explosives sent to sympathizers of Italian fascism living in the United States were likely sent by Fascists themselves as a means of garnering sympathy for their cause. "Al Smith Must Be President!," which seemed to shout from the front page of the 18 January 1932 *Brevities*, is the most curious of these headlines. Political endorsements were rare in the magazine and the article that followed was signed by "L. Simpson," president of the firm publishing *Brevities*. Whether Simpson had usurped Fuller's editorial role to impose a political preference or had found common cause with Fuller is unclear. The *Brevities* editorial refers to Smith as the most liberal of all aspirants to the Democratic nomination for the 1932 presidential election, a claim unlikely to have rung convincingly later in the year as the themes of Franklin Delano Roosevelt's campaign for the nomination became clearer. Mocking references to Hitler, Mussolini, and their American supporters would pop up regularly in *Brevities* columns long after Fuller left the publication, but the sharpest cluster of political commentary in the magazine may be found in the issues published during his brief period as editor.

Graft

In May 1932, after leaving *Brevities*, Hank Fuller turned up as editor of a newsprint publication called *Graft: A Tabloid For Those Who Can Take It*. *Graft* seemed clearly modelled on the tabloid *Brevities*, though it appeared to lack that publication's range of contributors, and it is easy to imagine Fuller having written most of each issue's content. The three issues I have seen combine relatively hard-hitting, progressive political commentary with satirical pieces on sexual fashions, gossipy bits on nightlife, and ribald cartoons. *Graft* was part of the explosion, in 1932, of tabloid weeklies, a phenomenon discussed at length in the next chapter.

NEW RACKET BRINGS DRUG IMPORTERS HEAVY JACK

See Page 5

GRAFT 15¢

A Tabloid For Those Who Can Take It

Vol. I, No. 1 NEW YORK, MAY 13, 1932 XXXX

CONGRESSMEN RUN WILD

Naked Solon Chases Woman in His Hotel

TAIL BOUND

Sex and Booze Cause Graft in Washington

By GERALDYN WASHINGTON

Congressmen can't take it. Many of them never even try to. Others go for the girls in a big way, but oh so feebly.

That's why those in the know around the House Office Building smile at the attempts at love making featured by our United States Representatives. Petty blackmailers annoy the old boys. But as a rule the grifters don't really know a darned thing. This is all to the good, both for the Congressmen, their families and the country.

Still people do become excited over the situation at times. When a tottering, white-haired old legislator becomes a little too liquored up and pulls a Harpo Marx act entirely in the nude during a quiet evening in one of Washington's more dignified hotels, people will talk. This is especially true of the women who are chased through the lobby and up and down stairs until the old gentleman is finally subdued.

LOVE LIVES LOST

Two years ago this peculiar incident served as my introduction to the sex life of, and the resultant petty grafting on, our United States Representatives. I had just become secretary to a Congressman and was somewhat surprised at the episode of the old "Colonel." But I soon learned a lot about our lawmakers.

More than 400 of them occupy the same office building while Congress is in session. Most of them leave their wives at home. They are no more moral or immoral than

(*Continued on page* 10)

Figure 7.5 First issue, *Graft*, 13 May 1932.

Like many of these titles, *Graft* was short-lived, and Fuller apparently went into mainstream newspaper work after its demise. During this period, he also maintained connections to political and journalistic circles in Harlem. Malcolm B. Fulcher, columnist for the *Afro-American*, wrote in his 6 August 1932 column that "I get a big kick when I hear Hank Fuller, former editor of Graft, and late of the Morning World, come into the office and discuss the race question. I guess if there were more men like him in the world there wouldn't be so much disorder."[34] In the same year, the *New York Amsterdam News* noted the presence of Fuller and his unnamed wife at Harlem's "Hamilton Lodge Ball" (the drag event also known as the "Faggot's Ball").[35]

Over the next few years, Hank Fuller's life seemed to be dominated by political work undertaken in the orbit of the Communist Party, with a strong focus on racial issues. We learn, from Christopher Phelps's study of the correspondence between Fuller and poet Muriel Rukeyser, that these two were in a romantic relationship during this period. Together, in April 1933, they travelled to Scottsboro, Alabama, to cover the trial of the eight African-American adolescents accused of assaulting a white woman – a trial that became a major focus of militant civil rights action. Fuller, described in one newspaper account as a "white representative of Southern Press," was arrested in Alabama on suspicion of being a Communist, then released and driven out of town.[36] The following month, in the magazine *Modern Monthly* (May 1933), Fuller published the article "Southern Golgotha," a hard-hitting account of the Scottsboro trial. Later that year, while apparently working for the African-American Communist newspaper *The Liberator*, he was arrested in New York for "disorderly conduct."[37] Thereafter, Fuller leaves few traces. Phelps shows how Fuller's letters to Rukeyser in 1934 reveal his growing involvement in Communist organizing, his sense of himself as failure, and his constant shortages of money. He would become, Phelps suggests, "one forgotten New York writer."[38] We are left with the outlines of an early life spent on the edges of Harlem society and a journalistic career that moved between the worlds of sensational tabloids, mainstream daily newspapers, and the militant press. Like Gordon Kahn, whose career took him from the original *Broadway Brevities* into the world of newspaper gossip columnists, and from there to a significant involvement in left-wing politics, Tom Davin and Hank Fuller exemplify a world of gossipy tabloid journalism not yet dominated by the thuggish, belligerent right-wing ethos that would characterize it in the decades after World War II.[39]

Morality Campaigns and Magazine Seizures

In January 1932, James F. Geraghty, licensing commissioner for the City of New York, forced city newsstands to cease selling *Brevities* (and two of the so-called sex pulps, *Paris Models* and *Artists' Notebook*) on the grounds that they were lewd and indecent. The Licensing Commission's power to stop the sale of magazines rested on its role in granting licences for newsstands operating in certain public locations (like subway stations.) The commissioner's action reverberated backward to the distributors of these magazines and from there to the publishers themselves. Immediately following Geraghty's attack on these three magazines, the Interborough News Company, a major distributor of periodicals in the city, acted voluntarily and immediately to withdraw those titles from newsstands that they supplied.[40] Commissioner Geraghty's attack on magazines was part of a broad campaign in the early 1930s against forms of cultural expression considered "indecent." New York's burlesque theatres were also targeted, in raids that prompted newspaper coverage full of jokey commentary about acceptable levels of nakedness and definitions of indecent behaviour.[41] Behind the city's actions was a group called the Citizens' Committee on Civic Decency, which was chaired by former United States attorney Charles H. Tuttle and included a number of religious leaders. At exactly the same time, New Jersey announced a clampdown on indecent magazines, with state Supreme Court Justice Clarence E. Case directing a county grand jury to indict those who sold or displayed them. "Sometimes these publications are offered under the guise of art," Case told reporters, "sometimes as literature, humorous or otherwise. On some of them the cloak is so thin that without difficulty one may determine that they are essentially obscene and indecent."[42]

The campaign against allegedly indecent magazines continued under Geraghty's successor, Paul Moss, who by 1934 had built a list of some forty magazines whose sale he sought to ban. By this point, *Brevities* was scarcely visible, and the list was dominated by sex pulps like *La Paree*, *Stolen Sweets*, and *Pep*, which combined racy sex-tinged fiction with inserts featuring images of nude women. Some of the publishers targeted by Moss's action contested it in the courts, arguing for an injunction that would stop the city from continuing its campaign. One of their arguments was that no independent authority – a court, for instance – had determined that these publications were obscene, and that the commissioner's actions were therefore unfounded. This request for an injunction was denied in May 1934 by New York State Supreme Court Justice Albert Cohn (father of the notorious right-wing lawyer Roy Cohn), who argued that the licensing commissioner was entirely within his rights to stop the sale of periodicals deemed by those in his orbit to be obscene.[43]

The Suit Against Warner Brothers

The anti-obscenity clampdown by New York's licensing commissioner was not *Brevities*' only entanglement with the legal system. In 1933, New-Broad Publishing Co. filed a suit in District Court against Warner Brothers Pictures, Inc. over the latter's use of the umbrella title "Broadway Brevities" for a series of short musical films it had begun releasing in 1931. By this point, Warner was distributing as many as twenty-five musical and dramatic shorts each year. While these were released under several series names (including "Vitaphone Musicals" and "Broadway Headliners"), many circulated as "Broadway Brevities," the name by which the film industry trade press generally referred to the series as a whole. These shorts were filmed in New York City and most showcased performances by Broadway actors and musicians. New-Broad Publishing Co.'s suit claimed that the title of the short film series "is closely similar to the plaintiff's names, THE NEW BROADWAY BREVITIES and BREVITIES, and the said name BROADWAY BREVITIES has the tendency and capacity to deceive the public and has deceived the public, into believing that the defendant's motion pictures so named, are connected with the plaintiff, all of which has been, and is, to the plaintiff's detriment, and constitutes an infringement upon, and is in violation of, the plaintiff's right as aforesaid."[44]

The suit seemed audacious. Warner Bros. was obviously a very powerful target, and the weekly *Brevities*, launched in 1931 when Warner began its film series, was hardly a high-profile national entity with which Warner Bros. might be expected to be familiar. (And, as we have seen, "Broadway Brevities" had already been the title of a high-profile theatrical production in 1920.) Warner's response to the New-Broad suit was to stonewall, and to hide any association with the "Broadway Brevities" film series behind a murky corporate structure. The film company's lawyers denied that any motion picture entertainment bearing the trademark or title "Broadway Brevities" had been released by the company known as Warner Bros. When New-Broad responded that Vitaphone Corporation was nominally responsible for the Brevities shorts and was clearly a subsidiary of Warner Bros., the Hollywood studio (quite astonishingly) denied any connection between the two entities, even as one of those submitting an affidavit on behalf of Warner's – the studio's assistant treasurer Samuel Carlisle – was revealed to hold the same role within Vitaphone Corporation. The studio denied "that it has ever distributed, or is now distributing, or that it has otherwise dealt with or is now otherwise dealing with, either as a series or otherwise, any motion picture or pictures bearing the name BROADWAY BREVITIES."[45] The periodical's suit against Warner Bros. was dismissed on technicalities. The major error of New-Broad Publishing Co. had been to go after Warner Bros. rather than Vitaphone Corporation. Additionally, as Warner Bros.' attorneys pointed out, the magazine had not applied for trademark protection until 27 August 1931. It had been granted on 17 May of the following year, when the film series was well underway.

If the magazine's lawsuit against Warner Bros. has any lasting importance, it is for the ways in which it helps us understand the magazine's financial condition. As part of the proceedings, New-Broad Publishing executive Elliot J. Simpson submitted an affidavit detailing some of the magazine's inner workings. He revealed that, in its first year, when it was a monthly (under the editorship of Stephen G. Clow, who was not mentioned), *Broadway Brevities* had sold roughly 50,000 copies in total. Over the following year – from August 1931 to August 1932 – and after switching to weekly publication and a tabloid format, it had sold a total of 2,801,762 copies. Then, from 22 August 1932 until its latest issue – representing a period of approximately six months – the New-Broad Publishing Co. had "published, distributed and sold about one million, five hundred nineteen thousand, ninety one (1,519,091) copies of its periodical." The magazine was sold, Simpson's affidavit claimed, in 450 towns and cities across the United States, until a recent advertising campaign had expanded that number to 1,000. The owners had spent $150,000 advertising the magazine, in campaigns that included display ads in New York's subway system.[46] These statistics all suggested a magazine doing reasonably well. Simple calculations point to a circulation per issue of roughly 50,000 for the weekly tabloid *Brevities* (the same as that claimed for the entire run of Clow's monthly precursor).

Brevities' Decline

It is unclear when sales began to decline, but even as the magazine was claiming high sales numbers for 1932, the signs of a struggle for survival could be glimpsed. *Variety* reported in June 1932 on the practice of publishers offloading unsold copies of magazines to brokers who sold them at cut-rate prices. Single back issues of *Brevities* and *Graft* – the publication edited by Hank Fuller – were apparently now going for a nickel.[47] By the spring of 1932, the tabloid *Brevities* was repackaging five older issues in bound volumes titled *Gems of Brevities*, priced at twenty-five cents.[48] A notice in the April issue of the professional magazine *Author and Journalist* warned writers that *Brevities* had failed to pay a contributor whose story had been published "without the formality of acceptance."[49] In September 1932, the Eastern Distributing Corporation – a key, independent handler of pulp magazines whose executives included people central to the imminent development of a comic book industry – declared bankruptcy, leaving the New-Broad Publishing Co. with a creditor's claim of $40,000.[50]

These financial problems were simultaneous with (and no doubt compounded by) ongoing monitoring of the magazine by city authorities. In 1933, a report on "Commercialized Prostitution in New York City in 1933" claimed that persons selling sexual services had turned from advertising in mainstream tabloid newspapers to placing ads in *Broadway Brevities* to evade police scrutiny. *Brevities*, described in the report as "a periodical which fairly reeks with 'double meaning' objectionable, indecent and suggestive articles and cartoons" allegedly ran advertisements for "massage parlours" that were disguised as dancing schools.[51] Indeed, *Brevities*' issues from 1933 and 1934 show lists of notices for dancing schools sitting in close proximity to others openly advertising massage services, as if their intended targets were the same. Such advertisements were gone from the magazine during its final months in 1935.

Confusion surrounding the magazine's health continued to spread. In October 1934, *Author and Journalist* claimed that publication of *Brevities* had been suspended in September 1933 and would soon be resumed.[52] However, this was clearly not the case – I have in my possession issues published on a weekly basis from the summer through December of that year. Two bits of reported news from 1934 suggest *Brevities*' publishers were looking to move in directions that were even more sensationalist. Bob Farrell, author of the "New York at Night" column in *Women's Wear Daily*, wrote in January that "the publisher of Brevities is readying another that will sell for a jitney [a nickel] and will look like what got Steve Clow in a jam"[53] (the original *Broadway Brevities*, presumably). In *Writer's Digest*, a writer's market report suggested *Brevities* (or a companion magazine) would join the sex-pulps wave: "The New Broad Publishing Company which puts out Brevities Weekly at 381 Fourth Avenue, is in the market for sexy love stories of 1,500 words and up; also snappy tales in which golddiggers, gunmolls, women detectives, etc., figure and drag in the sex angle."[54] Traces of these magazines have proved impossible to find.

The last issue of *Brevities* whose existence may be confirmed is dated 16 May 1935, and there is good reason to believe the magazine did not last much longer. In June of that year, *Author and Journalist* reported on a "reorganization" of the magazine at a new home at 254 Water Street. Those owed money were invited to write to the magazine's editor, L. Simpson, at that address, which suggested some continuity of ownership. In the same month, however, *Writer's Digest* reported that *Brevities* had disappeared and left no forwarding address for mail; by August the trade magazine was warning writers that they would not be paid.[55]

If the 16 May 1935 issue was the last, it offered few signs of a magazine in crisis. All the elements that had distinguished the tabloid since its debut in August 1931 could be found here. A naughty front-page headline, "Lads Lamp Nifty Nudes," led into a story about women who, having posed for nude photographs in their youth, later found these images back in circulation once they had achieved some level of show business celebrity. "Strictly Business," "In One Ear," and "Swinging Wide" (Juanyta Clivette's original column, now by an Edwina Sinclair) all featured tightly packed, up-to-the-minute gossip. While the many advertisements

Trackwise Tips Take Plenty Dough from Bothered Bookies!

See Page 13

BREVITIES

America's First National Tabloid Weekly

Vol. XIII, No. 9 :-: May 16, 1935 :-: Price 15 cents

LADS LAMP NIFTY NUDES!

Posing Beauties Get Boots from Angry Papas; Love Scrams as Daddies See Mamas Exposed

Read:
Clark Stable Mobbed
SEE PAGE 8

Girlies Hooked by Picture Release Gag Hide Heads as Wise Boys Give He-Haw

NO BULL ABOUT IT

"Who trew de panzee?"

By FRANKLYN KAMMERTON

Hundreds of Nifty Nellies are due for a look at themselves. And what they'll see won't please them. These kids wore a happy smile and a don't-care manner, plus precious little else, when they faced the camera. Today dozens are hiding pretty heads in corners. Too many others will be doing the act tomorrow.

There isn't a thing that can stop it.

Fate has nabbed them in the all-together. They are doomed to parade in that condition for every sap who can swap two bits for an eyeful of America's best girl-flesh.

Of course, the biz is a racket from start to finish. But it's as legal as the foreclosure on Uncle Silas' farm in Boobyville. This fact doesn't keep girlies from blubbering or husbands from getting hotter than a radiator should be in zero weather.

Trust the Boys

Gals who now wish they hadn't are everywhere in the country. Most of them are still living in big towns where they faced the seeing camera eye. Others, after a fling at stage or club life, have beat it back to the haven of home sweet home. But they didn't take their nudie pictures with them. These were left behind with the boys. Trust the boys to know what to do next.

Howls go up when a gang of slickers fake a photo by patching the head of a Name gal onto the body of some baby who has been posing for dirty pix. Of course, the howls and the long stretch that one mob, recently nabbed in this act, face, are justified. But this patching of smut pictures is nothing like as serious as the legal angles biz.

Those who know and don't tell too much about it still remember how one of the ace femme writers of Gotham retired one evening to find her nude torso staring at her from the pages of an "art" sheet. And the worst, or in this case perhaps the best of it, was that her husband saw the book first.

The kid had been playing here and there with

(*Continued on page* 12)

Figure 7.6 Last issue (?), *Brevities*, 16 May 1935.

for horse racing tips and pornographic mail-order materials offered some indication of how far the magazine had fallen, there were few of the usual signs of a magazine dealing with shrunken resources: no reprints from earlier issues and no obvious examples of generic content, like cartoons and jokes, bought at low prices on the open market.

The tabloid *Brevities* of the 1930s is best understood as the first in a wave of scandalous weekly tabloids that rose and fell in the years between 1930 and 1935. That it was also the last of these to die says something about its pre-eminence in this wave and testifies, perhaps, to the ongoing cultural weight of a title that was now almost twenty years old. Still, the weekly tabloid was just one among several trends in magazine publishing that took off quickly after 1930 and then burned out in the face of too many competing titles, ongoing struggles with censorship, and a weak market overall for consumer goods of any kind. The next chapter focuses on other publications in the crowded landscape of New York periodical publishing in the early 1930s.

EIGHT

THE NEW YORK MAGAZINE LANDSCAPE OF THE EARLY 1930S

People must have time to fool with typewriters, for the newsstands are breaking out with new things like a case of measles.

Unsigned item, *Writer's Digest*, February 1933, 25

The first half of the 1930s saw the rise and fall of several waves of sensational periodicals in and around New York City. New publications seemed to arrive in an unbroken stream, though few lasted more than a year and most did not make it to six months. Some disappeared when authorities in municipal or state government, often working in tandem with moral crusaders, hastened their campaigns to "clean up" newsstands. Others were the victims of intense competition within crowded niches (like that of the Broadway gossip sheet) or of shifting fashions that saw certain genres (like the satirical cartoon magazine) explode in popularity then quickly fade away. For editors and writers working at the lower, more disreputable levels of New York publishing, this was a period of ongoing experimentation and nearly constant risk.

Most of the magazines discussed in this chapter were launched between 1931 and 1933, during years commonly understood to have been among the worst of the Great Depression.[1] This context added to the precarity of a publishing sector long accustomed to failed trial launches of new titles and hasty attempts to capitalize on new trends. In other respects, however, the gossipy weekly tabloids and racy sex-and-humour magazines discussed here were better suited to the economic crisis than other kinds of periodical. Few of these publications relied on advertising for a significant portion of their revenues, so the weakness of the broader market for consumer goods was not a major concern. And while more middle-of-the-road magazines (like the *New Yorker*) carried the financial burden of weighty editorial teams and bureaucracies, these sensational publications were often produced by small firms with lower overhead. The primary activity of many of these firms was in the printing or newsstand distribution sectors, where volume and the variety of titles produced and handled were key to survival.

This chapter traces the life cycle of several clusters of sensational publishing in New York (and adjacent cities) between 1931 and 1935. The most prominent of these was the wave of satire magazines that followed the unexpected success of Dell Publishing Company's *Ballyhoo*, launched with a cover date of August 1931. Then, beginning in 1932, three publishers entered the market for scandal-filled weekly or monthly tabloid papers. One was Moses ("Moe") Annenberg, who built a roster of lurid city papers to supplement his publication of horse racing tipsheets. Just as these papers disappeared, in late 1932, a Manhattan publisher named Theodore Epstein launched a monthly scandal paper *Broadway Tattler*, which joined the roster of pulp fiction magazines and horse racing tipsheets produced on his premises in the Spinning Wheel Building on West 22nd Street in Manhattan. Finally, in mid-1933, a one-time football star and Greenwich Village bohemian named Joseph A. "Cap'n Joey" Burten announced a series of new magazines that mixed the tabloid format with the sex-and-satire formula popular among pulp magazine publishers in the early 1930s.

Clow's New Projects

In August 1931, when Stephen G. Clow left the *New Broadway Brevities*, *Variety* reported on his newest editorial venture, a collaboration with a prolific young writer and publicist named Noel Meadow. The magazine, to be called *Gotham Follies*, was described as the "World's First Baby Tabloid," and *Variety* noted that, while it was being launched as a semi-monthly, there were plans to make it weekly as soon as possible. Ever supportive, the show business trade paper added that the first issue would carry "some nice advertising as a friendly gesture towards Clow."[2] By September, different columnists were suggesting that a new Clow–Meadow magazine might be called "Persons," "Personals," or "Gotham Gossip."[3] It is not clear whether these titles were for different projects or for successive stages in the planning of a magazine that was announced but never realized. In any case, no magazines bearing these titles seem to have survived.

The earliest tangible evidence I have seen of Clow's publishing activities after he left the *New Broadway Brevities* is a curious artefact. The first issue of a magazine called *Boloney* was published on thick, high-quality paper and carried a cover date of November 1931. The front page offered what was clearly a parody of a tabloid headline ("Angry Jane Bites Dog"). Fake, sensational headlines (like "Night Club Coat Room Thrown into State of Wild Panic") filled the magazine's two-page centrefold and back cover.

Ballyhoo, *Boloney*, and the Satirical Magazine Wave

Boloney seemed designed to join the ranks of satirical magazines gathering momentum in the final months of 1931. In August of that year, Dell Publishing Company had launched a bold new periodical called *Ballyhoo,* unexpectedly kicking off a busy cycle of humour magazines. *Ballyhoo*'s main genre of content was the cartoon, but what distinguished it from other humour magazines was its relentless mockery of the advertisements, publicity stunts, and general hype of the media culture of the time. *Ballyhoo*'s first issue sold 150,000 copies in three days, and by February 1932 the publisher was printing a million copies of each issue.[4] Anticipating imitators, Dell rushed out another magazine of similar format and purpose, with the title *Hullabaloo*. Between them, *Ballyhoo* and *Hullabaloo* established the template for a wave of magazines that would follow from other publishers. The formula involved titles that borrowed words used in the worlds of the carnival sideshow and advertising to describe excessive hype or nonsense. Within a year of *Ballyoo*'s success, magazines with titles like *Aw Nerts*, *Bunk*, *Bushwa*, *Haywire*, *Hokum*, *Kookoo*, *Slapstick*, and *Blah* hit the market. While

BOLONEY

VOL. 1—NO. 1 BROADWAY—NOVEMBER, 1931 15 CENTS

ANGRY JANE BITES DOG

Near-Riot at 47th St. as Pooch Mistakes Gent's Leg for Lamp-Post

● ● ●

THE long-wished for but really little-expected has happened! A human being (that is, if you can call a chorine human) has upped and bitten a dog! This momentous piece of "news" broke at 2:37 P.M., September 28, at the corner of 47th street and Seventh avenue—right where it ought to break, where there were a lot of standees around to see it.

For years dogs have been biting men with a partiality (by the way) virtually maddening, for we have longed for the mongrels to orientate themselves properly, also do a little plain and fancy retributive work by biting a few of their dog-crazy mistresses. So far as we know, none of the demented pooch-doting sisterhood have, so far, received —what they damn well deserve—any canine incisors in their persons, but are all still galivanting around the streets of the residence section, leash-tethered to their infernal mutts.

Well, on September 28, above-named, things went completely haywire on our ardent hopes. For instead of the mutt biting the dame (our fondest dream) the dame bit the mutt.

How it all happened can easily be told, for we happened to be, by some quirk of fate, right on the spot.

The afternoon was sunny, with that opalescent haze in the air which foretells the advent of Autumn and rock-and-rye. It was just abaft of the Palace entrance that our eye was caught by a raggedy mongrel, evidently broken away temporarily from its carmined mistress, in the very act as we glanced of balancing itself against a stout gentleman's pant-leg. Some unhappy resemblance in this pant-leg to the usual lamp-post, ash-can or other receptacle must have tricked the pooch; moreover he was dealing with what to him assuredly appeared a fixed target, for the plethoric victim was standing stock still watching a moll make a long step onto a street car.

In any case, just as his mutt-ship was about the orgiastic middle of his brazen performance, his mistress's eye fell on him. Anger flaming in her cheeks, she dashed across the flags, seized the evacuating canine by the scruff of the neck, lifted it on a level with her lavalliere and—with a loud "Wherethehell do you think you are," sank her lovely incisors in one of its ears. Its shrieks could easily be heard in Leblang's cutrate office, full five blocks distant.

By this time an enormous crowd had gathered, so much so that the usual crowd of hangers-on at that corner had to give up their locations. Mounted police were to be

(Concluded last page)

Figure 8.1 First issue, *Boloney*, November 1931.

Figure 8.2 First issue, *Ballyhoo*, August 1931.

some were conventional cartoon magazines rather than sharp-edged takedowns of advertising and promotion, the coherence of the wave was impossible to miss. Then, no more than a year after the launch of *Ballyhoo*, observers were declaring that the satirical wave was over. *Brevities* itself, in April 1932, claimed that the "Ballyhooligan trend" was "nosediving into the basement," apparently, it suggested, because the Depression had made it difficult for people to laugh.[5] It was more likely that too many competing titles split the market too finely.

With no cartoons and a text-heavy cover, *Boloney* didn't look like other *Ballyhoo* imitators, but its title was drawn from the lexicon of hype and fraud. Its first issue is marked by an incoherence. suggesting its mission had shifted at midpoint in its conception – from offering the pleasures of a tabloid newspaper (like nightlife and gossip columns) to the suddenly fashionable project of mocking the genre for its excesses and absurdities. Smaller (at 8.5″ × 11″) than the tabloid *Brevities*, *Boloney* may have been the "baby tabloid" Clow had announced in August 1931. A tiny copyright notice on page four identifies the publisher of *Boloney* as Pix Publishing Co., 1133 Broadway, but there are no details of publishing frequency and no names of editors or other personnel. At the bottom of page five, two untitled paragraphs respond to a recent *New Yorker* piece by Alexander Woollcott about the novelist Frank Harris and his attitudes toward poetry. The author of the response writes as someone who knew Harris "intimately for years" and recalls arguing with him as to whether Matthew Arnold was "a minor bard."[6] The paragraph is signed "SGC." Given that Stephen G. Clow had on previous occasions touted his friendship with Harris, elsewhere made Alex Woollcott a target of his venom, and regularly inserted himself into debates over poets and poetry, there is no doubt that we have before us a trace of Clow's involvement in *Boloney*. The tabloid *Boloney* lasted no more than one issue. In January 1932, *Brevities* announced that "Hokum & Boloney will join Hooey pronto in the Fawcett group of adrazzing mag," suggesting that *Boloney*'s title, if nothing else, had been purchased.[7] An issue of *Boloney* dated Summer 1932 consists entirely of full-page cartoons and bears no traces of Clow's involvement.

Evelyn Nesbit, one of *Boloney*'s columnists, had been connected to Clow for several years.[8] Clow claimed to have been present at Madison Square Garden in 1906 when Nesbit's husband, Harry Thaw, shot and killed architect Stanford White, whom he suspected of having an affair with his wife.[9] Before and after these events, Nesbit pursued a lengthy career as a model and performer, and her portrait had appeared on the cover of the December 1920 issue of the original *Broadway Brevities*. She would soon be Clow's "associate" on a publication called *Broadway Tattler*, and *Variety* would speculate, in 1934, that either Stephen G. Clow or journalist Jack Lait had ghost-written her recent memoir, *Prodigal Days*.[10] Nesbit's column in *Boloney*'s first issue, "Comment and Recollection," was largely a rundown of nightlife venues in Atlantic City, where she resided at the time.

The Annenberg Tabloids

In 1932, less than a year after the relaunch of *Broadway Brevities* as a tabloid paper, other publishers rushed to bring out sensational, gossipy weeklies that shared its tone and format. First came a wave of city papers, whose titles anchored them in urban centres in the American Midwest and Northeast. *Washington Brevities*, *Baltimore Brevities*, *Philadelphia Brevities*, *Twin City Brevities*, *New York Hush*, and *Chicago Hush* were all launched in 1932. Despite their claims to local coverage, the papers were editorially coordinated from central offices, with the first four overseen from Baltimore and the last two claiming editorial offices in Manhattan. *Writer's Digest* noted the obvious similarities between these papers and the new weekly version of *Broadway Brevities*.[11] The city papers' use of the name "Brevities Publishing Co." to designate ownership of the Washington, Baltimore, Philadelphia, and Twin Cities titles reinforced these affinities.

The key figure behind these city tabloids was Moses Annenberg, father of Walter Annenberg (who would later launch *TV Guide*). Moe Annenberg was best known at this point in his career for his ownership of the *Daily Racing Form* and of what *Time* magazine called "a whole stableful of racing sheets," such as the *Daily Running Horse* and the *Sporting Times*.[12] He apparently printed the city tabloids when the presses used for the horse racing papers were idle.[13] The Annenberg tabloids dressed themselves up as papers crusading against government corruption and elite misbehaviour, but as weeklies with very limited reportorial resources, they offered little in the way of journalistic substance. Much of their content consisted of racy stories of moral transgression stretched to fill significant

'Yours Till Morning'—New Novel—Starts on Page 3

new york

5¢ HUSH 5¢

Vol. 1, No. 15 · New York, N. Y., Saturday, November 19, 1932 · Price 5 Cents

BUNIONS TRIP MITZI

Murder Rap Hangs On Tootsie Aches Of Blonde Lorelei

Only a **Weekly Paper** Can Give You the **LOWDOWN** on the Week's Big News Story. If you want the Inside on the story you read all week **Read It in HUSH**

Maybe Mitzi Downs wasn't so smart.

Sure the first part of the scheme worked all right. She made a monkey out of the district attorney and her jailbird husband, Victor Downs, was turned out on the first degree murder charge just as the doctor specified.

But after that Mitzi was worried.

It was all right for lawyers to assure her that her arrest on the first degree murder charge is just so much empty, angry gesturing. It was nice of them to get up in court and shout about a district attorney's dirty work inspired by political ambition. It was all right for them to say there was really nothing to worry about—THEY weren't in danger of the electric chair.

It was different with Mitzi. For the first few days after her coup had exonerated her husband of murder, she believed the attorneys when they told her not to worry, when they told her the prosecutor didn't have a thing on her. But now she began to remember things. She remembered, particularly, a certain line in her signed statement to the authorities. A line which read:

"I phoned Doc Tuthill and asked him to come over."

All that amounts to is a confession that she was an accessory before the fact; an accessory to the murder of Frank Tuthill, the shabby, wealthy, gun-toting itinerant who mixed his love with corn-plasters, in Quogue, Long Island.

Because, while she could—and did—prevent that statement from being used against her husband, she could not prevent it from being used against herself. True, such documents have been weakened by charges of third degree, but imagine Mitzi trying to prove that husky policeman beat her with rubber hose and jumped on her neck to extort a confession. And a

(Continued on Page Two)

JUNE ROSES couldn't be any sweeter than June Vlasek, Fox baby star, who's hiding her blonde tresses under that big hat. But she isn't hiding those walking appendages, so who could kick about a hat?

Figure 8.3 *Above and following three pages*
Annenberg city tabloids: *New York Hush*, 19 November 1932; *Chicago Hush*, 25 September 1932; *Washington Brevities*, 27 August 1932; *Baltimore Brevities*, 7 September 1932.

RADIO EXEC PREYS ON GIRLS

(Story on Page 2)

chicago HUSH

5¢ 5¢

Vol. 1. No. 2 · CHICAGO, Ill., Sunday, September 25, 1932 · Price 5 Cents

BERN SUICIDE Motive Bared for First Time

(Story on Page 3)

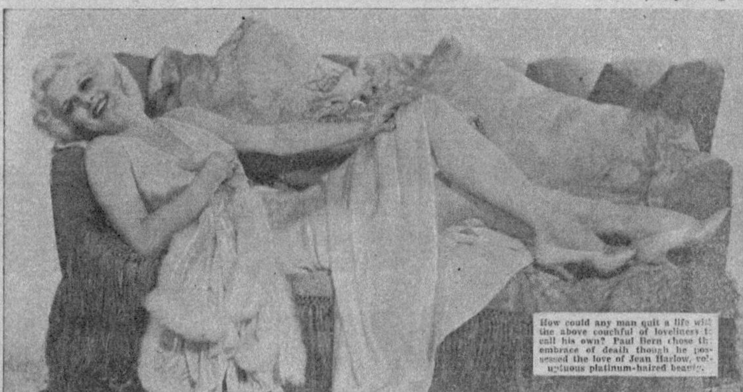

How could any man quit a life with the above couchful of loveliness to call his own? Paul Bern chose the embrace of death though he possessed the love of Jean Harlow, voluptuous platinum-haired beauty.

In this room Bern made his last decision. He held a pistol to his head and fell dead. His body can be seen where police found it.

5¢ WASHINGTON BREVITIES 5¢

Vol. 1. No. 13 WASHINGTON, D. C., Saturday, August 27, 1932 Price 5 Cents

TREASURY Official Stages ORGIES

Young Man Attacks Aged Mother After Dispute Over Girl

Charged with attacking his aged mother because she refused to eat with his ,sixteen-year-old sweetie, John Varner, twenty-nine, of Falls Church, Va., is languishing in the Fifth Precinct jug these days awaiting a hearing in Fairfax County Court.

The story has it that John wanted to invite his girl friend to dinner at the Varner home, but Mrs. Varner told him if he did so she would refuse to eat with her. After a short argument, it is claimed, John became angered and proceeded to smack mama all around the kitchen.

Mama therewith screamed and her husband, Joseph Varner, sixty, hearing, sped to the rescue. Arriving at the scene, he found that John had been joined by a companion, one James W. Morton, twenty-five.

Attack Father

Upon the arrival of the father, both youths turned on him. A brawl ensued which was heard by neighbors, who called in doughty Town Sergeant Paul Herrman. Herrman lost no time in arresting the boys.

Before taking his prisoners to the jail, however, Sergeant Herrman was asked by John if the latter might change his shirt. Upon Herrman's permission, John ducked into another room, returning a few minutes later with a gun.

Holding the weapon against the sergeant's ribs, he told the officer to release his companion. This done, he backed away and both youths precipitately fled from the house.

The sergeant noticed that they took a westerly course in leaving the Varner homestead and immediately notified District police. Descriptions were quickly radioed to all police scout cars and within a few hours the two fiery-tempered young men were wondering what it was all about as they fidgeted in a cell.

Warrants have been sworn out charging Varner with assault with intent to kill, resisting arrest, and the theft of an auto, which was commandered in their flight into the Capital. Morton is charged with assault.

BIG BREAD BROOD

Guiseppe, noted bricklayer, carpenter and decorator extraordinary, has a family, a large family, how large he really doesn't know unless he starts out methodically to count the individual members. When asked the other day how many children he had, Guiseppe replied:

"How many da kids? I don't know. Maybe nine, maybe ten. Alla I know is that they eat fifateen loaf bread a day."

Burlesque Favorite Vacationing

Lerinda Yancey, whose blonde beauty graces the burlesque stage in the big town, is now taking her annual summer rest. She will return to the Broadway stage next month.

In This Issue

AGED ROUE IS HOST AT WILD SEXUAL SPREES

Employes Threatened With Dismissal If They Whisper Story

A fantastic story of vice and intrigue in the United States Treasury Department, the tale of how a powerful executive terrorizes young girls working under him by weird love practices and threats of dismissal unless they cater to his senile, lustful whims, has been learned by the WASHINGTON BREVITIES.

This aged official, who is also an elder in one of the most fashionable churches in the Capital, has been carrying on his incredible practices for nearly a score of years. The story is familiar to employes of the Treasury Department and gossip concerning him is rampant.

Clerks and stenographers, however, have guarded their gossip closely for fear of instant dismissal once the executive learned of it. Attempts have been made on numerous occasions to bring action against the remarkable churchman, but in each instance, fear or powerful influences have pre-

(Continued on Page Thirteen)

M'CARL TOLD CONTRACTORS GYP WORKMEN

Building Trades Head Says Men Are Forced to Pay Rebates

Almost unbelievable charges that Government building contractors are maintaining fictitious wage scales by paying employes regular rates and then demanding rebates have been made to Comptroller General McCarl by Charles J. Columbus, executive secretary of the Building Trades Employers Association.

Charging that the Government is "being mulcted of thousands of dollars as a result of the failure of contracting officers of both the Federal and District governments to keep informed of the wage tendencies in the building construction industry of the District," Mr. Columbus has told stories of outrageous manipulations of employers to maintain apparent wage scales by tricking laborers into giving back large parts of their pay.

He has given data to the District Commissioners and Secretary of Labor Doak, only to learn that the latter has no power in the matter. One of the most recent examples of this manipulation was at Bolling Field, where it

(Continued on Page Thirteen)

BALTIMORE BREVITIES

5¢ 5¢

Vol. 1. No. 19 | BALTIMORE, Md., Wednesday, September 7, 1932 | Price 5 Cents

NUDE SLEEPS IN PARK

PEARL STREET HOUSE ESCAPES VICE CLEANUP

Other Joints Raided Following BREVITIES Expose of Conditions

Armed with the whereabouts of more than a score of disorderly houses in the western, northwestern and northern sections of the city, published in last week's BALTIMORE BREVITIES, police swooped down and closed the joints, making many arrests.

Baltimore, and especially the sections noted in the first installment of BREVITIES' exposure of vice conditions in the city, is closed tight today. True, there are several brothels operating, one large one in particular, but the "wide open" policy in force before the exposure is no more.

The one exception to this rule is probably the city's largest and best known disorderly house, located at **16 North Pearl Street**, where it has been operating for the past several years.

Still Running

According to reports from residents of the first block North Pearl Street, the house, mentioned in last week's issue of BREVITIES, suspended business for several nights following the publication of this paper but later reopened, doing business with "old customers" and turning down any strangers who they fear might turn out to be police.

"We neighbors of Pearl Street," says one letter received at this office, "are thanking your paper for coming out about the bawdy

(Continued on Page Seven)

Tailor Says Phooiey At Stork's Approach

Walter Winchell would call it a "blessed event" but that Roland Park tailor thinks it's a case of tough luck.

You see, dear pipples, the tailor, for several years, has been "carrying the torch" for a married woman who has long been a clerk in his shop.

They've carried on their not-very-clandestine romance in peace since Cupid first loosed his arrow at the tailor and his clerk. Of course, the clerk's husband let forth occasional yowls but he's the type who is easily hushed.

But now the "blessed event" is on the way and the clerk's husband has decided that enough's enough. He has threatened to sue for divorce and name the tailor as the slicker who stole his wife's affections. There'll probably be an alienation suit, too, and it'll take a lot of cleaning, pressing and dyeing to make up what the belatedly enraged husband is going to ask for his wounded heart.

Right From Russia

Nadja, "dancer extraordinary", who heads the season's opening bill at the Gayety, is wearing just the thing for these sultry days. Nadja comes well recommended from N'Yawk, where she was featured in various burlesque productions which had the customers pop-eyed.

Warning!

✳ ✳ ✳

Several persons were victimized during the past week by men representing themselves as reporters for BALTIMORE BREVITIES. We have repeatedly urged the public to demand credentials from anyone who says he is a representative of this newspaper. All BALTIMORE BREVITIES reporters or advertising solicitors carry credentials. Ask for them when you are approached. Never give a BALTIMORE BREVITIES reporter money to "keep a story out." If he accepts the money, he's not a legitimate reporter for this newspaper. Report all attempts on the part of fake representatives to get news or ads by calling Plaza 5819.

MARRIED MAN IS 'BEDFELLOW' OF NAKED GIRL

Cop Nabs Pair Asleep On Gwynns Falls Lawn; Both Dismissed

It's a shame that Baltimore has no recognized nudist cult because, if it had, Mrs. Christina Garrison wouldn't have had to stand the embarrassment of an appearance in Southwestern Police Station.

And, as far as that goes, Sergeant Emory Kopf, of the Southwestern District, wouldn't have had to hide behind a tree while the gorgeous Christina donned her garments in the merciless glare of a mid-day sun.

Christina, who is 22, and who lives in the 2900 block Frederick Avenue, says she doesn't remember much of what happened after she took the third—or was it the twenty-third—drink on the party she attended the night before she was found sans dress, sans stockings, sans shoes, sans undies—sans everything but her pearly white skin which was sizzling under the sun when Sergeant Emory Kopf happened to glimpse her, lying sound asleep on one of the greener swards of Gwynn Falls Park, at exactly eleven o'clock last Sunday morning.

Now Sergeant Kopf had read of nymphs, back in the days when he attended school and learned all about the lissome ladies who pranced about the forests of ancient Greece. He had dismissed those fables as products of some Greek baloney manufacturer and, therefore, he was surprised—nay, shocked—when he saw [illegible]tty Mrs. Garrison curled up in a [illegible]all on the Gwynns Falls grass, like [illegible] pink and white kitten, sound asleep, oblivious to the sign "KEEP [illegible]F THE GRASS"

(Continued on Page Thirteen)

Two Pick-up Girls Run Afoul of Law

Seen walking up to an [illegible]o in which were two young men whom they didn't know, two girls were arrested and fined five dollars and costs.

The girls, Pinky Manus, 24, 1318 W. Lombard Street, and Bettie Dyer, 24, of 434 Pulaski Street, paid the fine and were released. The two young men, William Harvey, 26, of 2538 Hollen Street, and Earl Alviker, 22, of 25 Franklintown Road, were dismissed.

The arrests were made by Officer George Mintiens, of the Western District, who saw the two girls approach the car in which the men were, about midnight recently.

portions of each issue. The 5 November 1932 issue of *New York Hush*, for example, devoted its entire front page and much of another to the scandal involving actress and singer Libby Holman, whose husband, tobacco heir Zachary Smith Reynolds, had died of gunshot wounds to the head during a drunken party. (Holman was initially charged with murder, but the charges were eventually dropped.) Elsewhere, stories in the same issue bore headlines like "Nude Girls Pinched at Stag Party: Raid Traps 300 Tired Husbands" and "Wifey in Bed Just to Keep Knees Warm." An issue of *Chicago Hush* with the same cover date carried an identical front page, but its interior pages were "localized" with Chicago-specific gossip columns and stories focusing on local scandals, such as the involvement of a group of Chicago university women in the sale of "smutty literature."[14]

Launched in the spring and summer of 1932, the Annenberg papers were almost immediately the target of government actions, which led to their disappearance by the end of the year. In July, the editor of *Philadelphia Brevities* was arrested, along with the paper's distributors and a newsdealer selling the title, on a charge of disseminating obscene material.[15] The attack on these papers then became a federal operation. In his history of the Annenberg family, Christopher Ogden claims that the Federal Bureau of Investigation had reacted badly to criticism of the agency, published in a September 1932 issue of *Baltimore Brevities*, and that J. Edgar Hoover himself opened a file on Moses Annenberg.[16] The FBI was clearly behind the November 1932 federal grand jury indictment of the Annenberg papers on charges of sending obscene matter through the mails and carrying out interstate commerce in such materials. Moses Annenberg was charged in the indictment, along with other officers of the papers.[17] Then, in December 1932, Annenberg's Brevities Publishing Company informed the United States Attorney's Office that it had ceased publishing all the tabloid weeklies.[18] The next month, fines totalling $40,000 were imposed on the various officers named in the federal indictment, though jail sentences for the editors and other personnel were "suspended conditionally."[19] In a little over a half-year since their launch, all the weekly tabloid titles linked to Moses Annenberg had been driven out of business by what seemed like heavy-handed judicial action. As with the *Brevities* indictment in 1924, federal action against the city weeklies rested on their alleged use of the mails, even though their circulation was principally through distribution to newsstands.

Beyond the Annenberg umbrella, other weekly city tabloids carried on into 1933. A company called the "H.E. Charles Publishing Co." launched *Baltimore Brevity* – identical in almost every respect to *Baltimore Brevities* – in early 1933. *Philadelphia Briefs*, from the Bis Publishing Co., lasted from early 1933 until May 1934, offering lurid headlines like "Torrid Love is $10 at 'Broker's Office'" (6 December 1933) and "Nordics and Sepias Swap Wives in Orgy" (4 April 1934). A Walter Gold of Philadelphia served as editor and publisher of two titles introduced in the autumn of 1933, *The Graphic News* (first issue, 29 September 1933) and *The Tabloid News* (first issue, 6 October 1933). All these shared the look and tone of the tabloid version of *Broadway Brevities*.

Epstein, *Broadway Tattler*, and the Spinning Wheel Building

A second cluster of tabloid titles, published in New York City in 1932–33, had more direct connections to the history of *Broadway Brevities* and would involve journalists, editors, and distributors who had passed through that title in its various incarnations. On 29 November 1932, *Variety* announced that "Steve Clow, with Evelyn Nesbitt as associate editor, is bringing out a tab style monthly called the 'Tattler.' Trying for a national circulation with a first edition of 100,000 copies. Hopes to go weekly by Feb."[20] A Business Certificate for *Broadway Tattler* (for so it was to be called) was dated 10 November 1932 and filed by Theodore Epstein and J.J. Harvey, who were conducting business as the Broadway Tattler Company. The headquarters for the new venture were at 7 West 22nd Street in Manhattan.[21] This address was part of a complex known as the Spinning Wheel Building, which had deep roots in New York City's media histories and has survived to the present day. The ten-storey edifice had been built in 1900 on a site that once included the home (at No. 5) of Samuel Morse, inventor of the single-line telegraph. Advertised at the time of its construction as perfect in its detail and modern in its features, the Spinning Wheel Building was the focus of press coverage in 1907 when an elevator fell six floors while carrying nineteen employees of *Broadway Magazine*, whose offices were briefly located there.[22]

By going to work with Theodore Epstein, Clow was tying his fortunes to a man whose career would eventually offer a through line linking key phases in

THE TABLOID NEWS — A BLUE EAGLE PAPER

10c

The TABLOID NEWS

10c

VOL. I.—No. 1 | OCTOBER 6, 1933 | 16 PAGES

EYELASH CURE BAD FOR EYES

"Lash-Lure" Called Eyebrow Remover As Women Tell Stories

By HARRY STANNING

Gullible ladies whose eyelashes look like the fringe on a Y.M.C.A. carpet have doled out thousands of dollars to support and make wealthy the proprietors of what has been branded as a notoriously quack nostrum for the beautification of the eyelashes.

But what is of more profound and serious aspect, in the opinion of the American Medical Association, is the fact that "LASH LURE," an eyelash dye, contains dangerous chemicals which often has the highly undesirable result of relieving its user of their blinkers entirely.

"Bring out the hidden loveliness of your eyes"; "Darken them naturally"; "Grow entrancing long lashes"—so read the advertisements. But the "hidden loveliness" might—and occasionally does—exhibit itself in the unfortunate loss of the lashes, followed by serious infection.

The bureau of investigation of the A. M. A., which has kept a record of the Lash Lure product for quite some time, announced last month, when the case of a woman whose eye lashes were burned away by the lotion was brought to its attention, that the concoction contains an aniline derivative and also large quantities of magnesium.

Continued on Page Nine

Demure Phyllis Barry, pretty R. K. O. starlet, spends most of her time on the sands of Malibu Beach, where her studio is on location for a sea picture in which Phyllis will play a leading part.

IT'S IN THE TABLOID-NEWS!

Figure 8.4 *Above and opposite*
Philadelphia tabloids published by Walter Gold: *The Graphic News*, 29 September 1933; *The Tabloid News*, 6 October 1933.

THE GRAPHIC-NEWS—A BLUE EAGLE NEWSPAPER

10c the GRAPHIC news 10c

VOL. I—No. 1 SEPTEMBER 29, 1933 16 PAGES

BROKEN NOSES FIXED BY GYPS

Bogus Beak Bender Banned By Farley When Bared As Gyp

By DON WESTWOOD

Does your nose droop dolefully about your chin? Are you one of those unfortunate suckers who have fallen for the blatant claims of uncontrolled quackery in an effort to make your beak resemble Clark Gable's?

Then you will be interested in learning that the widely touted "Sculptron," a device marketed by the Plastic Appliance Institute, heralded by exuberant ad writers as a boon to possessors of flopping smellers, has been barred from the mails by your Uncle Sam.

Likewise has the accompanying "mystery cream" known as "Velvex" been held up to public inspection and branded a fraud by no other authority than Postmaster General James A. Farley. Under date of August 19, 1933, the American Medical Journal records the decision of the postal authorities in putting the quietus on the mid-west Institutes' nation-wide operations.

Operations of the Plastic Appliance institute revealed an amazing audacity. Trial of the company head Paul Bieles revealed:

1. That Mr. Bieles offered to remodel to movie star beauty anyone's nose by the use of a few tapes and some mysterious "cream."
2. That Mr. Bieles had never undergone any medical training whatever.
3. That he decided to go into the nose remodeling business only after he had read how two other similar frauds had been barred from the mails.
4. That he knew his product was a fake since he had tried it out on his wife without any success at all.
5. That he marketed the fake nevertheless, offering for $6 something that cost 40 cents to manufacture.

The story of the self appointed nose remodeler and his fraud is graphically told in the Medical Journal as follows:

"During the past few years there have been advertised devices that the public has been led to believe could, by wearing, be made to change the shape of the adult nose. The post office department has already declared two of these concerns fraudulent and now reports another in the same class, the Plastic Appliance institute.

"According to a report by the Chicago Better Business bureau,

Continued on Page Fourteen

Sophisticated Ruth Chatterton, Hollywood social and screamie queen, pauses on the set while studying her scenario to gaze pensively at her GRAPHIC-News readers

IT'S IN THE GRAPHIC-NEWS!

the history of twentieth-century American periodicals. Epstein had briefly been circulation manager for the tabloid *Brevities* in the first few months following its launch in August 1931. With a base of operations in the Spinning Wheel Building, Epstein oversaw a series of interlocking companies handling periodicals of various kinds and in different phases of their production and circulation. These companies included the Newsstand Promotion Service (a distributor), New Ideas Publishing Co. (launched in 1932 to publish fiction magazines), Tab Printing Company, the aforementioned Broadway Tattler Company, and Tewhlel Publications (a joint venture formed to publish a magazine titled *Prison Life Stories*, with Sing Sing warden Lewis E. Lawes as co-editor). In 1935, Epstein expanded his occupancy on the street to include 32 West 22nd Street, which housed the offices of his horse racing paper, the *Daily Racing Tab*.[23] In the 1940s, Epstein was a co-owner of Crestwood Publications, a significant publisher of comic books now remembered for employing the writer-artist team of Joe Simon and Jack Kirby and for initiating the genre of "young romance" comics.

Run-ins with the law were not uncommon at Epstein's level of periodical publishing, but he found himself in legal jeopardy more often than many in the business. In 1922, when he was twenty-eight years old, he had been arrested after police seized copies of *Hot Dog*, a cartoon and joke magazine for which Epstein served as a distributor.[24] It was through his publication of the *Daily Racing Tab*, however, and his broader involvement in the world of horse racing, that Epstein found himself the target of two legal actions in the mid-1930s. In 1934, he was convicted of stealing information on the pre-race performance of horses (in so-called tryouts) from the Annenberg's *Daily Racing Form* and publishing it in his own *Daily Racing Tab*.[25] Annenberg trapped him by running fake results for horses with invented names in his papers; Epstein, unknowingly, reprinted them in his own paper. Then, in 1935, Epstein and associates were arraigned in Ballston Spa, New York, on widely publicized racketeering charges for running a horse racing tipster operation using fraudulent advertisements published in his paper. (These charges resulted in a fine.[26])

In 1932, when he hired Stephen G. Clow to edit *Broadway Tattler*, Theodore Epstein owned printing presses and newsstand distribution operations and probably, like Moses Annenberg, saw a sensational tabloid as an effective way of making fuller use of these. For his 1930 revival of *Broadway Brevities*, Clow had promised honesty and restraint, though these qualities had quickly faded as his preoccupation with the lurid exposure of queer lives seemed to edge out other interests. With *Broadway Tattler*, Clow clearly felt no need to be polite and respectable, and it is difficult to imagine Teddy Epstein wanting anything but the most sensational and attention-grabbing content Clow could assemble.

The debut issue of *Broadway Tattler*, with a cover date of November 1932, has proved impossible to find. However, in the fourteen that followed we see the lurid tone of *Brevities* equalled and often surpassed. An announcement in *Author and Journalist*, shortly after the new title was launched, offered a sense of the content *Broadway Tattler* was seeking: "The Broadway Tattler, 7 W. 22nd St., New York, writes that it is 'lying awake nights for highly racy cartoons (in line), gags, and exclusive "inside" stories of the theatrical, society, and business worlds' … Steve Clow, editor, is the boy to get into a huddle with."[27]

In his brief tenure with *Broadway Tattler*, Clow produced a magazine that was just as outrageous as any other bearing his name to this point. In the waning days of New York's pansy craze, Clow seemed to be convinced that a continued focus on queer people and places was the surest guarantee of attention, and by the third issue of the new title (January 1933), this obsession was unbridled. That issue's front-page headline, "Atlantic City Goes Pansy: Seashore Clubs a Riot of Hybrid Sex," leads into an article signed "S.G.C.," and Clow begins by establishing an atmosphere; queerness, it seemed, saturated even the natural environment of Atlantic City:

> The massy, whitecapped billows surge and retreat as though in torment. The emerald-hued mass that is Old Ocean finally flings itself into shallower depths and races in rollers up the yellow sands. Their swish and roar make the eternal monologue that is Atlantic City.
>
> Come closer, children. Now listen carefully, as we perch on the yellow beach. What are the wild waves saying? … Oh, say can you hear – right we are! – that sheer refrain, throated again and again, "Dearie, You Must Come Over."
>
> For even the breakers seem to have gone lavender at old Atlantic. America's imperial playground is winding up nance.[28]

15 Cents

EVELYN NESBIT Thaw **on Gin, Jazz, Sex—Page 3, In This Issue!**

JAN. 1933

BROADWAY TATTLER

~ The Lowdown on Everything ~

A National Publication

Vol. 1 — *Broadway, January, 1933* — No. 3

ATLANTIC CITY GOES PANSY

Hoops, Dearie! "Pansy Bugle" on Page 12

Seashore Night Clubs A Riot of Hybrid Sex

Broadway Hookers Clip a "Wise Guy" (Page 2)

THE massy, whitecapped billows surge and retreat as though in torment. The emerald-hued mass that is Old Ocean finally flings itself into shallower depths and races in rollers up the yellow sands. Their swish and roar make the eternal monotone that is Atlantic City.

Come closer, children. Now listen carefully, as we perch on the yellow beach. What are the wild waves saying? . . . . Oh, say can you hear—right we are!—that clear refrain, throated again and again, "Dearie, You Must Come Over."

For even the breakers seem to have gone lavender at old Atlantic. America's imperial playground is winding up nance.

And do you recall its heyday in '29 when about twenty swanky night-clubs catered to aristocratic visitors, and a week-end there had more thrills than Broadway could provide!

Don't believe it, eh? Well, let's take a stroll around the only night places left in

(Continued on Page 11)

Why Nudism is a Sure Flop

Figure 8.5 *Broadway Tattler*, January 1933.

As the article continues, Clow offers a tour of Atlantic City's nightspots: "First stop, all in, at that scrumptious North Carolina street Mecca of the Queens – the 'Pansy Club' (Winchell please write) that has a garish purple front … There's a female orchestra at the 'Pansy.' Scuse, pliss, did we make that last remark? For the orchestra is completely hybrid, and you ought to see those melting glances behind the big trombone and the trumpets."[29] Clow's writing, here and throughout his *Broadway Tattler* pieces, alternates between the old-fashioned erudition he had shown earlier in life and the effort to show himself at home with of-the-moment slang (like "pansy club") and fashionable rhythms of speech ("Scuse, pliss"). We may note, as well, the interjections suggesting that Clow still imagined himself to be bantering in print with Walter Winchell, though by this point in Clow's decline it is unlikely that Winchell was paying him much notice.

The first announcements of the launch of *Broadway Tattler* had promised an editorial collaboration between Clow and Evelyn Nesbit. The latter's period of greatest fame was behind her, but her name continued to circulate and elicit public interest. As it happened, Nesbit's involvement in the *Broadway Tattler* was delayed and short-lived. The magazine's second issue carries a display advertisement announcing that "Evelyn Nesbit (formerly Mrs Harry K. Thaw)" would come on board as Associate Editor in the following month."[30] She is finally listed as such in the masthead of the third issue (January 1933), in which her name and a photo portrait sit atop a feature with the title "Evelyn Nesbit Discusses Our Age of Sex, Gin and Jazz." In what turned out to be her single contribution to *Broadway Tattler,* Nesbit takes up the magazine's most high-profile obsession: "Twenty years ago, 'queens' were a rarity – today they are as plentiful as peanuts and quite the fashion. They are undoubtedly the heaviest drawing cards in the night clubs of today and draw the limousine trade." Nesbit continues: "As for the Lesbian – a decade ago one had to dash for the nearest book of reference to learn the term's meaning. Today – they are accepted with a cynical shoulder-shrug and the casual remark that many of them are to be found in the best social circles and that many stars of the theatre and screen are 'that way.'"[31] With this, Evelyn Nesbit's much-touted involvement in *Broadway Tattler* came to an end. By the next issue her name was gone from the masthead and, indeed, from the magazine overall. An announcement in the second issue had also told readers that Juanyta Clivette

Get the Number of That Truck, Dearie!

The PANSY BUGLE

My Gawd, Dearie, Here Comes a MAN!

Vol. I, No. 95 *"It'll be Just Plain and Dirty, Dearie!"* Feb. 41144

"YOUR BRASSIERE, CLARENCE, MIGOD, YOUR BRASSIERE!"

Here we see Hydrophobia, the Village Siren, calmly looking on while Cokie "Chuckles" and "Peach Blossom" do the new Flit Fandango in the Greek's on 4th Street, all in aid of the Home for Decayed Dikes at Lipstick-on-the-Hudson.

My dear, you oughta heard Gussie the other night! Taking a pose against the wormy old mantel, he draped his red bath-robe tight about his scraggy form and drawled, "My God, if I could only give birth to an idea!" Gussie you know writes poetry and is always hunting up ideas in his spare time between lampshade-sewing. But he almost killed us.

OH, GOD, MARGARET!

Well, here's the cutest thing—and how we girls have screamed! It's one on the straights, dearie—it's one on the straights. Seems that some stage hands were talking about meeting "Margaret" one night. Each had an appointment with Maggie. So the tenth one, who hadn't opened his darn mouth up to then, turned to a boy standing in the wings and said: "Oh, I suppose you've got an appointment with Margaret, too." And just listen to the answer the crude, crude man got: "Why, honey, I'm Margaret!"

•

My dear, just the other night we were reminiscing about the old Village places. Oh, dearie, what dirt-dishing. There was "Trilby's", on Greenwich avenue, steered by pudgy Diana Rose, and, my dear, there was the "Little Gray Hen" at No. 3—both in a cellar. Helen Dixon, fat and saucy, ran the latter. Oh, don't you remember the verse:

Said the Little Gray Hen
To the Little Red Rooster,
"Won't you please come over
Just like you useter."

It kills me, honey, it kills me. Then there was Dolly Judge's "Flower Pot" and "Paul & Joe's" on Worst 19th—oh, it slays me to speak of Paul and Joe's.

There was Leon, the fat brute, with skin like the bark on a cantaloupe, and Gus Fontaine and Jackie Law and the Lesbies and sloppy Paul and greasy Joe, showing the Bronxites and Statenites to tables—and didn't we shriek whenever a prizefighter came in! Oh, we had lots of big people come there—one night I actually saw Edna Leedom and Dave Stamper and that Steve fellow. Oh, we were scared, we were, of him for he wrote us up—and what a wicked, wicked pen he had!

•

Oh, mercy me, the fun we had after the Village closed and we all went—you know where, you hussies—to Mother Childs. Yes, right up the avenue—the Mother's was in the old Savoy then, you know. And will you ever—will you ever as long as you have a powder puff, dearie—forget that rheumatic night when the messy cops backed up their old patrol and took twenty of us away. Away, away, away! Oh, it was treacherous, it was.

•

And will you ever forget that wisecrack pulled by Gus one night at Trilby's. Some visitor asked Gus about the cat, was he a neuter. "My heavens, no—my heavens, no—don't you know the cat's just like the rest of us!" We all screamed so loud we drowned the three sleigh-bells jangling on the door. Oh, such dishin', my dear—every night, all night.

Figure 8.6 "The Pansy Bugle," *Broadway Tattler*, February 1933.

would be joining the magazine, though no pieces in *Broadway Tattler* identified her as author.

The third issue of *Broadway Tattler* introduced the feature that most clearly distinguished Clow's brief editorship. This was "The Pansy Bugle," disguised as the front page of an imagined newspaper inserted within *Broadway Tattler* and extending across two-thirds of a page. Its "motto" for this first instalment was "We deliciously dish," and in the text that follows (and in much of his writing in this period), we find Clow straining to master the campy cadences of speech he took to be typical of queer intimacy:

> "Oh, if I'd knew you were coming I'd have baked a cake." Oh, they had such a time after that honey, Bert Savoy died. You know they buried Bert up at Irvington or somewhere, and how their poor heads ached to get a proper line for his tombstone. Well, John Murray, poor thing, suggested, "You Must Come Over." But that mamma of Bert's wouldn't have it – so she scratched the line off the slab and put on, "He Made the World Laugh." ...
>
> Dolly Judge. My dear! There was a girl – 'scuse, plizz! – for you. Spite her bifurcations everyone liked Dolly. She carried the moniker of the "Prince of Wales." That is, Dolly resembled Princie. She had a long-time chum, Ruth West, who "went straight" and got married. That was when Dolly had the "Flower Pot" on Christopher – and didn't we roll our creaky old ankles around that place![32]

Dolly Judge and her "Flower Pot" had featured prominently in episodes 8 and 9 of "Nights in Fairyland" in 1924. It was in 1924, as well, that Bert Savoy, the cross-dressing stage performer sometimes described as "The Godfather of Camp," had been killed by lightning while walking with a friend.[33] Nostalgia for this period hangs over the three available instances of "Pansy Bugle" produced during Clow's editorship of *Broadway Tattler*. Two issues later, "Pansy Bugle" is devoted almost entirely to wistful reminiscences of the nightlife at Trilby's and Childs in the early 1920s. In contrast, the last "Pansy Bugle," in *Broadway Tattler*'s fifth issue (March 1933), is written as a more conventional gossip column, with brief items separated by ellipses, and offers no traces of Clow's voice or style.

By this point – and for reasons that are unknown – Clow's name was gone from the magazine's masthead. Nothing published in the ten remaining issues of *Broadway Tattler* referenced his name or suggests his involvement. Following Clow's departure, four issues of *Broadway Tattler* appeared with no designated editor. Then, with the July 1933 issue, Clifford Mack – a contributor to the magazine since its launch – was identified as such in the masthead. Mack would occupy the position until the magazine's demise. *Broadway Tattler* continued monthly publication until early 1934, with slow but steady shifts in its roster of contributors and range of features. Former *Brevities* cartoonist Henri Lamothe surfaced in the August 1933 issue, with a full-page, pansy-baiting comic strip, and cartoons by others assumed a more vicious, often racist tone as the year went on. With the April 1933 issue, Noel Meadow became a regular columnist with features titled "America 'tis of thee," "Strictly on the QT," and "Along the Main Stem."

The Many Lives of Noel Meadow

In 1931, Noel Meadow had been announced as Stephen G. Clow's collaborator on *Gotham Follies* and the two men clearly moved in overlapping circles during the early 1930s. Now forgotten, Noel Meadow was one of the most fascinating of the writer-publicists who passed through the worlds of sensational publishing in early 1930s New York. Like *Brevities* editors Tom Davin and Hank Fuller, Meadow would move from gossipy journalism into the realm of progressive politics, though he remained active as a show business publicist until the end of his life. Named Leon Blumenthal at birth, Meadow entered journalism at the age of seventeen, writing a series of celebrity profiles for the *Brooklyn Eagle* newspaper. In 1926, at the age of eighteen, he produced performances of two of his own plays and wrote to the recently launched *Time* magazine with the offer of a regular humour column, "Jest Around the Corner."[34] (*Time* declined the offer but published Meadow's letter, including some of the jokes he had sent as samples.) Around 1930, the busy young author reversed the letters of his first name and loosely translated the second from German to English. Leon Blumenthal became "Noel Meadow."

For most of his career, Noel Meadow would be identified as a press agent, but that professional label covered a wide range of activities. In the early 1930s, he wrote columns of New York nightlife gossip for a wide range of periodicals: *Brevities*-style tabloids like *Scandal*, joke-and-cartoon magazines like *Hot-Cha*, sex pulps like *Broadway Follies*, and the entertainment guides *Broadway* and *New York Amusements*.[35] For a few months in 1932 he contributed a joke column, "Gag and Double Gag," to the tabloid *Brevities*, joining the paper just as Terry Donoghue replaced Hank Fuller as editor. The other side of Meadow's career emerged on the eve of the United States's entry into World War II, and made of him a more serious figure, enmeshed in the political struggles of the time. Beginning in the early 1940s, Meadow would devote much of his energy to building American audiences for the art and culture of the Soviet Union. There is no clear evidence that Meadow was connected in any formal way to the US Communist Party – unlike Tom Davin and Hank Fuller, he left no clear traces of political involvements outside of the cultural realm. Nevertheless, in his tireless efforts to promote Soviet music and cinema to American audiences, with the clear aim of strengthening solidarity between the two nations during wartime, Meadow may be seen as an effective member of the Cultural Front, that broadly based, progressive coalition of the 1930s and 1940s whose history Michael Denning has traced in detail.[36] In the 1940s, while serving as executive editor of the New York–based trade paper *Writers' Journal*, Meadow also wrote regularly for *The Screenwriter*, the journal of the Screen Writers' Guild, during the period of that organization's most intense radicalism. This association would garner him brief mention in a Red Scare era investigation of *The Screenwriter* for its alleged Communist sympathies.[37]

In 1943, Noel Meadow bought the Stanley Theatre in Manhattan to exhibit wartime documentary films dealing with the Soviet Union. He assembled features out of Soviet newsreels and other available footage, showing them at the Stanley and distributing them throughout the United States.[38] After World War II, Meadow became a key force in expanding the audiences for "art" films in New York – and the United States more broadly – building upon the distribution circuits he had first established for wartime documentaries.[39] Though his output as a columnist had dropped sharply by the mid-1930s, Meadow was contributing the occasional compendium of New York show business news to *Variety* as late as 1966. In June 1968, two months before he died of a heart attack, Meadow worked as press agent for Andy Warhol's film *I, a Man*. A syndicated Broadway column told of him being besieged by reporters wanting stills from the film because one of its "stars," Valerie Solanis, had just shot Warhol. Meadow had apparently been working with such a small budget that none were left.[40]

Clifford Mack, the first editor of *Broadway Tattler* identified after Clow's departure, moved in the orbit of the Spinning Wheel Building for a time in the early 1930s.[41] In the *Broadway Tattler*, he authored several instalments of a column "'Neath the Harlem Moon," and he was clearly at home in African-American cultural circles in the city. In the second issue of the *Tattler*, Mack recounted a night spent in Harlem, beginning with dinner at Dominick's restaurant:

> 7:00 p.m. DINNER AT DOMINICK'S THE Sardi's of the Black Belt. Only occasional whites are seen in this resort of the bigger black folk. Here I have met men, prominent lawyers; a Haitian politico with a keen taste in ladies; a singer of hilarious unprintable songs; a high-toned gigolo for innumerable English and American dowagers; Bennie Butler, Winchell of the Inter-State Tattler; Effrom Duke, whose African drummers and dancers once disported at Belle Livingston's and the Roxy. About $2 per person will get you A-1 chow in an aura of Harlem celebs.[42]

Beginning in the late 1920s, the Harlem nightlife column had become a staple of African-American newspapers published across the United States. In the pages of the Harlem-based *Inter-State Tattler* (published under different names and incarnations from 1922 to 1932), we find virtually all the significant varieties of the nightlife column being tested and developed, from narratives of club-going through strung-together gossip hinting at misbehaviour among the rich and famous.[43] White-owned publications occasionally featured columns centred on Harlem nightlife; on even rarer occasions these were authored by African-American writers. The up-market magazine *Manhattan*, launched in 1939, carried the column "Harlem Town" by Michael Turner, who earlier had written the regular feature "Harlem Parade" for the African-American *New York Amsterdam News*.

One of Clifford Mack's strongest connections, it appears, was to the jazz and blues singer Monette Moore, who had emerged from the Kansas City music scene to pursue a lengthy career in New York. Mack devoted a paragraph to Moore's singing in his column for *Broadway Tattler*'s January 1933 issue, and in May his column described an encounter with her at the Lafayette club. Then, in the July 1933 issue of *Broadway Tattler*, presumably at Mack's invitation, Monette Moore was credited as the author of "'Neath the Harlem Moon." While she occupied this role for one issue only, hers may be the only contribution by an African-American writer across the entire corpus of weekly sensational tabloids discussed here. In the final paragraphs of Moore's full-page column, we find her capturing the racial dynamics of Harlem from a perspective otherwise missing in the magazine:

> WHO IS SHE? A little talented blonde cutie, rapidly climbing to Broadway stardom, has blood relatives in Harlem who are berry-brown. And, since the producer pushing her up hates the race, wild horses couldn't get us to mention her correct monicker and tincture together – she's much too deserving to be hampered by her real race! ... Funny part of it is, she's being dogged by one of this country's most distinguished blue-bloods who wants to marry her![44]

By the next issue, Moore was gone from the column, which now offered a lengthy profile of African-American businesswoman A'Lelia Walker, signed by "C.M." (presumably Clifford Mack). Thereafter, "Neath the Harlem Moon" was reduced to a multi-part fictional tale of Black chorus girls, credited to an obviously pseudonymous "Amanda Titzoff."

A defiantly anti-fascist political stance revealed itself slowly in *Broadway Tattler* over its final months of publication. A cartoon on the cover of the October 1933 issue showed a dachshund facing a picture of Adolf Hitler while a man with recognizable (but only lightly stereotypical) semitic features urges the dog to piss on the portrait: "Dachshund, spare that tree! (Here's a substitute for you.)" Inside, an article meanders through an account of its author's visit to Germany, then pauses near the end to note that Hitler is known to be a "pansy." The second

Political Pot Roast

THE CHALLENGE–

Johnstown, Pa.

To whom it may Concern
Broadway Tattler or Magazine like it

Listen you, there are readers of your Tattler who don't like the dope you are writing about Hitler—he is not in this Country. We are in America, to hell with what they are doing in France, or the Jews or anything else. Propaganda like yours got us in plenty of trouble in 1917. Cut it out. It is for your own good. As far as the Jews wanting to boycott German made goods, there is enough German decent people in the U. S. A. (51 million) to boycott Jew stores, it works both ways.

Be careful, this is a warning.

Yours truly, M. Marx.

THE ANSWER–

Figure 8.7 Letter from reader concerning Hitler story and cartoon response. *Broadway Tattler*, December 1933.

page of the following issue features a cartoon, unsigned, in which a brutish creature identified as "Nazism" is shown devouring the people of the United States.

The last issue of *Broadway Tattler* I have found is dated January 1934. Already, in mid-1933, Delo Publications, based at 7 West 22nd Street and presumably tied to Theodore Epstein, had launched another *Brevities* imitation – *Scandal: The Paprika Magazine* – with no editor identified. *Scandal*'s first issue (and I have seen no others) carried the headline "Married Mamas Melt: Lonesome Wives Warm Benches in Parks and Drive in Mad Quest of Romance," and if the rhythms of this title recalled those of the tabloid *Brevities*, so, too, did the article's quick fade into generalities. The same issue featured a column by Noel Meadow, "42nd Street," and a feature by Clifford Mack, "Harlem Heat," about the African-American blues singer Adelaide Hall.

In March 1934, a new tabloid, with the same dimensions and design as *Broadway Tattler*, appeared on newsstands. *New York Tattler* was edited by Clifford Mack, and the columns "Along the Main Stem" (credited to Joe Fabian) and "Sports of All Sorts" (by Paul Williams) were carried over from *Broadway Tattler*. Indeed, *New York Tattler* was almost certainly a successor to that title, though the new periodical gave its address as 39 West 67th Street, and a P. Rogers was identified as its publisher.[45] I have seen no issues of *New York Tattler* except the first, but this new title, packed with cartoons and satirical features about celebrities, seemed more calculated to amuse than its predecessor. This first issue contains a one-page short story, "It Happens This Way," by Sammy Fuller, the tabloid journalist who would emerge after World War II as a major film director.

Joe Burten and His Many Magazines

The man behind the final cluster of sensational periodicals to be examined here was an eccentric figure who emerged from Greenwich Village in the early 1920s to spend more than three decades as a purveyor of soft-core pornography. He was known, in different contexts, as Joseph Bernstein, Joseph Burten, Joseph Burton, Jo Burten, Joe Burten, and, in the editorial persona he had constructed for himself, Cap'n Joey. He is referred to here as Joe Burten, the name he used most often in print in the 1930s.

JULY Read "White Slave of Budapest"—Page 4 15c

SCANDALS

THE PAPRIKA MAGAZINE

Vol. 1—No. 1 New York July, 1933

MARRIED MAMAS MELT

Lonesome Wives Warm Benches in Parks and Drive in Mad Quest of Romance

On the Hunt

By H. G. Vermes

THE harpies have been complaining about the amateurs horning in on their regular trade ever since the depression began. But now they've got more competition than ever since the married mamas have been buzzing around outside the home hive. Of course, there have always been a few wedded women on the loose, but lately they are coming out in droves and are driving the sidewalk Sallys to distraction, particularly because these dizzy wiffs offer themselves as free gifts on the altar of love.

If you walk up the Drive on a sunny weekday afternoon you will fall over a dozen fraus who have their ankles stuck out in the aisle for no good reason. While they don't throw themselves into the arms of every passing pantaloon, they push over easily if given a little nudge.

Though it takes an eagle eye to tell these wilting wives from the masterful matrons, the reconnoitering ravisher works on the law of averages, as he knows that four out of five have it even if they haven't got IT. These deep-bosomed dames have to be careful of sharp-eyed husbands and friends, so they steer clear of the family neighborhood. But any place outside of that is their happy hunting ground and, as they have to play lone wolf for safety's sake, they can be found all over the Island. Besides the Drive, they are liberally sprinkled in spots like Bronx Park, Central Park, especially in the neighborhood of the West 72nd Street entrance, the River boats, and in the summer on the beaches during the hours when the old man is working. There are also the museums, and though it takes more than a speakeasy manner to hand a catalogue to a succulent dame while she's admiring a nude, it's being done every day with no visible casualties.

These errant wives are of all types but the prevalent kind is softig and has lots of embonpoint. They are easily isolated by the trained observer who invariably makes the rear approach, from which angle it is

(Continued on page 2)

Figure 8.8 First issue, *Scandals*, July 1933.

50,000 Tattler Readers Can't Be Wrong !!!

15¢
MARCH
1934
Vol. 1, No. 1.

NEW YORK TATTLER

Read the Latest *Gags*
Know all the *Gossip*
Follow the Amusement *Guide of Broadway! Hollywood! Harlem!*

"TO HELL WITH THE MULES
-I'LL TAKE THE BODY"

WHY RUDY FLOPPED!

By **DR. ALEXIS RACHMANOVICH**
(Freudian Psychiatrist & Student of Love)

¶ *"To hell with the mules, I'll take the body!"*
¶ *"Hug the pillow for me, dear!"*
¶ *"I mean we can do anything we want to DO in the back of my car!"*

WHAT DO THE ABOVE speakophone sizzlers mean? What kind of person do you figure they represent Fay Webb Vallee to be—if she actually spoke them, or listened with passion to them, as Rudy claims she did, in their forthcoming divorce suit.

What was the state of her heart when she allegedly cooed to Gary, the chivalrous adagio hoofer:

(Continued on Page 6)

Figure 8.9 First issue, *New York Tattler*, March 1934.

Born in 1893 in Elmira, New York, and given the name Joseph Bernstein, Burten joined the United States Army during World War I, rising to the rank of lieutenant. Before and after his military service, he attended Louisiana State University, where he played college football, and he continued in the game after moving to the University of Tulsa in 1920. In 1921, he played with the New York Giants in the America Professional Football League, then from 1923 to 1925 with the Rock Island Independents, an Illinois-based team that was part of the new National Football League.[46] Much of the available information on Burten's early life and career is to be found in the documentation by amateur historians of the careers of Jewish athletes.[47] Football history sources refer to him as "Joe Burten," suggesting he had already changed his name before going into magazine publishing in the early 1920s.

By the early 1920s, Burten was living at least part of the time in Greenwich Village, seemingly moving in bohemian circles that, while a rung or two below those of the neighbourhood's most celebrated writers and painters, were nevertheless part of a broader cultural ferment. In early 1922, Burten launched a small, digest-sized magazine called *Cap'n Joey's Jazza-Ka-Jazza*. The publication's inside front cover announced that it was "Dedicated to the elimination of the Blue Laws. Strong for personal rights of men and women. Edited by a World War Veteran." Burten's own, signed features for the magazine ranged from reflections on the football culture in which he was still involved to raunchy narratives of his travels – to places like Cuba – and comments on the behaviour of American flappers. These were interspersed with ribald poetry, jokes, and a variety of other forms of brief miscellany, usually but not always of a sexual character. The imagery in these first issues was sparse, with drawn silhouettes of possibly naked women on the covers of the first two issues and strings of such images used to separate sections. These were enough to get Burten arrested soon after the magazine's launch, following complaints from the New York Society for the Suppression of Vice, who charged that he was trafficking in "indecent humor" and other forms of allegedly offensive content.[48]

Through the mid- and late 1920s, Burten seemed to be forever revamping the magazine and building a roster of contributors, with the apparent aim of making it a commercially viable newsstand magazine rather than simply a vehicle for his own musings. In 1923, the magazine was renamed *Cap'n Joey's Follies* and then,

Figure 8.10 First issue, *Cap'n Joey's Jazza-Ka-Jazza*, February 1922.

by year's end, as *Burten's Follies*. It would keep this title, through changes of purpose, style, and ownership, until 1934. On a map of affinities linking the many varieties of sensational magazine published in the United States in the 1920s, *Burten's Follies* would sit at the intersection of several trends and traditions. As an outlet for his own social commentary, Burten's magazine shared traits with other small-sized periodicals of the decade dominated by strong editorial personalities who offered their opinions of passing fashions. Sam Clark's *Jim Jam Jems*, Wilford Fawcett's *Whiz Bang*, and Jack Dinsmore's *Hot Dog* – all launched far from Greenwich Village – resembled *Burten's Follies* in layout and size but lacked the latter's jazzy, urbane editorial voice. Burten's sense of himself as a cosmopolitan Greenwich Village bohemian also positioned his magazines in a different cultural space, which overlapped with those of Bobby Edwards's *Greenwich Village Quill* and, on occasion, the original *Broadway Brevities*.[49] The sporting side of Joseph Burten's persona found a specialized outlet in the boxing magazine *Self-Defense*, which Burten edited for a company called Ringside Publishers from 1927 through the early 1930s.

In the mid-1920s, *Burten's Follies* became one of the key print venues in which the image of the female flapper was commercialized, in the artwork of rising male illustrators like Worth Carnahan and John Decker, both of whom contributed to the magazine. Later, *Burten's Follies* published paintings of women's bodies by Alberto Vargas, a pin-up artist who later worked for both *Esquire* and *Playboy*. While this sexualized treatment of women's bodies offered (and justified) itself as artistic experimentation and social observation, it anticipated Burten's slow descent into those worlds of printed pornography in which the later phases of his career would unfold. By the end of the 1920s, a good deal of Burten's publishing activity seemed invisible, as he joined with others in publishing or editing the sex pulps that proliferated during this period. In his study of Jewish-American involvement in the pulp magazine industry, Gerald Jones writes of business ventures connecting Burten to figures like Harry Donenfeld (later a key player in the founding of DC Comics) and Henry Marcus (publisher of sexy pulps like *Parisian Life*, *Hollywood Nights*, and *French Follies*).[50] *Variety* noted that Burten had worked on the "artistic" sex magazines published in the mid-1920s under the Ramer Reviews imprint, with titles like *Art and Beauty Magazine*.[51] In fact, many of the images published in *Burten's Follies* in the second half of the 1920s shared stylistic

Figure 8.11 *Burten's Follies*, February 1925.

features with such magazines – titles like *Art Classics*, *Art and Life*, or *Edwin Besser's Art Monthly Pictorial* – which sought to circumvent morality campaigns by offering images (mostly photographic) of naked women in "artistic" poses.

In the summer and fall of 1933, Burten launched three new magazines – *Razzberries*, *Squawkies*, and *New York Life*. The first two looked like modified versions of the satirical magazines that had followed *Ballyhoo*, in 1931, but they featured fiction more typical of the sex pulps and sensational exposés not unlike those that filled the weekly scandal tabloids. Early announcements and advertisements for these magazines said that *Razzberries* would be edited by Wayne Sabbath, a long-time associate of Burten. Joe Burten himself, it seemed, would edit *Squawkies*. And Stephen Clow, *Variety* announced, would be responsible for a magazine titled *New York Life*, "patterned after the old Broadway Brevities."[52]

Stephen G. Clow's announced responsibilities in the new Burten magazines centred on editing *New York Life*, but his touch could be seen elsewhere. *Razzberries*, ostensibly devoted to satirizing the world of radio entertainment, nevertheless found room to resurrect Clow's excursions into queer Manhattan nightlife. The magazine's second issue featured a long article with the title "Tales of Fairyland: Being a True Story of the Goings-On of the Famous Androgynes of Greenwich Village." While the article was unsigned, everything about the piece pointed to Clow. The Village queer scene, the article suggested, had moved to Macdougall Street:

> Let's descend the stairs this Saturday night. But before you do so, let's have a look-see. Across the street, at 244, in the garret, is the home of Bobby Edwards, the bard of Greenwich Village. Down the corner blinks the light of Hank's, famous throughout New York. At the corner is the Open Door, the answer of how a waiter at The Pepper Pot got himself fired. At the turn of the corner can be seen Washington Square. Looking at you, in the dim light, the brownstone houses of a century ago, house the few remaining aristocrats of old Knickerbocker.
>
> What a setting for this nest of wastrels and libertines![53]

If the familiar Village territory covered in this piece didn't confirm Clow's authorship, the lengthy attack on "Horsewomen" with which the article concluded left little doubt. Another lengthy piece, in the December 1933 *Razzberries*, begins with a rundown of Greenwich Village places already visited in the original "Nights in Fairyland" series, recycling observations and anecdotes from that source. It then goes on to a detailed look at Sheridan Square, one of whose restaurants, unnamed, is identified as the home of "Fairyland's nobility today."

New York Life, the magazine touted as a successor to *Broadway Brevities*, was the Burten project most associated, in advertisements and promotional notices, with Stephen G. Clow. That said, Clow's name did not appear in the magazine until its third issue and it is uncertain whether a fourth was ever published. *New York Life* No. 1, dated June 1933 and published by Burten at 1027 Metropolitan Avenue in Brooklyn, has little to do with the gossipy, Broadway-focused magazine promised in advertisements. In fact, it is a sixteen-page exposé of Adolf Hitler and his atrocities, most of it written by a journalist named Tony Sarr. The title of the "dossier" assembled here – "The Truth about Hitler" – fills the top half of the cover, obscuring the information that this is the first issue of a magazine called *New York Life*. Inside, pages packed tight with text, and illustrated by stark photographs of Germany under Nazism, offer a detailed, relentless attack on Hitler and his regime. Sections bear the headings "Women for Breeding Says Hitler," "Rape of German Jew," and "Hitler the Butcher," and while in other contexts these might have promised the lurid exploitation of sex and violence, the tone here is of an outraged journalism burning with urgency. A subtitle on the cover notes that "Samuel Untermeyer [*sic*] Urges Anti-Nazi Boycott," and several paragraphs inside are devoted to the efforts by Untermyer, a US banker and Jewish activist, to end dealings between US firms and German interests.[54]

Burten's broadside against Adolph Hitler joined briefer expressions of alarm at the man's rise that could be found in *Broadway Tattler*, *Graft*, *Scandal*, and the *New Broadway Brevities* between 1932 and 1934. Sometimes, as in *Brevities*' regular references to him as "La Hitler," these items milked rumours of Hitler's homosexuality,[55] but they regularly described the dangers facing German Jews and condemned the postures of prominent Americans who seemed enchanted by German's emerging new order. We have already seen how, among those who worked in this world of sensational tabloids, Tom Davin, Hank Fuller, and (eventually) Noel Meadow would distinguish themselves through explicitly anti-fascist political work. Others in this world, and especially Jewish-identified publishers like Theodore Epstein and Joseph Burten, would also make a place in their magazines for anti-fascist sentiments that, in the early 1930s, were not uncontroversial.

The second issue of *New York Life* was edited by Burten's long-time collaborator Wayne Sabbath, delaying Clow's much-touted involvement a little longer. With the third issue (October 1933), Steve Clow was finally identified as the magazine's editor, and his personality runs all through its sixteen pages. Cartoons by the magazine's art director, Leo Manso, appear on almost every page, including the back cover.[56] The front-page headline, "Yep – I'm a Nudist!," credited to an Alice Bunyan Godiva, is written in the first person and recounts the adventures of a Times Square habituée who applies by mail to join a nudist club and, once accepted, ventures to their rural camp in an unspecified location. Other short pieces, mocking Evelyn "Evvie" Nesbit, Walter Winchell, Mark Hellinger, and Tallulah Bankhead, are more obviously by Clow, though these are unsigned.

The fullest flowering of Clow's sensibility comes on the magazine's back cover, under the cascading headlines "Lespers and Lesbies Infect Broadway – Greenwich Village Cellars Swarm With Rouged, Screaming Inverts – Fairyland in Full Bloom Again." The article begins by suggesting that "Broadway and Greenwich Village seem to be in for a new gold rush of Sapphos, sissies and streetwalkers." Quickly, though, we are taken back to the days of Paul and Joe's, Trilby's, and Dolly Judge's, and to the "fag cellars" of Macdougall Street a few years later. The single paragraph that seems intended to capture a contemporary queer scene also seems a very belated attempt to answer the charge that so clearly stung Clow in 1924 – that he knew nothing about the gay and lesbian lives of those of higher standing who lived north of Times Square. Here, Clow changes focus, in a paragraph that seems to condense his claims to familiarity with present-day (and upscale) queerdom, his disdain for Manhattan's cultural elites, and his preoccupation with the predatory lesbian:

> None of this takes account of the myriad hideouts frequented by the somewhat higher order of fags often in exotic apartments on the Drive or Park Avenue. Here, at "daisy chain" fiestas, you'll find personalities of New York's publishing, literary and musical world you'd gasp at encountering ... There will be a few Lesbies – but this old brood, infinitely more cunning

NEW YORK LIFE

A NATIONAL MONTHLY PUBLICATION

BREEZY — BUBBLING — OCTOBER, 1933 — SATIRICAL — SPICY

LISPERS AND LESBIES

INFEST BROADWAY

Greenwich Village Cellars Swarm With Rouged, Screaming Inverts— Fairyland in Full Bloom Again

BROADWAY and Greenwich Village seem to be in for a new gold rush of Sapphos, sissies and street-walkers.

Maybe it's dat ole debbil depression, or the new beer or the heat, or just the general lid-lifting which presages return of red liquor that is to blame. Go ask your Aunt Charlotte—we're bug.

All we can say is, if you don't believe it just sprint your dogs around Times Square or along Macdougall Street any midnight and watch the hussies, male and female, doing their stuff.

Not far from the Palace Theatre is a hot spot recalling the hybrid days of Paul & Joe's, Trilby's, Dolly Judge's downtown—or the departed "Pansy" or Calais clubs near Longacre. Or the old Lesbie "Double R" on Worst 46th., or old Mother Childs at the Circle, front of which the sailors used to sock the punks, after liberties, and grab all the dough they had. Those were the days of "rough trade." Oh, dearie!

But get a load of the fag cellars on good old Macdougall *strasse* which, strangely enough, margins on Washington Sq., vivid with innocent greenery. Captain Masterson chased the buttercups out of the Village ten yawhs ago, and Chief Mulrooney put the burners on them in recent times — but, take our word for it, the "queens" are now all back, with their rouged lips, passionate eyelashes and obscene chanteys—"Come in and creak your rusty old hips, dearie —you know you're just as queer as we are!"

Likes 'Em Tall, Eh?

"Gee, Gertie, your sweetie makes mine look like a runt."

"Sure—I'm nuts for height. I guess my Jack has at least six more inches than your Harry."

None of this takes account of the myriad hideouts frequented by the somewhat higher order of fags, often in exotic apartments on the Drive or Park Avenue. Here, at "daisy chain" fiestas, you'll find personalities of New York's publishing, literary and musical world you'd gasp at encountering! Half the weird crowd will probably consist of interior decorators, whose fixed fate seems to be sex-abnormalcy. Maybe it's from fingering so much silk and satin. Or they were born that way—and the fabrics just pep them up! There'll be a few Lesbies —but this odd brood, infinitely more cunning and dangerous than the fag, prefer secretive places and contacts. Wells of Loneliness!—from these, only, they quaff their nauseous nectars.

Want to see the psychos in full swing without much cruising around? All right, just park any time after 1 a.m. at Broadway and 42nd Street, northeast corner. Here the queers gather in screaming groups, "dishing the dirt," meeting old cronies, ogling pedestrians—and occasionally giving a hooker friend a lift with her work!

(For further fascinating revelations on the Queer Gang read Nov. issue of NEW YORK LIFE.)

Figure 8.12 Back cover, *New York Life*, no. 3, October 1933.

and dangerous than the fag, prefers secretive places and contacts. Wells of Loneliness – from these, only, they quaff their nauseous nectars.[57]

By early 1934, *Razzberries*, *Squawkies*, *Burten's Follies*, and *New York Life* had all ceased publication. As we shall see in the next chapter, it is possible they were all terminated in response to the threat of action by the New York Society for the Suppression of Vice, which had carefully followed Burten's activities since the early 1920s. A certificate dated 18 October 1937 and deposited with the New York County Clerk's Office indicated that Joe Burten, with his brother Morris D. Bernstein, had founded the Burten Magazine Distribution Co. on West 44th Street in Manhattan.[58] This corporate name would surface in 1945 as the identified publisher of at least two comic books, *Miss Liberty* and *Roly Poly*, both of which claimed their place of publication as Dearborn, Michigan, but otherwise contained no information on editorial staff.

In the 1940s, with Wayne Sabbath credited as his managing editor, Joe Burten launched a large number of digest-sized men's magazines, full of pin-up photographs and racy jokes and presumably directed at men serving in the armed forces. The firm behind most of these was the Greenwich Features Syndicate, located at 15 Park Row in New York. These publications, many of them one-shots, had titles like *Argentine Nights*, *Artists and Models*, *Gay Broadway*, *Gay Parisian*, *Hollywood Follies*, *Hollywood Scandals*, *La Paree*, and *Life in Rio*. In 1960, a syndicated news report listed Burten among several distributors of pornographic materials who had been indicted in Dallas, Texas, on charges of sending materials through the mail to newsstands in that city. "The book distributors," the report stated, "are Max Goldstein and Dominion News Company, Inc., of Newport News, and the W.F. Hall Printing co., and Joseph Burten of Chicago."[59] *Variety*'s coverage of this story noted that Burten actually lived in Oxford, New Jersey (in the state in which he would die in 1967).[60]

■■■

With Annenberg's city tabloids gone at the end of 1932, and with the disappearance of Epstein's *Tattlers* and Burten's *New York Life* by early 1934, *Brevities: America's First National Weekly Tabloid* would outlast all its imitators before itself vanishing in 1935. By mid-decade, the various genres of sensational content that had marked the tabloid wave could each be found in other kinds of magazines. Rude cartoons by the hundreds filled magazines like *Lulu*, *Gee Whiz*, or revamped versions of *Ballyhoo* and those which more and more specialized in these. Racy stories were abundant in sex pulps and in those lingering titles from the 1920s, like *Capt. Billy's Whiz Bang* and *Hot Dog*, which now strained to copy them. In addition, New York entertainment guides like *New York Amusements*, *Cue*, *Day and Night*, *East Side – West Side*, *Gotham Life*, *The Metropolitan Host*, and *New York: Where To Go* all had their nightlife gossip columns. While these were invariably more polite than those that had made the weekly tabloids so notorious, they were a defining feature of a dense media environment in which gossip and sensation were no longer scarce commodities.

NINE

BROADWAY BREVITIES IN CANADA

O John S., in thy hours of ease,
Uncertain, coy and slow to please;
Alas! When sex-pulps knot thy brow
A devastating angel, thou!

Stephen G. Clow. "The Arbiter of Smut," Author and Journalist, November 1934, 9.

"The Arbiter of Smut," published in the November 1934 issue of the trade magazine *Author and Journalist*, stands almost alone among Clow's writings of the 1930s in making its author appear to be a principled, sympathetic individual. In a gently mocking tone, Clow denounces the relentless efforts of John S. Sumner, "militant secretary of the New York Society for the Prevention of Vice,"[1] to keep sensational, spicy printed materials of all kinds off the newsstands. Clow's article clearly spoke on behalf of a great many publishers of sex pulps and scandal tabloids who had faced Sumner and his society. It also hints at a possible reason for the quick death of some of the publications in which Clow himself had been involved over the previous three years. During this period, the offices of the New York Society for the Prevention of Vice were located on West 22nd Street, not far from the Spinning Wheel Building and the busy pulp and tabloid factory of Theodore Epstein, for whom Clow had worked briefly in 1932.

In his *Author and Journalist* piece, Clow describes the "safety" system set in place by Sumner and the society:

> So heavily does his menacing shadow fall across the counting rooms of the magazine distributors in New York that, within the past three years, a "safety" system has been founded by them. The big wholesalers now submit to Mr Sumner advance copies of all doubtful issues, as well as first issues of any publication inspected. The patient gentleman inspects every line of every page, as well as the engravings and cartoons and the advertisements as well. Should he return the samples to the distributors adversely blue-pencilled, the publication is refused or withdrawn as the case may be. This is merely a self-preservation gesture, for in case of prosecutions, both publisher and distributor are included.[2]

Clow goes on to note that, while the society's campaigns against indecent books had regularly failed, its moves to ban magazines had proved devastating to those publishing and distributing them. We may suspect that the municipal government's regulation of newsstands made magazines an easier target than books, given the frequency with which city officials collaborated with organizations like Sumner's. Clow's article also offers what might be the clearest reason for the hasty disappearance of the three magazines introduced by Joe Burten the year before: "But he [Sumner] sent at least three over-spicy tabloid 'tabs' to Davy Jones' locker since September, 1933, via the distributors' deadly advance-copy route. This prophylactic technique has prosecution beaten all hollow; the evil-minded publishers are licked before they start."[3]

By late 1934, when Clow's article appeared, he may well have been offering one reason for the apparent dead end he had reached in his own publishing career. One month earlier, in the same magazine, a small advertisement showed Clow, presumably now unemployed, looking – indeed, pleading – for editing work: "I Sold $10,000 Worth of my own writings (1927–34), simply as side-line to my editing work … Published books for 12 years … Edited three national magazines … Have read, revised, 'ghosted' and corrected hundreds of scripts … Don't you think I could help you? Stephen G. Clow, Leona Studios, 335 W 57, N. Y. City."[4] How Clow supported himself in the period immediately following the collapse of the Burten magazines is unclear, though we may guess that it involved some combination of behind-the-scenes editorial work and handouts from old friends. *New York Life*, which Clow edited briefly for Joe Burten, almost certainly represented his last opportunity in New York to publish a magazine reminiscent in any way of the original *Broadway Brevities*. The tabloid *Brevities*, as we have seen, had disappeared in 1935, and the second half of the decade saw few new attempts to perpetuate the format in New York.

Then, in 1937, *Broadway Brevities* would be relaunched one last time, with Stephen G. Clow as its editor. This new incarnation would be published in Canada, by a young entrepreneur who saw opportunity in repackaging, for Canadian readers, the format, style, and original content of sensational American periodicals of the previous decade. In Toronto, Clow found employment with a publisher who, like Theodore Epstein and Joe Burten, seemed to recognize his talents and perhaps sense the value of his lingering notoriety.

Clow in Toronto

On 16 December 1937, newspapers in Toronto reported that a man named Stephen G. Clow had been arrested in that city, charged with publishing obscene matter tending to corrupt morals. The arrest followed a police raid on a printing shop at 10 St Patrick Street, where authorities seized copies of three magazines published on the premises – *Broadway Brevities*, *Canadian Tattler*, and *Garter Girls*. Soon after, police also arrested a man named Morris Rubin, identified in the press as the "manager, owner and publisher" of the magazines seized.[5] Clow was remanded until 4 January 1938 on bail set at $1,000.[6] From press coverage of the trail, which began on 14 January 1938, we learn that Clow was being paid $35 per week for his editorial duties on the three titles. Morris Rubin, identified as his employer, apparently wept during the proceedings, and "said that he had put his all into the venture."[7] In any event, the charges were dismissed by the presiding magistrate on 14 January – in part, it seemed, because the defence was able to prove that the magazines in question were much less obscene than many others currently available on newsstands.[8]

The circumstances that led a Toronto-based publisher to launch a new version of *Broadway Brevities* in 1937 had much to do with the complicated, constantly shifting traffic in magazines between the United States and Canada in the 1930s. Early in that decade, the New York tabloid version of *Brevities* had appeared on a regularly updated list of "Prohibited Publications" maintained by the Canadian government. These were magazines deemed obscene and denied entry into Canada.[9] The titles appearing on this annual list offer a useful index of shifting fashions within US periodical publishing at the time. Alongside the confession and true crime magazines launched in the 1920s, we see a variety of titles testifying to the later explosion of the US "spicy" periodical. The "spicy" label assumed a loose coherence around 1930, when a variety of magazines seeming to serve distinct interests (gossip about Hollywood celebrities, ribald humour for men, lightly pornographic "French" sex stories, etc.) began more and more to resemble one other, each offering slightly different combinations of pin-up imagery, cartoons with sexual content, and risqué fiction. Among those whose importation into Canada was blocked were *Film Fun*, *Paree*, *Stocking Parade*, *Calgary Eye Opener*, and *Stolen Sweets*. In 1931, *Brevities* appeared on the list, alongside the many satirical magazines launched following the success of *Ballyhoo*.[10]

Despite these prohibitions, it was common, by the end of the decade, for Canadian publishers to acquire the content of certain kinds of US magazines (spicy cartoons and sex stories, for example) and package it in titles printed in Canada for the domestic market. While this offered a way of avoiding seizures of magazines at the Canadian border, publication of these materials in Canada brought the threat of arrest and confiscation by lower levels of government within Canada that constantly monitored the public sale of obscene materials. Under pressure from Canadian civic groups like the Knights of Columbus and the National Council of Women, the government of the Province of Ontario actively responded to citizen complaints about obscene materials being sold on newsstands. The morality squads of municipal police forces (like that in Ottawa) regularly confiscated allegedly obscene magazines from city newsstands.[11]

This was the context in which Stephen G. Clow began an association with Morris Rubin. Rubin changed his name by deed poll to "Morris Ruby" in October 1937, and it was under this new name that he built his reputation in Canadian periodical publishing. Since early 1937, Ruby, originally from Montreal, had begun doing business as the Union Publishing Company. Just before his arrest with Clow, he had released the three titles seized by police in December. *Broadway Brevities*, launched with its April 1937 issue, seems to have been the first of Ruby's magazines. *Garter Girls* (whose first issue carried no date) and *Canadian Tattler* (registered for second class mail in July) were introduced very shortly thereafter.

The first issue of the Toronto *Broadway Brevities* was published on 8½" × 11" newsprint and carried the subtitle "Humor With a Million Laughs!" Its title was printed in red, and the typeface and spacing used for the title were the same as those used on the cover of the New York tabloid version of *Brevities* earlier in the decade. The sixteen pages of the first issue consist entirely of cartoons and short jokes; there is no masthead nor any text that might be construed as direct address to the magazine's readership. Nothing here suggests Clow's influence or authorship, and all of the materials appear to have been lifted from US joke books and humour magazines of the previous decade. A single line on the final page lists the publisher as "Union Publishing Co., 446 Spadina Ave., Toronto, Ontario."

Then, in the magazine's second issue, dated May 1937, a "Publisher's Announcement" tells the reader that "[we] take great pleasure in informing our readers of the interesting, indeed rather thrilling fact that we have been able to secure the editorial services of Stephen G. Clow, the founder of "Broadway Brevities" in 1917 (*sic*). Mr. Clow happens to be Canadian-born and is thus especially fitted to gauge the tastes of Canadian readers."[12] Clow's involvement in this second issue is easily identifiable. A piece with the title "Among the Grenwich [*sic*] Villagers," attributed to a "Sheridan D. Square," revisits the same queer establishments as the "Nights in Fairyland" series of 1924–25 (and, indeed, draws on content already recycled in the magazine *Razzberries* in 1934). This allows Clow to return, with brief barbs, to some of his familiar targets – modernist writer Max Bodenheim and *Greenwich Village Quill* editor Bobby Edwards – though one wonders whether these names would have resonated with Canadian readers

Figure 9.1 First Canadian edition, *Broadway Brevities*, April 1937.

of the late 1930s. A brief mention of Juanyta Clivette serves to extoll her talents, and Evelyn Nesbit's name is dropped on more than one occasion. New pieces clearly written by Clow offer some relatively current Broadway gossip, but their up-to-date quality seems less important than the broader tone Clow seems to be seeking: to offer Canadian readers an insider's taste of New York and its sensations. A notice in this second issue makes it clear that Clow would be returning to some of his earlier preoccupations in the issues to come: "Flash! Keep your eye peeled for our June issue! Which begins a series of inside stories, from a non-sensational, clinical standpoint of that strange set of humans grouped under the head of THE THIRD SEX."[13]

It had been obvious, from the 1930s revival of *Brevities* through Clow's contributions to *Broadway Tattler* and *New York Life*, that he believed he had much to gain from endlessly recycling the sensations of the original "Nights in Fairyland" series of 1924–25. By the time of his relocation to Toronto in 1937, that series seemed the only part of *Brevities*' original content that might still hold interest and currency. Blocks of text from the original series, lightly updated and revised to render them more contemporary, run through these early issues of the Canadian *Broadway Brevities*. The sixth issue contains an unsigned piece whose title cascades down several subheadings: "When the Fags Shriek; In Wicked Greenwich Village, New York and 'Dearie' was the word for 'Carrie'; Continuing the story of the strange tribe of abnormals in Greenwich Village 15 years Ago – But Who lispingly infest it today; Exchanging the Jibes at Leon's Epidermis." The article reprints several paragraphs of "Night No. 7 in Fairyland" (from the July 1924 issue of the original *Brevities*). The next few issues of the Canadian *Brevities* would continue to pull from the original series, albeit in misnumbered episodes with misleading titles. By this point, however, Clow's exposés of queer New York read more and more as nostalgic looks back at a world of wonder rather than as outraged accounts of depravity.

While Clow's voice, threaded through the earliest issues of the Canadian *Broadway Brevities*, gives the magazine something of a coherent editorial personality, we can already see the Toronto magazines becoming little more than chaotic assemblages of purloined materials. In the first issue of another of Ruby's titles, *Canadian Tattler*, the publisher's scattershot entry into the market is even clearer.

Figure 9.2 First issue, *Canadian Tattler*, May 1937.

This issue bears a cover date of May 1937, but the year is covered over in black ink, presumably to facilitate its continued circulation in later years. Inside, the masthead identifies the magazine as "Broadway Tattler," suggesting it is a revival of Clow's early 1930s tabloid, but the decision was clearly made at one point to "Canadianize" the title appearing on the cover. Otherwise, thirty-four of the thirty-six pages of *Canadian Tattler* No. 1 are identical to those released the previous month as *Broadway Brevities* No. 2, suggesting that most of it was printed from the same plates.

Joe Burten and Cross-Border Traffic

A 1938 letter from the Crown attorney for the City of Toronto to the office of the attorney general for the Province of Ontario offered further details on Morris Ruby's methods:

> Dear Mr Common:
> Certain magazines published in foreign countries are denied the right of entry into Canada by the authorities at Ottawa. Magazines are then published in Canada which contain virtually the same material. The magazines, "Garter Girl," "Broadway Brevities," and "Canadian Tatler" [*sic*] have such an origin. Some of the features in these magazines were taken from the "Calgary Eye Opener" published in Minneapolis and banned for many years, although the supposed jokes, pictures, etc., may have a different heading.[14]

A more mysterious development, perhaps implicating Clow more directly, involved the Canadian activities of Joe Burten. Traces of Joe Burten flit in and out of the legal record and publishing history of Canadian magazines in the late 1930s and 1940s. The first (and probably only) issue of a sex-fiction magazine called *Saucy* was published by a "Premier Publications" in the Canadian border city of Windsor in 1939. Its editorship was credited to a Wayne Sabbath and authorship of one article to a "Celestine Vichy," both long-time associates of Burten (and possibly his own pseudonyms). In the same year, a magazine called *Keyhole Hu-*

mour, full of jokes, cartoons, and sex stories, was issued by a Toronto-based Empire Magazine Company. A private letter to the Ontario attorney general from solicitor C.P. Hope claimed that both *Saucy* and *Keyhole Humour* were edited and owned by "one Joe Burton [*sic*] who left Toronto last year and is now residing in New York City."[15] If, like Stephen Clow, Joe Burten had gone to Toronto in the late 1930s in search of opportunity, it was no doubt because a ban on the direct importation of certain kinds of magazines from the United States encouraged the recycling of their content in periodicals printed just across the border. Other titles in Morris Ruby's growing roster of magazines included a *Capt. Joey's Tattler Winter Annual*, full of materials that had originally appeared in Burten's New York magazines or in Fawcett titles like *Smokehouse Monthly*.

The Ontario government would use its failure to obtain a conviction against Ruby and Clow in 1938 to justify judicial restraint in dealing with other similar magazines.[16] As it happened, *Garter Girls* and *Canadian Tattler* would both disappear in early 1939, while *Brevities*, as we shall see, lasted several more years. The interests that produced these magazines would find new purpose and respectability over the course of World War II, which Canada entered in September 1939, one week after Great Britain's Declaration of War on Germany. On 4 December 1940, the Canadian minister of finance introduced measures intended to prevent the flow of Canadian currency outside the country. These included a ban on the importation of a whole range of popular periodicals, including those featuring "detective, sex, western and alleged true or confession stories."[17] The importation ban stimulated the quick emergence of a Canadian industry producing popular magazines across several genres – crime, romance, western and aviation stories, science fiction and fantasy, and so on – and several series of comic books.[18]

In a summary of promising local business developments for the month of October 1940, the *Toronto Daily Star* noted the launch of Duchess Printing and Publishing Company.[19] This was the name now used by Morris Ruby for an ambitious new publishing venture. Very quickly, Duchess launched a number of new titles and formats – pulp fiction magazines, paperback novels, comic books, and magazines devoted to humour, true crime, and romance. Most of these bore logos for "Superior Publishing" or "Superior Publishers," the new imprints under which Ruby and his associates now operated. While it had several competitors during the 1940s, Superior would emerge as the most respectable of publishers who had moved to exploit the ban on imported magazines. By 1942, most of its magazines announced that they were "edited, illustrated and produced in Canada by Canadians on Canadian paper without foreign affiliation." One of Superior's most long-lasting titles was *Brevities*.

In late 1938 or early 1939, Canadian *Broadway Brevities* changed its name to *Brevities*. By 1942, *Brevities* was touting itself on its covers as "Canada's Oldest Humour Magazine." This ludicrously self-important claim may have been technically accurate, but it obscured both the newness of the title and its links to one of the most notorious scandal magazines in US publishing history. In fact, the Canadian version of *Broadway Brevities* would last eleven years, longer than all previous incarnations of the magazine. Like the tabloid *Brevities* of the 1930s, the Canadian *Brevities* would live out most of its run without any involvement from Stephen G. Clow, whose name would soon disappear from the magazine. Before it ceased publication (I have seen no issues dated later than 1948), it was one of a number of Superior magazines (like *Halt*, *Zippy*, and *Paree*) specializing in mildly impolite cartoons clearly directed at a military readership. *Brevities*' final skirmish with the law came in 1945, when Duchess Printing and Publishing Company was fined $400 for using eleven tons of paper more than allowed by wartime quotas to publish the magazine.[20]

Clow's Death

In January 1938, following the Toronto court hearing at which the charges against him were dropped, Stephen G. Clow returned to New York. In response to a query, a member of Ruby's extended family remembered Morris Rubin, later in life, having spoken of a New York–based editor he had hired in the late 1930s to come and help him with the launch of several magazines. The man wrote beautifully, the publisher apparently said, but drank too much to be reliable, and so the partnership did not last.[21] On 16 March 1938, back in New York, Clow wrote a desperate letter to New York entertainment columnist Louis Sobol, asking for help in obtaining a handout from Jules Brulatour, the one-time movie mogul turned wealthy New York socialite:

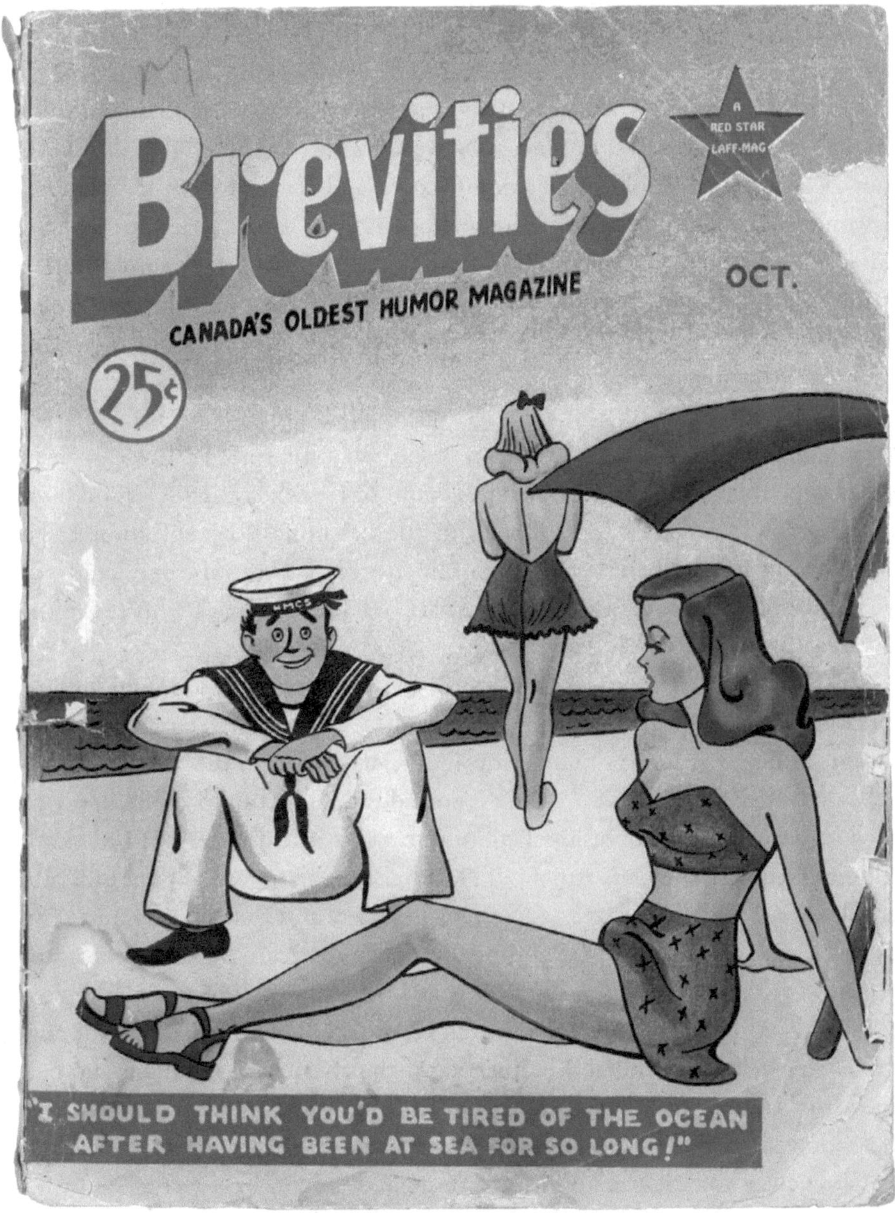

Figure 9.3 Last issue (?), Canadian *Brevities*, October 1948.

> Dear Louis:
> If I have not worn your kind heart to shreds – PLEASE do send that little note to Jules Brulatour about me. You know how to word it so as not to implicate yourself and yet put in a good word for me, as I am in dire distress now. I so wish you would strain a point, Louis, and do this for me for which I would bless you. Unless something happens I am now headed for what looks like the final round-up. I am trying night and day to get something without avail. If Mr B. would let me have a moderate amount, I plan to put most of it in ads for editing work – and have a good chance of survival. Please do this for me.[22]

The outcome of this plea is not known. Sobol, who reprinted Clow's letter in his memoirs, then added the following account of Clow's last days: "In other of his final letters to me, he offered thanks for another minor loan and hinted that at last a break for the better seemed imminent. He was certain he would not have to trouble me again and would, in fact, be able at long last to repay the loans. Death took him four days later."[23]

On 6 June 1941, at the age of sixty-seven, Clow died of an abdominal tumour in New York's Bellevue Hospital, having gone there by himself in a taxi. His body went unclaimed by friends or family until officials took it to the morgue. In his last few months, the *New York Times* reported, Clow had lived alone in a furnished room, selling the occasional column to a race track tipsheet.[24] The death certificate filed with the Department of Health, Borough of Manhattan, indicates that Clow had been living at 102 West 54th Street, and that he was buried in Flushing Cemetery.[25] In his 1948 compendium of American show business scandal, *Hollywood Without Make-Up*, Pete Martin claims that the journalist (now Hollywood producer) Mark Hellinger, an ongoing source of financial support for Clow, paid for his funeral in a final act of charity toward the man who had helped him launch his journalistic career. Martin also suggests that only three people showed up at Clow's funeral: "Mark's secretary, the Federal attorney who'd sent Clow away to Atlanta, and a superannuated lady of easy virtue."[26] In his 1968 autobiography, Louis Sobol names four people as having attended the burial. These included Maxwell S. Mattuck (the prosecutor in Clow's 1925 trial) and Evelyn Nesbit Thaw (almost certainly the "superannuated lady" mentioned by

Martin). Sobol also notes the presence of Broadway columnist, publicist, and producer S. Jay Kaufman and Juanyta Clivette, the "Sappho Poet" and bohemian journalist of the 1920s and 1930s who seems to have been one of Clow's most loyal friends.[27]

Most New York newspapers reported on Clow's death in a perfunctory manner, typically making his 1925 conviction for blackmail the key event for which he was remembered.[28] A few days after his death, Hearst columnist Westbrook Pegler (who in the same year would win a Pulitzer Prize) spent his entire column suggesting that Stephen G. Clow was more responsible than anyone for all that was wrong with contemporary journalism: "Some old-timers will probably vote for Col. William D'Alton Mann of the old Town Topics, but he was just a cur, whereas Clow was all of that and a purveyor of filth as well. Up to his time he was the most versatile and diligent rotter of them all, and it must have depressed him horribly in his later years to see in print material which made his foulest and proudest efforts seem demure if not a little priggish."[29]

Pegler's lengthy piece offered an overarching framework for understanding Clow's place in the development of sensational journalism in New York since the 1920s. It began with the claim that, if only indirectly, Clow had engineered the descent of New York's most high-profile daily newspaper into an amoral sensationalism that would eventually corrupt the profession. In Pegler's account, Clow's friendship with Phil Payne, managing editor of the *Daily News*, had brought Payne into the world of gangster-ridden speakeasies in which his newspaper more and more found its inspiration. Before meeting Clow, Pegler suggested, Payne was a "native rube" with little experience of big-city life and its sensations. Clow led him to embrace, as suitable topics for a big-city newspaper, "the enormous exploitation of the social and carnal affairs of criminals and the drunken rich and the well-dressed moocher."[30] At the same time, Pegler argued, the gossipy sensations of *Broadway Brevities* had come with time to seem timid when set against the unrestrained scandalmongering of journalism in the early 1940s. Clow, he suggested, had simply lived too long – so long, in fact, that "by the time he died developments in the craft had made him seem decent, and this must have been a bitter end for someone who for so long had stood alone." Already, in the late 1920s, as we have seen, observers like *Variety*'s Sime Silverman had suggested that a steady decline of American journalism into sensationalism made the excesses of the original *Broadway Brevities*, and of its editor, seem tame in retrospect.

Westbrook Pegler used the death of Stephen G. Clow to bemoan journalism's decline into ever greater levels of degradation and sensationalism following the closure of the original *Broadway Brevities*. To believe that this descent is a constant and unidirectional feature in the history of US journalism, we would have to be convinced that later periodicals selling gossip, like *Confidential* magazine and the so-called supermarket tabloid *National Enquirer*, were more cruel and destructive of reputations than *Broadway Brevities* at its worst. As with claims about the ever-worsening "personalization" and defamatory tone of political campaigns in the United States, the diagnosis of a steady descent of journalism into the swamp of ever greater sensationalism does not survive historical examination.[31] Remembering *Brevities*' calls for the burning of queer-infected cities, its mocking of substance-addicted theatre stars, and its fantasies of film crews beheaded by guillotine, the notion of a constant irreversible decline across the last hundred years does not seem so easily defended.

CONCLUSION

THE SHIFTING TERRAINS OF MEDIA GOSSIP

Across its different incarnations, the gossipy sensationalism of *Broadway Brevities* shows us the very different forms that printed gossip might take. As suggested in the preface, gossip both whispers and shouts. It whispers in the oral transmission of innuendo from one ear to another, but also in the printed forms of the columnist's hushed brief item. Gossip also finds its ways of shouting, in the exclamatory tone of the tabloid headline ("Sapphic Sisters Scram!") or the stark assault on privacy captured in the candid celebrity photo. The distinction between these two treatments allows us to note a key difference between the first version of *Broadway Brevities* (1916–24) and the tabloid *Brevities* of 1931–35. The first, in the manner of society magazines before it, concealed lurid gossip behind covers featuring images of untainted glamour or luxury. The second filled its covers with headlines that screamed loudly, exaggerating the secrets offered inside and misrepresenting editorial content that was, much of the time, formulaic and unsensational. It is tempting to suggest that the difference between these two kinds of gossip allows us to distinguish between phases in its history – from Victorian discretion, as it is imagined today, to what many might perceive as the noisy attention-mongering of twentieth-century tabloid culture. The continued circulation in the present day of restrained, coy gossip, in email newsletters like the British *Popbitch* or Instagram threads reporting conversations "Overheard" in different cities, suggests that this transformation has never been completed.

Gossip and the Law

There are other ways in which we may chart differences in printed gossip and the ways in which it has been treated. The history of gossip journalism in the United States is also a history of how sensational publications have been brought down by the law. *Broadway Brevities*, like *Town Topics*, faced courts because they used information as the basis of blackmail, a practice made possible by the intimate relations between editors and targets that were typical of the worlds in which these magazines were published and circulated. In the 1930s, the tabloids discussed here were more likely to be the object of campaigns aimed at eradicating obscenity. Their gossipy items were viewed, much of the time, as little more than rhetorical devices that gave periodicals a pretext for speaking of sex. Municipal campaigns to "clean up" newsstands, typically fuelled by electoral politics and carried out in collaboration with civil society groups, targeted sensational tabloids for their general air of moral degradation rather than for their revelations about specific individuals. Personalized gossip itself, however much it wove its way through the pages of 1930s tabloids like the *New Broadway Brevities*, did not itself elicit much attention from governments and was rarely, if ever, revealed to be a tool within schemes to extort or blackmail.

Then, from the 1950s through the present, in a history that runs from *Confidential* magazine to modern-day tabloid journalism (in its American and British varieties), the charge of libel has been the key legal instrument through which gossip has been controlled.[1] The practice of blackmail, if it persists, is almost never brought to trial in cases that produce high-profile criminal proceedings.[2] The charge of obscenity, once wielded so effectively by governments at all levels, has been weakened by court decisions or has found its targets elsewhere than on newsstands and magazine racks.

Personal Gossip and Collective Morality

An additional shift, more cyclical than linear, may be found in the different versions of *Broadway Brevities*, and across the career of Stephen G. Clow. Through it, we may understand some of the broader transitions in American sensational journalism of the twentieth century. I am referring here to the movement back and forth between personalized gossip focused on individual lives and the broader exposure of collective immorality. The original *Brevities*, in its last year of publication, pulled back from items that named (or hinted at) specific personalities, preferring to offer its readers the vision of a broader depravity supposedly infecting New York City as a whole. Likewise, the tabloid *Brevities* launched in 1931 – and its imitators, like *Graft*, *Broadway Tattler*, and *Scandals* – scattered brief gossipy items about individuals on its inside pages but devoted its public face (its headlines and cover graphics) to exposing new kinds of collective behaviour that extended far beyond the simply personal.

In the years after Stephen G. Clow's death, this back and forth between personal scandal and social exposé would drive key developments in the history of scandalous journalism in the United States. In 1948, journalists Jack Lait and Lee Mortimer published the book *New York Confidential*, the first in a series of four volumes concerned with exposing the moral condition of American cities.[3] For Lee Mortimer, in particular, the *Confidential* books offered an alternative to the celebrity-focused nightlife columns with which he had made his name (and as a result of which, on at least one occasion, he was the victim of physical violence[4]). The journalism of social exposé offered several advantages to those who had hitherto devoted themselves to celebrity gossip. The long forms of the exposé lent themselves more easily to publication in book form, and thus promised higher returns, a benefit that Mortimer exploited (and that Clow, who once promised a book-length study of queer life, might have imagined). And as suggested in chapter 2, *Broadway Brevities*' dive into Manhattan's queer geographies in 1924 was one way of avoiding the ostracism, threats of physical violence, and possible libel suits that a more personalized gossip might provoke. Finally, exposés of urban vice and nonconformity typically had a longer shelf life than celebrity-focused gossip – the generalities of the former did not date so quickly, and they were easily adjusted to accommodate new developments or future uses. Clow, as we have seen, recycled entire paragraphs from "Nights in Fairyland" fifteen years after their original publication, while insinuations about the private lives of Tallulah Bankhead or Elisabeth Marbury had long ceased to interest most readers. The city confidential books of Lait and Mortimer lent themselves to regular updates and film adaptations that extended their commercial lives considerably.

The passage from personalized gossip to a broader social commentary was not unidirectional, however, and it is in the back and forth between the two that the history of gossip and sensation might be understood. In 1952, a one-time publisher of pin-up magazines launched *Confidential*, arguably the first American gossip magazine whose notoriety in its time exceeded that of *Broadway Brevities*. In its years of greatest fame and influence, between 1952 and 1957, *Confidential* ran stories on show business celebrities – on their drug use, their interracial romances, and their suspected homosexuality – that stand today as among the most invasive and lurid examples of gossip journalism ever. *Confidential* magazine took its title from the urban exposé books written by Jack Lait and Lee Mortimer, but its editor, Robert Harrison, was influenced as well by the set of US Senate hearings (also known as the Kefauver Committee) that travelled the country in 1950 and 1951, looking for evidence of municipal corruption and rampant vice.[5] For Harrison, the high levels of public interest in these hearings stood as proof of a fascination with the private lives of people in the headlines.[6]

While *Broadway Brevities*, in its first incarnation, moved from personalized gossip into social commentary, *Confidential* was born in the effort to convert a panic over collective morality into a fascination with personal transgression. Less well known is Robert Harrison's later turn away from celebrity gossip, when faced with libel suits and censorship, back to the less risky genre of urban exposé. A 1959 letter from Lee Mortimer to Walter Winchell's secretary bemoans the fact that, having sold the rights to the city *Confidential* books to a publisher intending to bring them out in magazine format, Mortimer discovered that Harrison was now the secret owner of those rights.[7] Published in 1959, a new, magazine-sized edition of *New York Confidential*, claiming on its cover to be "based on the Best-Seller by Jack Lait and Lee Mortimer," but otherwise featuring new, salacious content, was one of the titles offering Harrison a pathway out of celebrity gossip. In 1961, under his own name, Harrison published the book *Naked New York*, a mildly titillating exposé of the city's sensations and subcultures that nevertheless dodged the risks of libel by avoiding direct reference to individuals. Harrison, it seemed, had followed a pathway etched earlier by Stephen G. Clow. Both men had begun by revealing personal secrets, then moved to exploit a broader fascination with urban communities and their behaviours.

The Tabloid Revolution of the 1960s

In 1957, a publisher named Gordon Pope transformed a failing New York daily newspaper, the *New York Enquirer*, into a nationally distributed weekly, the *National Enquirer*. Between 1957 and 1962, as Jeannette Walls recounts, some forty imitations of the *National Enquirer* began publication in the United States. Pope had determined that, with migration to the suburbs and the decline of the urban newsstand, new venues for selling news periodicals were required. And so, in the late 1950s, Pope decided to reorient his weekly paper toward supermarket sales and a predominantly female readership.[8] Display at supermarket checkouts required that the *National Enquirer* play down the themes that had driven its success in the beginning – violent crime and lurid vice. Instead, the *National Enquirer* would establish itself as the pre-eminent vehicle for celebrity gossip.

In fact, this shift was never complete. A great many issues of the *National Enquirer* filled their covers with headlines like "Yes! Flying Saucers Come From Other Planets" (10 1967 01) or "9-Year-Old Arrested 200 Times" (11 1964 15), offering stories that carried on, albeit in eccentric form, the paper's early focus on human interest stories and tales of unusual phenomena. This miscellany would characterize the paper in the public mind as much as its ongoing fascination with Jackie Onassis or Frank Sinatra. Nevertheless, in a look at several dozen of the supermarket tabloids from the 1960s, one of their striking features is the persistence of the show business gossip column. The *National Enquirer* carried, for a time, "Inside and Straight" by Alex Freeman, and other tabloid weeklies had similar columns (in the *National Tattler*, Terry O'Neill's "Behind the Scene;" in the *National Bulletin*, Mike Winsor's "The Hot Line"; in the *National Informer*, Dale Roberts's "New York Inside Informer," and so on).The celebrity gossip column, with its three-dot ellipses and short paragraphs, became as predictable a feature of these papers as astrology columns and classified advertisements offering companionship or sexual connections.

By this point, the form and substance of the tabloid gossip column had become highly standardized, with most columns seeming to offer little more than rewritten press releases to which a vaguely familiar name was attached. A columnist of long standing, Louis Sobol, contributed his column "New York

Cavalcade" to the quasi-pornographic tabloid *Tab International*, where it seemed quaintly respectable and old-fashioned alongside articles that described newly observed (or invented) sexual practices and habits.[9] Indeed, by the end of the 1960s, the tabloid gossip columnist's announcement of a celebrity's minor career moves or changes in marital status would come across as tame and polite alongside illustrated features detailing the moral transgressions of persons who were usually unnamed.

A 1966 issue of the *National Limelight*, whose cover headline read "I Sold My Body To Pay For My Lover's Funeral," featured "In the Limelight," a gossip column whose authorship was attributed to African-American performer Diahann Carroll. Some of its items (reporting a romance between Jean-Paul Belmondo and "German sexpot Christine Schmidter," and the rise of the neo-Nazi NPD party in West Germany) expressed a cosmopolitanism out of line with the paper's overall tone. Most, however, performed the work of promotional press releases, including one that clarified the state of the author's own personal life: "Diahann Carroll and Sidney Poitier resumed – for now at least, but both insist it's just 'platonic' … It was good to see Otto Preminger back in artistic harness again when he appeared as 'Mr Freeze' on a recent 'Batman' segment. It was the first appearance he's turned in in 12 years. Nowhere, but nowhere can a more frightening villain be found … The Rock Hudson-Judy Garland idyll has apparently ended. Rock's latest interest is shapely Jill St John."[10]

Surrounded as it was by lurid tales, probably invented, of sexual entrapment or horrendous personal tragedies, Carroll's *National Limelight* column, with its recognizable names and innocuous announcements, might be seen as calming its readers rather than exciting them. The gossip column, in these contexts, offered a space of refuge filled with the familiar and predictable, rather than capturing, as had *Broadway Brevities* in the 1920s, a world in which moral standards might no longer be certain. For a time, from the late 1950s through the 1970s, gossip columns in American tabloids conveyed the sense that they were lingering features of an earlier time. Gossip would be reinvigorated in later decades, of course, in the various versions of "Page Six"[11] associated with globally circulating tabloid media, and in the frequently queer-inflected nightlife columns carried by the alternative weekly newspapers that flourished in cities from the 1970s until recently. With the ongoing disappearance of print media, these, too, have come to be remembered as endearing features of an age in which seasoned professionals shared, in columns of familiar style and regularity, the sensations of the social worlds through which they moved.

NOTES

Introduction

1 "Girl Thief Calm in Cell," *Sunday News* (New York), 1 November 1925, 3.
2 "Jackie Reveals Crime Lure," *Daily News* (New York), 2 November 1925, 4. The reference to "effeminate men" and "masculine women" appeared in only one of the paper's editions on that date and was dropped from the version of the article carried in others.
3 "Night No. 3 in Fairyland," *Broadway Brevities*, March 1924, 12.
4 "Jackie Reveals Crime Lure," 4.
5 For more on the ways in which "exposés" of the places of illicit sexuality might serve as guides for those seeking such places, see Lucy Santé, *Low Life: Lures and Snares of Old New York* (New York: Farrar, Strauss, Giroux, 1991), 257–8.
6 Jim Bishop, *The Mark Hellinger Story* (New York: Appleton-Century-Crofts, 1952), 55.
7 "Brevities Trial Greatest Show on Earth – and Admission's Free," *Sunday News*, 1 February 1925, 1.
8 "The Press," *Time*, 11 August 1930, 23.
9 Gershon Legman, "Toward a Motif-Index of Erotic Humor," *The Journal of American Folklore* 75 (July–September 1962): 227–48.
10 For a contemporary account of the tabloid newspapers' rise to market dominance, see Simon Bessie, *Jazz Journalism: The Story of the Tabloid Newspapers* (New York: E.P. Dutton, 1938).
11 Louis Sobol, *The Longest Street: A Memoir* (New York: Crown Publishers, 1968), 334.

12 See, in addition to the memoirs and biographies mentioned elsewhere in this chapter, Pete Martin, *Hollywood Without Make-Up* (Philadelphia and New York: J.B. Lippincott, 1948); Neal Gabler, *Winchell: Gossip, Power and the Culture of Celebrity* (New York: Alfred A. Knopf, 1994); and the overview Abel Green and Joe Laurie Jr, *Showbiz: From Vaudeville to Video* (New York: Henry Holt & Company, 1951).

13 Jim Bishop, *The Mark Hellinger Story* (New York: Appleton-Century-Crofts, 1952), 55.

14 Richard Jean So, "Literary Information Warfare: Eileen Chang, the US State Department, and Cold War Media Aesthetics," *American Literature* 85, no. 4 (2013): 733.

15 Clive Scott, *Street Photography: From Atget to Cartier-Bresson* (London and New York: I.B. Taurus, 2007), 164.

16 Patricia Meyer Spacks, *Gossip* (Chicago: The University of Chicago Press, 1985), 34.

17 See, for a useful summary of these arguments, Nicholas Baer and Maggie Hennefeld, "All the Rumors Are True: An Introduction," *NECSUS* 11, no. 1 (Spring 2022): 4–17.

Chapter One

1 For genealogical details concerning the family, see "The Descendants and Kin of William Graham of Lockerbie, Scotland," accessed 3 February 2020, www.islandregister.com/graham.html#google_vignette; and "Reid-Schroeder Genealogies," accessed 30 October 2024, www.reidgen.com/search.php?myfirstname=Clow.

2 See, among many accounts, "The Late Mr James Clow," *The Guardian* (Charlottetown, Prince Edward Island), 4 April 1901, 4.

3 "Teachers' Provincial Institute: The Annual Meeting," *Daily Examiner*, 10 October 1891, 2.

4 The only confirmation I have found of any postsecondary education Clow might have received took the form of a letter by Clow, published in the Charlottetown *Daily Examiner*, recommending a teacher of stenography at the Charlottetown Business College for an award. Clow wrote as "one of the members of Mr Moren's shorthand class in your College." S.G. Clow, "Letter," *Daily Examiner*, 31 December 1896, 3.

5 *Who's Who in New York City and State* (New York: L.R. Hamersly & Company, 1909), 286. In answer to a request for information from the staff of the Parliamentary Press Gallery in Ottawa, I was told that, while the gallery had a database

of all its members, Clow's name did not appear in it (Shane Séguin, Canadian Press Gallery, email communication, 5 May 2018). *The Daily Examiner* did report that "Mr S.G. Clow has returned from Ottawa" in July 1897 but did not provide further details. "Personal," *The Daily Examiner*, 2 July 1897, 3.

6 While there is no reason to doubt the *Guardian*'s own claim that Clow had been its city editor, his name appears nowhere in the *Guardian* in connection with that role during the years in which his age would have made it possible.

7 Census of Canada, 1901, item number 770030, Library and Archives Canada.

8 Stephen G. Clow, "Broadway Yesterday and To-Day," *Broadway Brevities*, July 1917, 22. United States Federal Census, 1910, Year: 1910; Census Place: Manhattan Ward 18, New York, New York; Roll: T624_1037; Page: 4A.

9 Personal communication to Will Straw, 18 August 2009. The name of the source of this information is withheld at their request.

10 Nick Mount, *Moved When Canadian Literature to New York* (Toronto: University of Toronto Press, 2005), 19–21.

11 Dean Irvine. "'Little Magazines' in English Canada," in Peter Brooker and Andrew Thacker, eds., *The Oxford Critical and Cultural History of Modernist Magazines. Volume II: North America 1894–1960*, 602 (Oxford, UK: Oxford University Press, 2012).

12 See Irene Gammel, *Looking for Anne of Green Gables* (New York: St Martin's Press, 2009), 26–7.

13 "Personal Mention," *Charlottetown Guardian*, 24 August 1900, 8.

14 Stephen G. Clow, letter, in "About Mr Markham's Poetry: A Fresh Batch of Letters from His Severe Critics and His Enthusiastic Audiences," *New York Times Saturday Review of Books*, 19 August 1905, 24. "The Poet's Hard Pathway," *The Globe* (Toronto), 8 July 1905, A5; Stephen G. Clow, Letter: "Poetry vs Civilization," *New York Times Saturday Review of Books*, 11 March 1905, 27.

15 Unsigned, "The Saunterer," *Town Talks* (San Francisco), 28 October 1905, 17.

16 Louis Sobol. *The Longest Street*, 334.

17 A 1904 notice of a suit for bankruptcy against the Broadway Magazine Company claims that this firm had taken over the business of the original Broadway Publishing Company, including its debts, in 1903. "Petitions in Bankruptcy," *New York Times*, 13 April 1904, 11.

18 Helen Kenny, "Stephen Clow – the Poet-Publisher," *Broadway Weekly*, 17 March 1904, 5.

19 Dayton Stoddart, *Lord Broadway: Variety's Sime* (New York: Wilfred Funk, 1941), 109–19; 338–40. Dayton Stoddart's main activity was as a journalist and press agent, but he was the author of one novel, *Prelude to Night* (1947), which served

as the basis of the film *Ruthless*, directed by Edgar G. Ulmer and released in 1948. Stoddart had a co-author credit for the film's screenplay with Gordon Kahn, who had worked with Stephen G. Clow on *Broadway Brevities* in the 1920s.

20 Stoddart, *Lord Broadway*, 148. The will of James Clow, who died on 2 April 1901, was approved and rendered public on 19 April of the same year. It left $1,000 to James's daughter, identified as Mrs Leslie Poole, and $500 each to his two grandchildren, Ella and Lucy Hoyt. The rest of the estate (of unspecified value) went to James's wife (and Stephen's mother) Lucy, but with instructions that it be "for the use and benefit" of his two sons, Stephen and Benjamin, with the latter to receive a slightly larger share. "Mr James Clow's Will," *The Guardian*, 11 May 1901, 5.

21 "The Hollywood Bookshelf," *The Courier-Journal* (Louisville, Kentucky), 19 December 1903, 4.

22 Display advertisement, *New York Time Saturday Review of Books*, 4 September 1909, 27.

23 Stoddart, *Lord Broadway*, 111.

24 Ibid., 151–3.

25 Ibid., 147–51; George Fuller Golden, *My Lady Vaudeville and Her White Rats* (New York: Broadway Publishing Company, 1909).

26 Advertisement, "Our New Baltimore Branch," *New York Times Saturday Review of Books*, 29 May 1909, BR345. Eugene L. Didier's book *The Poe Cult And other Poe Papers* was published by the Broadway Publishing Company in 1909.

27 Stephen G. Clow, "How I Blackmailed the Stars of Society and the Stage," chapter 1, *The Orlando Sentinel* (Orlando, Florida), 8 January 1928, 26.

28 State of New York, Certificate of Incorporation of Broadway Publishing Co., Inc., dated 21 October 1912, no. 4814. Under the terms of this incorporation Clow was to retain 998 shares while partners named Edwin B. Sibley and Aimee Gibbon held one each.

29 "Dissolutions," *New York Times*, 9 November 1913, 8.

30 *Who's Who In New York City and State*, 1909 edition, 286; "The Semi-Monthly Record of Books," *The Bookseller, Newsdealer and Stationer*, 15 November 1907, 370. The status of "The Decay of Poetry" remains a mystery. While it was announced as a stand-alone publication, advertisements for new releases by the Broadway Publishing Company in 1907 suggest it was Clow's introduction to a volume featuring an essay on the British poet Robert Montgomery by the poet and historian Thomas Babington "Lord" Macaulay, whom Clow held in great esteem. Display advertisement, "Broadway Publishing Co.," *The New York Times Saturday Review of Books*, 19 October 1907, RB669.

31 "3 One-Act Plays on Triangle Theater Bill," *New York Tribune*, 18 March 1924, 12.

32 "Is It as Bad as This?," letter to the editor, *The Sun* [New York], 10 December 1917, 6.

33 "'Broadway Brevities. A magazine typical of Broadway," *Catalog of Copyright Entries by the Library of Congress*, 20 April 1916, B359666.

34 Clow, "How I Blackmailed the Stars of Society and the Stage," chapter 1, *The Orlando Sentinel Sun,* 8 January 1928, 26. While the first issue of *Broadway Brevities* was, indeed, printed in the small 7½″ × 4¾″ size, by the time of its September 1916 issue, it had grown to dimensions of 9″ × 6″, which remained consistent until the magazine ceased publication in 1925.

35 Library of Congress, *Catalog of Copyright Entries*, 20 April 1916, B359666.

36 "Along the Line," *Broadway Brevities*, January 1917, 25.

37 Broadway Brevities Inc. File 07061 16C, *Certificate of Corporation of Broadway Brevities, Inc.*, State of New York, 2 December 1916.

38 "Cabaret Managers Hauled into Court: Wallick's and Rector's Accused of Giving Theatrical Shows," *New York Times*, 29 May 1915, 20.

39 "Late New York State Incorporations," *Billboard*, 5 February 1910, 5. Cacciola's appointment as commissioner of deeds is recorded in *New York, The City Record*, 19 November 1915, 8759.

40 The certificate of incorporation of *Brevities* lists a "C. Nicholas Reinhardt," and it is as "C.N. Reinhardt" that he appears on *Brevities*' masthead during his time with the magazine. In his 1928 memoirs, Clow refers to him as "Charles D. Reinhardt." Clow, "How I Blackmailed the Stars of Society and the Stage," chapter 1. Well-known columnist O.O. McIntyre, in a 1920 item noting Reinhardt's new role as a passenger agent for the aviation company Aero, Inc., describes "Charles A. Reinhardt" as "an old newspaper man [who] started Broadway Brevities." O.O. McIntyre, "Bits of New York Life," *The Atlanta Constitution*, 5 July 1920, 4.

41 O.O. McIntyre, "New York Day-By-Day," *Passaic Daily News*, 13 April 1917, 9.

42 Clow, "How I Blackmailed the Stars of Society and the Stage," chapter 10, *The Orlando Sentinel Sun*, 11 March 1928, 27.

43 "Along the Line," *Broadway Brevities*, September 1916, 14.

44 The accusation that Kingsley fed gossip items to *Broadway Brevities* is made in "'Brevities' Investigated," *Variety*, 5 October 1917, 5.

45 For a usefully detailed history of society columns in New York City newspapers, Eric Homberger, *Mrs Astor's New York: Money and Social Power in a Gilded Age* (New Haven and London: Yale University Press, 2002), 205. Homberger suggests that 1880 was a key year in the emergence of the society column, with *The Sun* newspaper introducing a column of "society chat" and other newspapers following. I discuss the role of names in social columns in Will Straw, "Gathering Up

the Social: Nightlife Columns in the African-American Press," *Ethnologies* 44, no. 1 (2022): 40–59.

46 "Editorially speaking," *Broadway Brevities*, 15 September 1917, 18–19.

47 "The Whole Staff Goes to the Front: The Five Little Editors of Broadway Brevities Do Their Bit in Khaki," *Vanity Fair*, January 1918, 88b.

48 Ibid.

49 In 1920, the word "Broadway" disappeared from the magazine's covers, leaving "Brevities" to sit there alone – in an effort, perhaps, to build a readership outside of New York. However, the full name, "Broadway Brevities," was still used on the magazine's interior masthead throughout its history and would return to the cover in early 1922.

50 "'Brevities' Investigated," 5.

51 "Libel Suit Started," *Variety*, 12 October 1917, 4.

52 "The Whole Staff Goes to the Front," 88b.

53 Clow, "How I Blackmailed the Stars of Society and the Stage," chapter 1, 26.

54 In 1920, New York–based syndicated columnist O.O. McIntyre wrote of bumping into Reinhardt at the Fifth Avenue offices of an aviation company called the Aero, Ltd, at which the former editor was now working as a "passenger agent." O.O. McIntyre, "Bits of New York Life," *Atlanta Constitution*, 5 July 1920, 4.

55 Stephen G. Clow, "Broadway Yesterday and To-Day," *Broadway Brevities*, May 1917, 17–18.

56 George Jessel, *So Help Me: The Autobiography of George Jessel* (Cleveland and New York: The World Publishing Company, 1943), 49.

57 "Impertinent Questions," *Broadway Brevities*, April 1917, 32.

58 "Impertinent Questions," *Broadway Brevities*, August 1921, 32–3.

59 "Gum-shoeing along the Old Street," *Broadway Brevities,* April 1921, 12.

60 "Rhymes of a Broadway Bum," *Broadway Brevities*, August 1921, 16.

61 "The Nuts in a Nutshell," *Broadway Brevities*, August 1921, 32–4.

62 Ibid., 33, 32.

63 "H.U.," "At the Cabarets," *New York Tribune*, 8 May 1919, c6.

64 Richard Abel, "Harriette Underhill," *Women Film Pioneers Project*, 2020, accessed 7 February 2021, https://wfpp.columbia.edu/pioneer/harriette-underhill/. For further details on Underhill's career, see Anthony Slide, *Inside the Hollywood Fan Magazine,* 40.

65 A particularly vicious, unsigned item about Underhill from 1921 claims "Harriett annoys us severely" and belittles her attempts at humour, claiming she is "as funny as a medical almanac." "Hattie Terrifies Us," *Broadway Brevities*, November 1921, 10.

66 Stephen Clow, "How I Blackmailed the Stars of Society and the Stage," chapter 2, *The Orlando Sentinel*, 15 January 1928, 21.

67 Clow, "How I Blackmailed the Stars of Society and the Stage," chapter 1, 27.

68 "'Broadway Brevities' Revue,'" *Broadway Brevities*, September 1919, 42.

69 Heywood Broun, "Broadway Brevities Is Produced at the Winter Garden: George LeMaire's Production Dull, with a Single Scene by Eddie Cantor as the Only Redeeming Feature," *New York Tribune*, 30 September 1920, 8; Jack Lait, "Broadway Brevities," *Variety*, 8 October 1920, 17.

70 "Chorus Girl Contest," *Variety*, 20 February 1920, 1.

71 State of New York. Certificate and Record of Marriage. No. of Certificate 32796.

72 Clow's death certificate in 1941 reverted to his real age – sixty-seven – but the marriage certificate maintained the fiction that he was five years younger.

73 The name of the second witness is illegible on the certificate.

74 "Hated Women, But – He's Married Now," *The Kane Republican*, 26 November 1920, 1.

75 Obituary, "Janice A. Clow," *Bradford Era* (Pennsylvania), 29 December 1967, 2.

76 "The Clique of Craps," *Broadway Brevities*, August 1921, 18.

77 See, for one confirmation of Clow's authorship of the attacks on New York critics, Burton Rascoe's account of a meeting with Clow, which the former organized in an attempt to patch things up. Burton Rascoe, "A Bookman's Day Book," *New York Tribune*, 3 June 1923, SM22.

78 "The New York Log-Rollers, Inc.," *Broadway Brevities*, December 1922, 30.

79 Burton Rascoe (1892–1957) was a literary critic who had achieved his first success at *The Chicago Tribune* in the 1910s. Known for being highly opinionated and making enemies of authors and critics, Rascoe was dismissed from the *Tribune* in 1920. He then moved to New York, where he took up a position at the *New York Tribune*, contributing a regular, widely read feature, "A Bookman's Daybook." (Rascoe remained at the *Tribune* until 1924, when he was let go following that newspaper's merger with the *New York World*.)[97] "Burton Rascoe Papers," University of Philadelphia Finding Aids, accessed 2 June 2020, https://findingaids.library.upenn.edu/records/UPENN_RBML_PUSP.MS.COLL.1145.

80 Other members of the group, listed in Clow's diatribe, included R.W. Fisher, Edmund Wilson Jr, Rafael Sabatini, Alfred Harcourt, Arthur Carnes, Caryl Frink, C.G. Ross, R.N. Linscott, Thomas C. Chubb, Charley MacArthur, John Cournos, and Stuart Sherman.

81 In her detailed history of the Algonquin Round Table, which draws on much of her own experience as daughter of its manager and herself a journalist, Margaret Case Harriman mentions Burton Rascoe only once and notes that he was not a

member of the Round Table. *The Vicious Circle: The Story of the Algonquin Round Table* (New York: Rinehart and Company, 1951), 161.

Chapter Two

1 Stephen Clow, "How I Blackmailed the Stars of Society and the Stage," chapter 1, *The Orlando Sentinel*, 8 January 1928, 27.

2 One possible exception is the magazine's unsuccessful attempt to extort money from owners of the Childs restaurants, but the details of that effort are not available.

3 "Leavin' Em Where They Fell," *Broadway Brevities*, February 1922, 25.

4 "The New York Log-Rollers, Inc.," *Broadway Brevities*, December 1922, 30.

5 Joel Lobenthal, *Tallulah! The Life and Times of a Leading Lady* (New York: Harper, 2004), 43.

6 "Discord Among the Horsewomen!" *Broadway Brevities*, January 1923, 23.

7 See, among many other mentions, "jtoconnell69," "Tallulah Bankhead," *It's a Big Gay World Out There*, 13 July 2018, https://jtoconnell69.wordpress.com.

8 "Tryin' to Be Cordial for a Minute," *Broadway Brevities*, August 1923, 29.

9 See, for coverage, "Strap Beating Told by Wife," *Los Angeles Evening Post-Record*, 12 December 1921, 2; "L.A. Society Beauty Wins Rights to Sons," *Los Angeles Evening Express*, 4 August 1921, 6.

10 This description of the book is based in part on the article on Beery in *Broadway Brevities*, and on newspaper accounts of the scandal it generated.

11 See "Authorless Gets Local Color for Novel on Jails," *The Los Angeles Times*, 26 September 1923, 21; "Playwright Asks Divorce: Florence Beery Merrick Tells of Being Jailed by Husband in Complaint Filed," *The Los Angeles Times*, 29 September 1923, 15.

12 "Woman Writer Withdraws Book Called Obscene," *Daily News* (New York), 6 January 1924, 99.

13 Ibid.

14 "'Insides' on the Life of Florence Beery," *Broadway Brevities*, February 1924, 12.

15 Ibid.

16 An entry in WorldCat indicates that *For Love of Women* was published in 1923 by Associated Publishing and ran to thirty-three pages. The same entry also notes that "no libraries with the specified item were found."

17 "'Insides' on the Life of Florence Beery," 12.

18 Ibid.

19 See, among other sources, Chapter Eight, "The 8080 Club," in Gavin Lambert, *Nazimova: A Biography* (New York: Alfred A. Knopf, 1997), 199–249.

20 This "Helen Hammond Sterling" is perhaps the woman profiled in a "Detroit Diary" column published in 1942 in the *Detroit Free Press*. It describes Sterling as the author of several unpublished books, a convert to Islam who had lived in Morocco for eighteen years, and an expert on "Arab" cultures who had lived in Carmel, California; New York City; and Detroit. Marjorie Avery, "Detroit Diary," *Detroit Free Press*, 9 January 1942, 9. A very detailed entry on the genealogy site Wikitree indicates that Sterling was born in 1896. "Helen Esselstyn (Hammond) Sterling (1896 – aft. 1953)," accessed 15 January 2024, www.wikitree.com/wiki/Hammond-3719.

21 "'Insides' on the Life of Florence Beery," 14.

22 Ibid., 15.

23 Florence Beery, "The Psyche of the Intermediate Sex." *The Medico-Legal Journal* 41, no. 1 (January–February 1925), 4–9.

24 For more on Herzog, see Hugh Ryan, *When Brooklyn Was Queer* (New York: St Martin's Press, 2019), 83–5.

25 Beery, "The Psyche of the Intermediate Sex," 5.

26 Ibid.

27 Margaret Gibson, "The Masculine Degenerate: American Doctors' Portrayals of the Lesbian Intellect, 1880–1949," *Journal of Women's History* 9, no. 4 (1998): 78–103.

28 "Our Bow to Society," *Broadway Brevities*, January 1923, 3.

29 Stephen Clow, "How I Blackmailed the Stars of Society and the Stage," chapter 3, *The Orlando Sentinel*, 22 January 1928, 24–5.

30 For a detailed discussion of Fitch's sexuality, see "Who Was Clyde Fitch?," *The Clyde Fitch Report*, accessed 17 January 2023, www.clydefitchreport.com.

31 "The Mirrors of Mayfair," *Broadway Brevities*, April 1924, 39–40.

32 Archie Bell, *The Clyde Fitch I Knew* (New York: Broadway Publishing Company, 1909).

33 "The Mirrors of Mayfair," *Broadway Brevities*, November 1924, 44.

34 See, for example, "Elizabeth Marbury & Elsie de Wolfe Residence," NYC LGBT Historic Sites Project, March 2007, www.nyclgbtsites.org/site/elisabeth-marbury-elsie-de-wolfe-residence/. A full account of the lives and relationships of Elisabeth Marbury and Elsie de Wolfe may be found in Alfred Allan Lewis, *Ladies and Not-So-Gentle Women* (New York: Viking, 2000).

35 This is clear from a reading of Gavin Lambert, *Nazimova: A Biography* (New

York: Alfred A. Knopf, 1997), 153–5. See also, the discussion of Marbury's overlapping circles in Lisa Cohen, *All We Know: Three Lives* (New York: Farrar, Straus and Giroux, 2012), Kindle location 2407.

36 See, for example, the item in "Giving the Eskimo Pie Kids the Once-Over," *Broadway Brevities*, July 1922, 18, which speaks of Nazimova's "rupture" with Jean Acker; untitled item, *Broadway Brevities,* October 1922, 36, on Rudolph Valentino's "taking" Jean Acker from Nazimova, to marry her; and the item "We Repeat – A Find," *Broadway Brevities*, August 1923, 32, in which Nazimova's one-time relationship with Marie Doro is recalled.

37 "Women's Criticism Is Costly," *The Times* (Munster, Indiana), 17 October 1924, 9.

38 "The Mirrors of Mayfair," *Broadway Brevities*, November 1924, 44–5.

39 Ibid.

40 For a detailed summary of the Poillon sisters' lives, looking back from 1948, see Charles L. Mooney, "The City Editor Reminisces," *The Knickerbocker News* (Albany), 4 September 1948, 2nd section, 1. For later profiles of the Poillon sisters, see Carl Sifakis, *American Eccentrics* (New York: Facts on File Pub., 1984), 232–5; Scott MacEachron "The 'Amazonian' Sisters Who Terrorized the Men of 20th-Century New York," *Vice Media*, 4 December 2015. www.vice.com/en/article/the-amazonian-sisters-who-terrorized-the-men-of-20th-century-new-york/é.

41 See, for example, "Dismisses Charge Against Clow," *New York Times*, 17 February 1933, 20.

42 *Brevities* referred to the Palais Royale at least twice as a "fairyland," in a use of the term free of sexual connotations. See "Restaurant Review," *Broadway Brevities*, May 1917, 29; Untitled item, *Broadway Brevities*, October 1920, 21.

43 "Alice in Wonderland: A True Story of Alice's New Adventures," *Broadway Brevities*, May 1923, 36–7.

44 *Broadway Brevities*, October 1923, 45.

45 Marcelle Earle, *Midnight Frolic: A Ziegfeld Girl's True Story* (Basking Ridge, New Jersey: Twin Oaks Publishing Company, 1980), 249.

46 "Startling Revelations of Broadway Perversion," *Broadway Brevities*, November 1923, 16.

47 Ibid.

48 Ibid.

49 Arrests Made on Two Questionable Papers," *Variety*, 16 April 1924, 12.

50 Ibid.; Stephen Clow, "How I Blackmailed the Stars of Society and the Stage," chapter 2, *The Orlando Sentinel*, 15 January 1928, 21.

Chapter Three

1 Charles W. Gardner, *The Doctor and the Devil: Mid-Night Adventures of Dr Pankhurst* (New York: Gardner & Co., 1894). For a historian's account of Pankhurst's investigations and their effects, see Daniel Czitrom, *New York Exposed: The Gilded Age Police Scandal That Launched the Progressive Era* (Oxford: Oxford University Press, 2016). The visit by Comstock's investigators to the Black Rabbit is described in Amy Werbel, *Lust on Trial: Censorship and the Rise of American Obscenity in the Age of Anthony Comstock* (New York: Columbia University Press, 2018), 257–8. The scholarly literature on investigations of New York vice and morality in the late nineteenth and twentieth centuries is vast. See, for an overview of "sin tours," Richard Zacks, *Island of Vice: Theodore Roosevelt's Quest to Clean Up Sin-loving New York* (New York: Anchor Books, 2012), 7–24; and, for other aspects, Timothy J. Gilfoyle, *City of Eros: New York City, Prostitution and the Commercialization of Sex, 1790–1920* (New York: Norton, 1992); Kevin J. Mumford, *Interzones: Black/White Sex Districts in Chicago and New York in the Early Twentieth Century* (New York: Columbia University Press, 1996); Hugh Ryan, *When Brooklyn Was Queer* (New York: St Martin's Press, 2019); Mara Laura Keire, *For Business and Pleasure: Red-Light Districts and the Regulation of Vice in the United States, 1890–1933* (Baltimore: Johns Hopkins University Press, 2010); and Anna Lvovsky, *Vice Patrol: Cops, Courts, and the Struggle over Urban Gay Life before Stonewall* (Chicago: The University of Chicago Press, 2021).

2 Stephen Clow, "How I Blackmailed the Stars of Society and the Stage," chapter 2, *The Orlando Sentinel*, 15 January 1928, 21.

3 In 1921, Rostacher sued "Philadelphia Jack" for $100,000 after the latter claimed Rostacher had been impersonating him for financial gain. See "Gentleman Jack O'Brien Sues Philadelphia Jack," *New York Tribune*, 3 August 1921, 4.

4 "JACK O'BRIEN AGAIN," *Variety*, 22 October 1920, 3.

5 For an overview of the "flash" papers, see Patricia Cline Cohen, Timothy J. Gilfoyle, and Helen Lefrowitz Horowitz, *The Flash Press: Sporting Male Weeklies in 1840s New York* (Chicago: Chicago University Press, 2008); for useful commentary on the Broadway mythologizing of Damon Runyon, see William R. Taylor, *In Pursuit of Gotham: Culture and Commerce in New York* (New York and Oxford: Oxford University Press, 1992), 177.

6 "Gentleman Jack O'Brien Will Divulge His Secrets of Beauty," *Broadway Brevities*, August 1924, 30.

7 "Gentleman Jack O'Brien Chats on Many Different Subjects," *Broadway Brevities*, August 1924, 34.

8 "A Night in Fairyland," *Broadway Brevities*, January 1924, 12. "Battleship" Kate "Diamond Tooth" May is not mentioned again in the article, and it is unclear whom she might have been.

9 Ibid.

10 The best-known study of the "arrival scene" in anthropological writing is Mary Louise Pratt, "Fieldwork in Common Places," in James Clifford and George E. Marcus, eds., *Writing Culture* (Berkeley: University of California Press, 1986), 27–50.

11 I discuss this kind of opening sequence briefly in my article on nightlife columns in African-American newspapers of the 1920s and 1930s. See Will Straw, "Gathering Up the Social: Nightlife Columns in the African-American Press," *Ethnologies* 44, no. 1 (2022): 40–59.

12 "A Night in Fairyland," *Broadway Brevities*, January 1924, 14.

13 Ibid., 16.

14 "A Night in Fairyland," *Broadway Brevities*, February 1924, 24.

15 Ibid., 28.

16 "Night No. 3 in Fairyland," *Broadway Brevities*, March 1924, 12.

17 Chauncey, *Gay New York*, [Updated Edition] (New York: Basic Books, 2019), 239.

18 See, for example, "Cafés in 'Village' Included in Day's 15 Volstead Raids," *New York Tribune*, 25 October 1921, 7.

19 Chauncey, *Gay New York*, 239–40.

20 "Night No. 3 in Fairyland," 14.

21 Ibid., 16. Clow appeared to take pride in his talent for cataloguing queer catchphrases and cadences of speech; as discussed in chapter 8, he would recycle many of these examples in the 1930s in a publication called *Broadway Tattler*.

22 "Night No. 3 in Fairyland," 18.

23 Ibid., 20–1.

24 Ibid., 21.

25 "Night No. 4 in Fairyland," *Broadway Brevities*, April 1924, 10.

26 Ibid., 10–11.

27 Ibid., 11.

28 Ibid., 21.

29 Ibid., 14–15.

30 Ibid.

31 "Splashing Around in the 'Turkish Baths,'" *Broadway Brevities*, May 1924, 28.

32 "Night No. 5 in Fairyland," *Broadway Brevities*, May 1924, 10.

33 Ibid., 11.

34 Ibid.

35 The description of Trilby's appears in "Night No. 5 in Fairyland," 11; the "dim lights of Dolly Judge's Flower Pot" are noted in "Night No. 9 in Fairyland," September 1924, 14.
36 "Night No. 5 in Fairyland," 11.
37 Ibid., 15.
38 "Night No. 6 in Fairyland," *Broadway Brevities*, June 1925, 22.
39 Ibid., 24. One reviewer of the manuscript of this book offered the tantalizing suggestion that Chloé was really Clow, but this would assume that the address and profession of the host of the party were altered and would require that Clow be capable of extravagances of dress and behaviour that are not to be found in any other descriptions of the man. It is true that none of these conditions are beyond the realm of possibility.
40 "Night No. 6 in Fairyland," 25.
41 Ibid., 26.
42 "Night No. 7 in Fairyland," 11.
43 Ibid.,15.
44 "Night No. 8 in Fairland," *Broadway Brevities*, August 1924, 11.
45 Ibid.,12.
46 Night No. 8 in Fairland," 14.
47 Ibid., 15.
48 "Night no. 9 in Fairyland," 15.
49 Ibid.,15–16.
50 Ibid.,19.
51 "Night No. 10 in Fairyland," *Broadway Brevities*, October 1924, 47.
52 Ibid., 53.
53 The letter was published in the August 1924 issue under the headline "A Pansy From Our Mail-Bag." *Broadway Brevities*, August 1924, 26.
54 "Night No. 10 in Fairyland," 46–7.
55 Ibid., 47.
56 "Night No. 11 in Fairyland," *Broadway Brevities*, November 1924, 32.
57 "Editorial: BREVITIES FEARLESS EXPOSES OF JOURNALISM JUSTIFIED," *Broadway Brevities*, July 1924, 20.
58 Ibid.
59 Unsigned, "Chatter for Lowbrows," *Greenwich Village Quill*, June 1924, 26.
60 "BREVITIES FEARLESS EXPOSES OF JOURNALISM JUSTIFIED," 21.
61 "Night No. 12 in Fairyland," *Broadway Brevities*, December 1924, 31.
62 Ibid.
63 Ibid., 36.

64 Ibid.

65 "Night No. 13 in Fairyland," *Broadway Brevities*, January 1925, 40.

66 Ibid.

67 For more information on Jazz and similar English-language magazines published in Paris in the 1920s, see Céline Mansanti, "Where Cuckoos Nest: Jazz and The Night Light, Two Risqué English-language Periodicals in Interwar Paris and Their Relationships with the French Entertainment Press," *Revista Internacional de Historia de la Comunicación* 23 (2024): 66–80.

68 "Between Ourselves," *Jazz: A Flippant Magazine*, 15 November 1924, 3.

69 I am very grateful to Gary Elsby for noticing this image swipe. The *Jazz* article in which it appeared was "Some Berlin Nights, no. 2," *Jazz: A Flippant Magazine*, 15 March 1925, 4.

70 The Lounger, "Here and There," *Jazz: A Flippant Magazine*, 15 February 1925, 8.

Chapter Four

1 Patricia Cline Cohen, Timothy J. Gilfoyle, and Helen Lefkowitz Horowitz, *The Flash Press: Sporting Male Weeklies in 1840s New York* (Chicago: Chicago University Press, 2008), 51–2. Donna Douglas writes of *New York Tribune* editor Horace Greeley's testimony to a British parliamentary committee, in which he spoke in detail of the role played by blackmail in the business model employed by the "flash" editor-publishers. Donna Dennis, *Licentious Gotham: Erotic Publishing and Its Prosecution in Nineteenth-Century New York* (Cambridge, MA.: Harvard University Press, 2009), 52. Scholarship on the role of blackmail in newspaper publishing in other countries is extensive – for France, see, for example, Dominique Pinsolle, *Le Matin (1884–1944): Une presse d'argent et de chantage* (Rennes, France: Presses universitaires de Rennes, 2012).

2 The most detailed account of the history of *Town Topics* is Andy Logan, *The Man Who Robbed the Robber Barons* (Pleasantville, New York: Akadine Press, 2001; first published 1965); see also Eric Homberger, *Mrs Astor's New York: Money and Social Power in a Gilded Age* (New Haven and London: Yale University Press, 2002), 204–5; and Susan Hamilton, "The New York Gossip Magazine in 'The Great Gatsby,'" *The F. Scott Fitzgerald Review* 8 (2010): 34–56.

3 "'Town Topics' Suspends after Inquiry by State," *New York Herald Tribune*, 8 January 1932, 15.

4 William Schack, *And He Sat among the Ashes: A Biography of Louis M. Eilshemius* (New York: American Artists Group, 1939), 161.

5 "Clow Accused by Edith Bobe,' *The Sun*, 26 January 1925, 2(a).

6 Stephen G. Clow, "How I Blackmailed the Stars of Society and the Stage," Chapter Two, *The Orlando Sentinel* (Orlando, Florida), 15 January 1928, 20–1.

7 The literature on the film industry scandals of this period is vast and of highly uneven quality. See, for example, Greg Merritt, *Room 1219: The Life of Fatty Arbuckle, the Mysterious Death of Virginia Rappe, and the Scandal That Changed Hollywood* (Chicago: Chicago Review Press, 2013); Timothy Dean Lefler, *Mabel Normand: The Life and Career of a Hollywood Madca* (Jefferson, North Carolina: McFarland and Company, 2016); Laini Giles, *The Forgotten Flapper: A Novel of Olive Thomas* (N.p.: Sepia Stories Publishing, 2015).

8 See, for one example of the "too beautiful" comment, "Filmland Faces New Scandal in Writer's Death," *The Washington Times*, 21 September 1921, 3.

9 "The Finger of Fate," *Syracuse Daily Journal,* 29 October 1921, 11.

10 "Inside Stuff," "On Pictures," *Variety*, 9 July 1921, 29. Some writings on Hollywood scandals repeat the claim that Zelda Crosby's highly placed film industry lover had been William Desmond Taylor, who would be found murdered in Hollywood in February 1922. See, for example, Alex Madsen, *The Sewing Circle: Hollywood's Greatest Secret – Female Stars Who Loved Other Women* (New York: Citadel, 1994), 136; Jennifer Chase, "Mysterious Death of a Casting-couch Director," *Venture Galleries*, 1 February 2016, https://venturegalleries.com/. The well-regarded online publication devoted to Taylor, Bruce Long's *Taylorology*, refuted any claims to a connection between Taylor and Crosby, and Crosby's name is not even mentioned in three extended studies of the William Desmond Taylor case. See *Taylorology* (archived postings), *Silent Era,* accessed 3 February 2019, www.silentera.com/taylorology/index.html. See, as well, for additional commentary and speculation, William J. Mann, *Tinseltown: Murder, Morphine, and Madness at the Dawn of Hollywood* (New York: Harper Collins, 2014); Sidney K. Kirkpatrick, *A Cast of Killers* (New York: E. Dutton, 1986).

11 "Zelda Crosby's Death Reason Still Mystery," *New York American*, 22 September 1921, 11.

12 "Cinema Scandal May Be Revealed," *Los Angeles Times*, 22 August 1921, 16. See, among many instances of coverage of the revived 1917 case, "Movie Men's Revel Bared in Court," *Evening Public Ledger* (Philadelphia, Pennsylvania), 13 July 1921, 2.

13 The extent of the belief that Crosby's lover had been Adolph Zukor – a hypothesis that even entered into Federal Trade Commission investigations of Zukor and Famous Players – is discussed in Mark Lynn Anderson, "The Historian Is Paramount," *Film History* 26, no. 2 (2014): 9–10. Newspaper reports in August 1921, albeit based on Clow's own pronouncements and those of others identified only

as "in the know," said that Crosby's lover was one of those who had attended the "million dollar" orgy in Massachusetts in 1917. "Film Magnate Is Blamed for Girl's Suicide," *Chicago Daily Tribune*, 22 August 1921, 5.

14 "Film Magnate Is Blamed for Girl's Suicide."

15 "Cinema Scandal May Be Revealed," *Los Angeles Times*, 21 August 1921, 16.

16 "Girl's Death Bares Romance in Movies," *Daily News* (New York), 22 August 1921, 3.

17 See, among others, "Hushed Movie Scandal," *Lincoln State Journal*, 27 August 1921, 3.

18 Several press accounts say that only three people were asked to testify and name Schuster, Gross, and Hollywood. One example is "Poison Inquiry May Bare Film Scandals Here: Arbuckle Case Causes New Probe into Mysterious Death Last June of Zelda Crosby, Scenario Writer," *New York Tribune*, 21 September 1921, 6.

19 "Scandal in Broadway Beauty Probed," *New York American*, 21 September 1921, 1.

20 "Tell-Tale Letters in Movie Writer's Death Start Probe," *Daily News* (New York), 21 September 1921, 2.

21 "Zelda Crosby's Death Reason Still Mystery," *New York American*, 22 September 1921, 11.

22 "The 'Brownie' Scandal," *Broadway Brevities*, September 1921, 9.

23 "Inside Stuff on Pictures," *Variety*, 8 July 1921, 29; see, as well, Anderson, "The Historian Is Paramount."

24 The story claiming that an "entire edition of a weekly periodical" had been bought by unnamed interests was carried widely. See, for example, "'Hush' A Movie Scandal," *Kansas City Star*, 24 August 1921, 2.

25 Slide, *Inside the Hollywood Fan Magazine*, 56.

26 I am grateful to Bruce Long for this suggestion. In 1922, a magazine called *Camera! The Digest of the Film Industry* claimed that *Film Truth* had been purchased, "a year or so ago," to stop publication of "a certain story." Ted Taylor, "It's Not Our Sins; It's Our Stupidities," *Camera!* 5, no. 30 (4 November 1922): 3. For a brief history of *Film Truth*, see Mary Mallory, "Hollywood Heights – Film Truth Tells It Like It Is," *The Daily Mirror*, 14 October 2013. https://ladailymirror.com/2013/10/14/mary-mallory-hollywood-heights-film-truth-tells-it-like-it-is/.

27 "Brevities Publisher Denies 'Hush' Graft," *New York Evening Post*, 29 January 1925, 6; "Clow Denies Threats Got Ads," *Daily News* (New York), 29 January 1925 (Afternoon Edition), 2; "Brevities Editor Denies Blackmail," *New York World*, 29 January 1925, 1.

28 See, for example, the wire service story "Tragedies of 'Everybody's Secret,'" *Philadelphia Enquirer*, 2 October 1921, 3; "Her Own Tragic Fade-Out Reverses the

'Happy Ending' of All Her Pretty Photoplays," *The Kansas City Star*, 4 September 1921, 1.

29 "The Root of It," *The Atlanta Constitution*, 18 September 1921, E4.

30 Western Union Telegram, "Broadway Brecites" (*sic*) to David W. Griffith, 2 September 1921, *D.W. Griffith papers, 1897–1954*, Frederick, MD: University Publications of America, 1982, Box One, "Business and Personal Correspondence."

31 Charles Affron, *Lillian Gish: Her Legend, Her Life* (Berkeley: University of California Press, 2001), 141.

32 Richard Schickel, *D.W. Griffith: An American Life* (New York: Simon & Schuster, 1984), 435–6; Robert M. Henderson, *D.W. Griffith: His Life and Work* (New York: Oxford University Press, 1979), 212.

33 Sokorra Lewis, "The Dark Age of Hollywood (1/2)," *The Creative Ramblings*, 17 January 2009, https://sokorralewis.com.

34 Handwritten note, "dictated by Mr Lloyd," David W. Griffith, 2 September 1921, *D.W. Griffith papers, 1897–1954*, Box One, "Business and Personal Correspondence."

35 Western Union Telegram, "S G Clow Publisher of Brevities" to David W. Griffith, 8 September 1921, David W. Griffith, *D.W. Griffith papers, 1897–1954*, Box One, "Business and Personal Correspondence."

36 Unsigned note, "Oct. 13, 1921 – mailed to D W G," *D.W. Griffith papers, 1897–1954*, Box One, "Business and Personal Correspondence."

37 "Tales of Addie, Hagop and the Old Doc," *Broadway Brevities*, October 1921, 21.

38 "Head of Broadway Brevities Said to Capitalize Fear," *New York World*, 21 January 1925, 1.

39 "Karr Tells of Blackmail Plan," *New York Sun*, 20 January 1925, 3(a).

40 "Betty Jewel," *Broadway Brevities*, August 1922, 9.

41 "Griffith's 'Orphans of the Storm,'" *Broadway Brevities*, October 1922, 43.

42 "David W. Griffith's Epochal Picture Creation 'One Exciting Night,'" *Broadway Brevities*, January 1923, 46–7.

43 Display advertisement, *Broadway Brevities*, July 1923, 8

44 "Another Masterpiece from Griffith," *Broadway Brevities*, October 1923, 5.

45 In other circumstances, *Brevities* might have been charged under the Comstock Act, which criminalized the distribution of obscene materials through the mail, but obscenity was not a focus of the 1924 Grand Jury action.

46 "Brevities' Editor Held on Blackmail Allegation. Treasurer and 'Ad' Manager Accused of Using Mails to Defraud," *New York Herald Tribune*, 10 April 1924, 9; "Charge Blackmail in Broadway Paper," *New York Times*, 10 April 1924, 8; "Broadway Editor Held in Mail Fraud," *Daily News* (New York), 10 April 1924, 57.

47 "Charge Blackmail in Broadway Paper," *New York Times*, 10 April 1924, 8.
48 Ibid.
49 Roger J.R. Hynes and Alana Callender, "The Sauchelli Affair: A Bit of Ballyhoo," *Chiropractic History* 33, no. 1 (2013): 29–47.
50 Stephen G. Clow, "Joshua Bartlett Palmer, the Shylock of Chiropractic," Article II, *Brevities*, October 1922, 11.
51 Stephen G. Clow, "Joshua Bartlett Palmer, the Shylock of Chiropractic," Article III, *Brevities*, November 1922, 11, 13.
52 "Brevities Trial Greatest Show on Earth – and Admission's Free," *Sunday News*, 1 February 1925, 1.
53 "Brevities' Editor Held on Blackmail Allegation. Treasurer and 'Ad' Manager Accused of Using Mails to Defraud." The *New York Times* reported that the men had been indicted on 9 April, then corrected this two days later, noting that they were merely being held on bail pending a trial later in the month. "Three Held for Hearing: Error Made in Report of Indictment in Broadway Paper Case," *New York Times*, 12 April 1924, 10.
54 "'Wolf of Broadway' Nabbed: First Time in Long Career," *Atlanta Constitution*, 10 April 1924, 1.
55 "Brevities' Got $2,500 Lasky Ad, Galli Paid $250," *New York Herald Tribune*, 28 January 1925, 9.
56 "Arrests Made on Two Questionable Papers," *Variety*, 16 April 1924, 12.
57 Quoted in "'Wolf of Broadway' Nabbed: First Time in Long Career."
58 "Charge Blackmail in Broadway Paper," *New York Times*, 10 April 1924, 8.
59 "Arrests Made on Two Questionable Papers," *Variety*, 16 April 1924, 12.
60 See, for example, "'Not Guilty,' Says 'B'Way Brevities,'" *New York Clipper*, 15 May 1924, 1.
61 "Indictment," "The United States of America vs Stephen G. Clow, Andrew S. Brown, Charles J. Green, Nat Kunnes and Brevities, Inc.," 5 May 1924, United States District Court, no. 15,569 38–126.
62 "'Not Guilty,' Says 'B'Way Brevities.'"

Chapter Five

1 "Announcement," *Broadway Brevities*, November 1924, 52. In the trial, Clow would brag that the circulation of *Brevities* had increased from 2,000 to 3,000 following the indictment.

2 Stephen G. Clow, "How I Blackmailed the Stars of Society and the Stage," chapter 1, *The Orlando Sentinel*, 9 January 1928, 26–7.

3 Characters modelled on Fallon's public persona have appeared in such films as *The Mouthpiece* (1932), *The Man Who Talked Too Much* (1940), *Illegal* (1955), and *Chicago* (2002). David Aaron Baker played Fallon in six episodes of the television series *Boardwalk Empire* in 2010–11.

4 Westbrook Pegler, "Alleged Arch Blackmailer on Trial in Federal Court; Steve Clow, Editor of Broadway Brevities, Charged with Using Mails to Defraud; Celebrities May Testify," *The Evening Independent*, 22 January 1925, 34.

5 "US Begins Fierce Fire on 'Brevities,'" *Daily News (*New York), 21 January 1925, 2.

6 "Clow of Brevities Guilty," *Daily News* (New York), 30 January 1925, Pink edition, 1; "Brevities Publisher Gets 6 Years: Fined $6000 in Mail Fraud," *New York Evening Post*, 31 January 1925, 1; "Clow Sentenced to 6 Years and Fined $11,000," *New York Herald Tribune*, 1 February 1925, 1.

7 "US Begins Fierce Fire on 'Brevities.'"

8 "Head of Broadway Brevities Said to Capitalize Fear," *New York World*, 21 January 1925, 1.

9 "How About a Clean-Up at the Biltmore?," *Broadway Brevities*, August 1922, 31.

10 "US Begins Fierce Fire on 'Brevities.'"

11 "Charge Magazine Hit Beauty Clay after Ad Refusal," *Brooklyn Eagle,* 21 January 1925, 2.

12 "$1,000 Paid to Get Letter Broadway Brevities Offered," *New York World*, 23 January 1925, 15. The original Brevities piece was "Hey! Victor Gherson, Mumma Wants to See You," *Broadway Brevities*, September 1923, 40.

13 "'Dempsey Is Named in Brevities Suit. Defense Says Pugilist Was Paid $10,000 to Endorse a Preparation He Never Used; Others Tell of Threats/Declare That Derogatory Articles Followed Their Refusal to Insert Advertisements," *New York Times*, 24 January 1925, 28. The phrase *Brevities* used was "terrifying preparation" – untitled item, *Broadway Brevities*, September 1922, 26.

14 "Look Out, Gert, Your Ears Are Showing," *Broadway Brevities*, February 1923, 46.

15 "Frank E. Campbell" was the funeral director listed on Stephen G. Clow's 1941 death certificate as having handled his body.

16 "Follies Girl Says She Paid to Stop Scandal Monger," *New York World*, 22 January 1925, 3-star edition, 3.

17 "Picture's Price," *Daily News* (New York), 22 January 1925, 1.

18 "Follies Girl Says She Paid to Stop Scandal Monger."

19 "Clow at Brevities," *Daily News* (New York), 27 January 1925, 1.
20 "Thrilling Broadway Tales," *Daily News* (New York), 27 January 1925, 3.
21 "Alleged Arch Blackmailer on Trial in Federal Court; Steve Clow, Editor of Broadway Brevities, Charged with Using Mails to Defraud; Celebrities May Testify," *The Evening Independent*, 22 January 1925, 34.
22 In fact, the published item was a three-liner: "Must look into this reported Mlle Bobe – Bobby Haig [*sic*] imbroglio! Sounds durn sensational! And a married gent, at that." "Kiss Her Yerself," *Broadway Brevities*, January 1924, 26.
23 "Madame Bobe to the Bar," *Broadway Brevities*, February 1924, 32.
24 Joyce's treatment by the press is well covered throughout Constance Rosenblum, *Gold Digger: The Outrageous Life and Times of Peggy Hopkins Joyce* (New York: Metropolitan Books, 2000).
25 "And Peg's Don't Look Like Chicken Either," *Broadway Brevities*, February 1921, 26. The reference to Morosco placing "forceps" on Joyce's bankroll may suggest little more than that Morosco had access to Joyce's funds. However, Joyce was believed to be indirectly responsible for the death of one of Morosco's infant daughters, by giving her a string of pearls that caused a fatal rash, and *Brevities* may have sought to invoke this tragedy as well.
26 Donald Henderson Clarke, *In the Reign of Rothstein* (New York: Grosset and Dunlap, 1929), 233.
27 *Broadway Brevities*, October 1923, 5–6.
28 *Broadway Brevities*, December 1923, 19.
29 Clarke, *In the Reign of Rothstein*, 233; Constance Rosenblum, *Gold Digger: The Outrageous Life and Times of Peggy Hopkins Joyce* (New York: Metropolitan Books, 2000), Kindle location 1067.
30 "'Gave Hush Money Says Peggy Joyce,'" 23; "Clow on Stand Denies Blackmail of Broadwayites," *Brooklyn Eagle*, 28 January 1925, 3.
31 "Stars Cite High Cost of Silence In 'Brevities,'" *New York Herald Tribune*, 27 January 1925, 13. The item "Richard the Great" appeared in *Broadway Brevities*, February 1924, 6.
32 "Scandal Hunters Blocked by Judge. 'Inner Secrets' of White Way Celebrities Not Given in Court," *The Scranton Republican* (Scranton, Pennsylvania), 28 January 1925, 2. This report is credited to Edna Marshall of the Consolidated Press Association.
33 See, for example, "Judge Limits Clow's Defense," *New York Sun*, 22 January 1925, 3.
34 "Notables Helped Brevities Prosper," *New York World*, 28 January 1925, 1.

35 This specific wording of the list was published in "'Brevities' Got Prominent Aid," *The Sun*, 27 January 1925, 2(a).
36 Earlier in the trial, Gordon Kahn, *Brevities* staffer turned prosecution witness, had claimed Brown bragged of being able to "lay sufficient filth on the doorstep … [of Otto Kahn]." "Head of Broadway Brevities Said to Capitalize Fear." Julius Fleischmann, who died of heart disease a week after the trial closed, was widely believed to be experiencing "marital difficulties."
37 "'Brevities' Got $2,500 Lasky Ad, Galli Paid $250," *The New York Herald Tribune*, 29 January 1925, 9.
38 Ibid.
39 "Owner of 'Brevities' Denies All," *The Sun*, 28 January 1925, 2(a). *The New York Evening Post* said Clow was "gray of hair and face." "'Brevities' Publisher Denies He Forced People to Advertise," *New York Evening Post*, 29 January 1925, 6.
40 "Owner of 'Brevities' Denies All," 2(a).
41 Ibid.
42 "Brevities Publisher Denies 'Hush' Graft," *New York Evening Post*, 29 January 1925, 6.
43 "Owner of 'Brevities' Denies All," 2(a); "Clow Denies Threats Got Ads," *Daily News* (New York), 29 January 1925, Afternoon Edition, 2.
44 Pete Martin, *Hollywood Without Make-Up* (Philadelphia and New York: J.B. Lippincott, 1948), 90.
45 "Owner of 'Brevities' Denies All," 2(a).
46 "Clow Denies Threats Got Ads."
47 "Prosecution Is Aid to Defense," *Los Angeles Times*, 29 January 1925, 7.
48 Ibid.
49 Ibid.
50 "Fallon Pictures Clow as Martyr,' *New York Evening Post*, 29 January 1925, 5.
51 "Brevities' Ways Hotly Assailed."
52 "Fallon Pictures Clow as Martyr."
53 "'Brevities' Ways Hotly Assailed."
54 "Clow and 2 Others in Brevities Trial to Jail Tomorrow," *Brooklyn Daily Eagle*, 30 January 1925, 22.
55 "Brevities Publisher Gets 6 Years: Fined $6000 in Mail Fraud," *New York Evening Post*, 31 January 1925, 1.
56 United States District Court, Proceedings C38-126, Docket 928.
57 "Publications Similar to Brevities Now to Face Similar Prosecution," *Brooklyn Eagle*, 1 February 1925, 4.

58 "Brevities' Solicitor Insane," *Billboard*, 7 March 1925, 7.

59 Stephen G. Clow, "How I Blackmailed the Stars of Society and the Stage," Chapter Seven, *The Orlando Sentinel* (Orlando, Florida), 19 February 1928, 33.

60 In 2025, on his last full day in office, outgoing president Joe Biden pardoned Garvey on these mail fraud charges. See, for a recent revisiting of this case, "Marcus Garvey Convicted of Mail Fraud 100 Years Ago in Black Star Line Case Sinking His 'Back to Africa' Campaign," *Richardson Reports*, 18 June 2023, https://richardsonreports.wordpress.com/2023/06/18/marcus-garvey-convicted-of-mail-fraud-100-years-ago-in-black-star-line-case-sinking-his-back-to-africa-campaign/.

61 See, for a lengthy account of Tresca's trial and conviction, Nunzio Pernicone, *Carlo Tresca: Portrait of a Rebel* (New York and Houndmills: Palgrave MacMillan, 2005), 151–6.

62 "Inside Stuff on Vaudeville," *Variety*, 1 April 1925, 18.

Chapter Six

1 See, among others, "Blood Suckers," *Arizona Daily Star*, 5 February 1925, 12; "Six Years for a Blackmailer," *Pittsburgh Daily Post*, 2 February 1925, 6; "Parasites Convicted," *The Sheboygan Press* (Sheboygan, Wisconsin), 2 February 1925, 16; "Broadway Brevities," *Ashbury Park Press*, 6 February 1925, 10.

2 "Blackmailing for Righteousness," *St Louis Post-Dispatch*, 2 February 1925, 18.

3 Clow, "How I Blackmailed the Stars of Society and the Stage," chapter 5, *The Orlando Sentinel*, 5 February 1928, 22–3.

4 "Inside Stuff on Vaudeville," *Variety*, 22 April 1925, 9.

5 That Clow may have been editor of *Good Words* is suggested by a *Variety* item from 1928 about the release from the Atlanta penitentiary of Ben Leven, described as a "formerly rich and advertising man and later high-powered promoter." The item claims that Leven had taken over as editor of *Good Words* from "Steve Clow." "Around the Square," *Variety*, 11 January 1928, 42.

6 "Making the Most of It," *Good Words*, 1 November 1925, 13.

7 SGC, "A Day in the Hospital," *Good Words*, 1 November 1925, 5.

8 SGC, "What Makes Men Criminals?," *Good Words*, April 1927, 1.

9 "May Parole New York Editor," *New York Times*, 3 April 1927, Second Section, 4.

10 Stephen G. Clow, "What Kind of Men Go to Prison?," *Plain Talk*, March 1928, 297–302.

11 See, in addition to Clow's article, the summary in "'Atlanta Houses Brilliant Minds,' says Ex-Prisoner," *The Brooklyn Daily Eagle*, 19 February 1928, 5F.

12 Dayton Stoddart, *Lord Broadway: Variety's Sime* (New York: Wilfred Funk, 1941),

339–40. See also the chapter "Sime's Square," in Abel Green and Joe Laurie Jr, *Showbiz: From Vaude to Video* (New York: Henry Holt & Company, 1951), xxiii. The extent of Sime's warmth toward Clow is unclear. An unsigned remembrance of Clow, published in *Variety* in 1956, claimed that "although he [Sime] despised Clow, and had himself been injured by the man, he sent for Clow and offered him a job reading proofs" following his release from prison. "Steve Clow: A Memory," *Variety*, 4 January 1956, 40.

13 "Literati," *Variety*, 30 November 1927, 25.

14 "Yesterday and Today," *Variety*, 13 August 1930, 64.

15 Some of the newspapers carrying the series gave it a different title. In the *Tulsa Tribune*, for example, it was titled "How I Blackmailed High New York Society."

16 Editor's note, Clow, "How I Blackmailed the Stars of Society and the Stage," chapter 1, *The Orlando Sentinel*, 4 December 1927, 56.

17 Clow, "How I Blackmailed the Stars of Society and the Stage," chapter 7, *The Orlando Sentinel*, 19 February 1928, 25.

18 Stephen G. Clow, "Broadway Angels," *Plain Talk*, January 1929, 82–8.

19 While I have no empirical proof of Clow selling materials to *Smokehouse Monthly*, the evidence of his authorship of multiple columns focusing on Broadway is strong. The style is very close to that of Clow's other writings, particularly in describing Manhattan's gay and lesbian spaces or events. At different points, the column makes reference to Walter Winchell, early in his career, having stolen much of his material from "a certain monthly Broadway 'scandal sheet' that was the talk of the city and town," an obvious reference to *Brevities*. Twice, the column offers anecdotes concerning author Gaston Means's stay in the Atlanta Federal Penitentiary in the years 1925–28, referring in one of them to the things Means talked about in prison. One of these columns spends a paragraph hinting at unreported stories about the recently deceased New York lawyer William Fallon, who had been Clow's lawyer in the *Brevities* fraud case. See, on Manhattan gay life, "Sweeping Up Broadway," *Smokehouse Monthly*, October 1932, n.p.; on Walter Winchell, "Sweeping Up Broadway," *Smokehouse Monthly*, January 1933, n.p.; on Gaston Means, "Abroad on Broadway," *Smokehouse Monthly*, April 1931, n.p. and "Sweeping Up Broadway," *Smokehouse Monthly*, August 1932, n.p.; on William Fallon, "Sweeping Up Broadway," *Smokehouse Monthly*, August 1932, n.p.

20 Other "tabloid novels" of this time are Clement Wood, *The Tabloid Murders* (New York: The Macaulay Company, 1930) and Mary Lee Dutcher, *Circulation: An Uncensored Story* (New York: William Faro, Inc., 1932).

21 Willard K. Smith, *Bowery Murder* (Garden City, New York: Doubleday, Doran and Company, Inc., 1929).

22 Neal Gabler, *Winchell: Gossip, Power and the Culture of Celebrity* (New York: Alfred A. Knopf, 1994), 64.

23 The *Evening Graphic*, popularly known as the "pornoGraphic," was the most lurid and exploitational of New York tabloid newspapers in the late 1920s and 1930s. Its editor, Emile Gauvreau, was of French-Canadian background and lived most of his childhood in Montreal. Almost all issues of the *Evening Graphic* have been lost.

24 The relationship between Clow, Payne, and Hellinger is described at length in Pete Martin, *Hollywood Without Make-Up* (Philadelphia and New York: J.B. Lippincott, 1948), 90–2.

25 In 1928, Kahn wrote at least one instalment of a Broadway column, "Meet the Town," for the entertainment guide *New York Amusements* (14 January 1928, 19). By 1931, he was contributing a column of "West Coast Chatter" to the same magazine ("Gordon Kahn in Hollywood," *New York Amusements*, 25 September1931, 28–9).

26 Stephen G. Clow, "How I Blackmailed the Stars of Society and the Stage," chapter 10, *The Orlando Sentinel*, 11 March 1928, 27.

27 "Clow's New 'B'way Brevs,'" *Variety*, 18 June 1930, 79.

28 "Certificate of Incorporation," State of New York, Office of the Secretary of State Corporation Bureau, Albany, 3 July 1930.

29 "The Press," *Time*, 11 August 1930, 23.

30 "Literati," *Variety*, 25 June 1930, 128.

31 "The Press," *Time*, 11 August 1930, 23.

32 "Kelcey Allen, "Amusements," *Women's Wear Daily*, 24 July 1930, 6.

33 "Clow's New 'B'way Brevs.'"

34 Renée Carroll, "Checking Up on Broadway," *New Broadway Brevities*, August 1930, 42.

35 Laurel Miller, "Seeing Stars," *New Broadway Brevities*, August 1930, 94.

36 "Peeps at Pineapple Parkway," *New Broadway Brevities*, August 1930, 15.

37 "See Aliens Dominate Here. Mrs Clivette Asks for Immigration Curb at League Meeting," *New York Times*, 27 November 1926, 5.

38 See, for example, Albert Parry, *Garrets and Pretenders: A History of Bohemianism in America* (New York: Dover Publications, 1933), 311, and more recently, Charles Hagen, "Village Bohemians from Another Era," *New York Times*, 2 September 1994, C1.

39 Michael David MacBride, *The Great Clivette* (N.p.: Salty Books Publishing, 2023).

40 "Mystery of 'Little Sappho,' of Greenwich Village," *Pittsburgh Press*, 12 September 1920, 92.

41 A video essay by Kaz Rowe, with the title "The Bizarre Story of the Girl Who Claimed to Be Sappho Reincarnated," posted to Youtube in 2021, argues quite plausibly that claims about Juanyta's reincarnation of Sappho were part of a hoax, engineered by her family to capitalize on the fascination with the figure of Sappho that had swept over the New York theatre world following production of Clive Fitch's play *Sappho* in 1899. Indeed, the video explains, a "Sappho craze" had been a key impulse within trans-Atlantic bohemian literary networks in the early twentieth century and seeped into the broader culture. "The Bizarre Story of the Girl Who Claimed to Be Sappho Reincarnated," Youtube, 29 July 2021, www.youtube.com/watch?v=2SpPx3D8RDU.

42 See, among others, Amy Whichmiller and Juanita Clivette, "Little Theatres," *The Quill*, May 1924, 12, and the poem "The Entrepot," by Juanita Clivette "Sappho of Greenwich Village," *The Quill*, December 1923, 19.

43 In 1936, Juanyta Clivette delivered the "main address," "Greenwich Village Poets from Edgar Allan Poe to John Masefield and Edna St Vincent Millay," at a meeting of her mother's Greenwich Village Historical Society. "Groups Will Honor Greenwich Village Poets," *New York Sun*, 28 May 1936, 2. In 1940, a poem, "The Once Over," was published in *The Washington Post* (10 July 1940, 7) and other papers.

44 "Juanyta Clivette," California Death Index, 1940–1997, Ancestry library edition.

45 "Notes at Protest," *New Broadway Brevities*, September 1930, 7.

46 Quoted in Unsigned, "The Enforcement of Laws against Obscenity in New York," *Columbia Law Review* 28, no. 7 (1928): 957; for an extended discussion of this panic, see Brett Gary, *Dirty Works: Obscenity on Trial in America's First Sexual Revolution* (Stanford, California: Stanford University Press, 2021), 125–6.

47 "Is Your Own Daughter Safe?" [Safe from what? Safe from the Lesbian]," *New Broadway Brevities*, November 1930, 7,

48 For a detailed overview of Malin's career, and of the "pansy craze," see George Chauncey, *Gay New York*, 314–21; and Chad Heap, *Slumming: Sexual and Racial Encounters in American Nightlife, 1885–1940* (Chicago: University of Chicago Press, 2009), 85–95. For an interesting overview of coverage of the "craze" in the New York–based African-American press, see Kim Gallon, *Pleasure in the News. African American Readership and Sexuality in the Black Press* (Urbana, Chicago, and Springfield: University of Illinois Press, 2020), chapter 5.

49 "The Lisping Lipstickers," *New Broadway Brevities*, November 1930, 28.

50 Ibid., 30.

51 "We're Certainly to the Fag End! Have YOU a Little Fairy in Your Home?," *New Broadway Brevities*, November 1930, 54.

52 Ibid.
53 Ibid., 56.
54 Walter Winchell, "In Memoriam," *Broadway Brevities*, December 1922, 44.
55 Untitled item, *Broadway Brevities*, January 1923, 22.
56 Walter Winchell, "Your Broadway and Mine," by Walter Winchell, *Broadway Brevities*, January 1923, 5.
57 "HELP YOURSELVES, ANYTIME, BOYS!" *Broadway Brevities*, January 1923, 22.
58 Walter Winchell, "Merciless Truth," *Vaudeville News*, 20 August 1920, 2.
59 Gabler, *Winchell: Gossip, Power and the Culture of Celebrity*, 80.
60 Dwight Macdonald, *Masscult and Midcult: Essays Against the American Grain* (New York: New York Review Books, 2011), 50.
61 Stephen G. Clow, "Parasites Who Have Fattened Off Brevities," *Broadway Brevities*, November 1921, 32.
62 Ibid., 34.
63 The recommendation came in Walter Winchell, "On Broadway," *Daily Mirror*, 29 July 1930, 18. The announcement that the magazine was folding appeared in Walter Winchell, "On Broadway," *The Wisconsin State Journal*, 20 October 1930, 3.
64 The suit was launched against Winchell on 13 November and the *New York Mirror* on 18 November 1932. "Mirror and Winchell Sued," *Editor & Publisher*, 22 November 1930, 8. For the Summons, see "104 – W Summons with Notice, New-Broad Publishing Co., Inc., Plaintiff vs Daily Mirror, Inc., and Walter Winchell, Defendants," no. 34826, Supreme Court of the State of New York, County of New York, 19 November 1930.
65 "Literati," *Variety*, 29 July 1931, 50. An intriguing one-line item in Winchell's column of 20 October 1923 said that "The B'Way Brevities suspension fib was started by dismissed employes [*sic*]," but as the lawsuit would be launched two weeks later, it is difficult to see this admission as part of a settlement with the magazine. Walter Winchell, "On Broadway," *Daily Mirror*, 20 October 2023, 20.

Chapter Seven

1 From the very beginning, there was confusion over the new publication's title. On its front cover, the first issue of this new incarnation presented itself as *New Broadway Brevities: America's First National Tabloid Weekly*. The back page (and inside masthead) kept the title *New Broadway Brevities,* while a banner running along the top of each inside page read "Broadway Brevities Weekly." With the 12 October 1931 issue, the magazine became simply *Brevities*, at least on its front

cover, possibly to downplay ties to earlier versions of the title associated with Stephen G. Clow, and perhaps to bolster the publisher's apparent ambition to be national in scope.

2 See, for example, Adrian Bingham and Martin Conboy, *Tabloid Century: The Popular Press in Britain, 1896 to the Present* (Oxford, UK: Peter Lang, 2015), 1–6.

3 The "tabloid revolution" in American newspaper publishing, and the role of New York papers in this revolution, are discussed at length in John D. Stevens, *Sensationalism and the New York Press* (New York: Columbia University Press, 1991). See also Kevin G. Barnhurst and John Nerone, *The Form of News: A History* (New York and London: The Guilford Press, 2001).

4 Bingham and Conboy, *Tabloid Century*, 1.

5 Roth's role as an important distributor of illicit literature is covered at length in two books by Jay A. Gertzman: *Bookleggers and Smuthounds: The Trade in Erotica, 1920–1940* (Philadelphia: University of Pennsylvania Press, 1999) and *Samuel Roth: Infamous Modernist* (Florida: University Press of Florida, 2013.).

6 "Thomas J. Davin" [death notice], *Variety*, 28 June 1961, 71.

7 "Brevities Weekly," *Writer's Digest*, October 1931, 56.

8 The cover of the 30 November 1931 issue is reproduced on the site Digital Transgender Archive, no date, accessed 3 February 2019, www.digitaltransgender archive.net; several other covers with queer themes are archived on the Queer Music Heritage site, accessed 5 January 2024, www.queermusicheritage.com/gayephemera5.html.

9 David Saunders, "Ken Browne (1900–1965)," *Field Guide to Wild American Pulp Artists*, 2014, accessed 3 December 2019, www.pulpartists.com/Browne.html.

10 Of these magazines, *Calgary Eye Opener* had the most convoluted history, one that exemplified the cross-border arrangements to be discussed in chapter 9. *Calgary Eye Opener* was born *c.* 1911 as a newspaper of political news and commentary based in Calgary, Alberta. Its editor and founder, Bob Edwards, died in 1922, and his wife, Kate Edwards, helped relaunch it as a digest-size humour magazine, based in Minneapolis and in partnership with Harvey Fawcett, brother of Wilford Fawcett, the editor and publisher of *Capt. Billy's Whiz Bang*. The title of the magazine carried the name of the Alberta city throughout its decade-long run, though, following their divorce, Wilford Fawcett's ex-wife, Annette Fawcett, purchased the magazine. The Minneapolis version of the title continued to be credited to Bob Edwards Publishing Co., as did various spinoffs of the mid-1930s, such as the *Eye Openers Red Pepper Annual.*

11 For Lamothe's claim to have invented the Lindy Hop, see "His Only Success Is a Perfect Clop," *People*, 22 April 1974, 22.

12 See, among many sources, "Boat Show Slates for Grand Rapids," *Evening Sentinel* (Holland, Michigan), 12 February 1970, 11; "Driving and Diving. A 72-Year Old Helps General Motors Study Safety," *Wall Street Journal*, 9 December 1975, 1; "TV Listings" (Henri Lamothe on the *Mike Douglas Show*), *New York Times*, 14 April 1976, 61; James F. Jerome, "His Only Success Is a Perfect Flop," *People*, 22 April 1974, 22–3.

13 Josephine Withers, "Jody Pinto," *Feminist Studies* 11, no. 2 (1985): 379–90.

14 Connie Lingle (*sic*), "Sapphic Sisters Scram," *Brevities*, 16 November 1931, 1.

15 Ibid.

16 Jim Downs, "Rediscovering Eve Adams, the Radical Lesbian Activist," *The New Yorker*, 26 June 2021, www.newyorker.com/culture/culture-desk/rediscovering-eve-adams-the-radical-lesbian-activist.

17 Anastasia Jones, "She Wolves: Feminine Sapphists and Liminal Sociosexual Categories in the US Urban Entertainment Industry, 1920–1940," *Journal of the History of Sexuality* 26, no. 2 (2017): 294–317.

18 "Schwanda Schwbik," "Chicago's Worlds Fairies," *Brevities*, 1931 December 7, 11.

19 "Fag Balls Exposed: 6,000 Crowd Huge Ball as Queer Men and Women Dance at 64th Annual Masquerade," *Brevities*, 14 March 1932, 1.

20 Ibid., 12.

21 John Swallow Martin, "Death Knell of Degeneracy? Police and Pansies No Longer Friends as Dirt Begins to Spread a Little Too Thick," *Brevities*, 5 October 1931, 1.

22 "See, respectively, the covers of "Sleeper Sex Sold," *Brevities*, 18 July 1932; "Love Boats Sale," *Brevities*, 25 July 1932; "Week-End Love Holes," *Brevities*, 1 August 1932; "Ninety Cent Love," *Brevities*, 28 August 1932.

23 Juanyta Clivette, "Six Little Columnists," *Brevities*, 17 August 1931, 4.

24 "R.J.D.," On the Bandwagon, *Brevities*, 25 April 1932, 5.

25 Louis Sobol, from the *New York Graphic*, excerpted in "Chips from the Quarry," *The Afro-American* (Baltimore), 11 January 1930, 6.

26 "Memo from Mr Winchell of the 'Mirror,'" appended to "Strictly Confidential," *Brevities*, 21 December 1931, 2.

27 Swan reported on Davin's new job in his column "In New York," *Frederick Maryland Post*, 6 January 1932, 4; the "topsy-turvey" comment came in a later column, "In New York," *Bismarck Tribune*, 9 May 1932, 4.

28 "Presenting the Plays of Broadway in Your Library," *New York Times*, 29 May 1936, BR. 25; "Book Notes," *New York Times*, 27 January 1937, 17; "The New Books for Boys and Girls," *New York Times*, 6 June 1937, 124.

29 "Thomas J. Davin" (death notice), 71.

30 Tom Davin, "Conversations with James P. Johnson," *The Jazz Review* 2, no. 5 (1959): 14–17; "Conversations with James P. Johnson, Part II, *The Jazz Review* 2, no. 6 (1959): 10–13.

31 "'American League' Uses New Method to Fool Public: 'Catholic Editor' Advertised to Speak for 'Peace and Democracy,'" *The Brooklyn Tablet*, 30 July 1938, 1.

32 "Readers Forum: Catholics and Loyalist Spain," *New Masses*, 24 January 1939, 20.

33 See references to Davin in Eric Smith, "The Communist Party, Cooptation, and Spanish Republican Aid," *American Communist History* 8, no. 2 (2009): 37–165.

34 Malcolm B. Fulcher, "Believe Me," *Afro-American*, 6 August 1932, 3.

35 "Hamilton Lodge Ball Draws 7,000: Men Step Out in Gorgeous Finery of Other Sex to Vie for Beauty Prize," *The New York Amsterdam News*, 2 March 1932, 2.

36 "County Chafing Under High Cost of Scottsboro Trials," *New Journal and Guide* (Norfolk, Virginia), 8 April 1933, A2; see also, Bernard Young, "Even Scottsboro Judge Uses Offensive Epithet Applied to Negroes," *Afro-American*, 9 April 1933, 3.

37 "White Reporter Fined $5," *New York Age*, 12 August 1933, 2.

38 Christopher Phelps, "The Communist Party," in Ichiro Takayoshi, ed., *American Literature in Transition, 1930–1940*, 425–7 (Cambridge, UK: Cambridge University Press, 2018).

39 The place of post-war gossip in American journalism after World War II is examined in detail in Christopher M. Elias, *Gossip Men: J. Edgar Hoover, Joe McCarthy, Roy Cohn, and the Politics of Insinuation* (Chicago: University of Chicago Press, 2021).

40 See, among many reports, "400 Stands Ban 3 Periodicals as Questionable. Interborough Company Acts voluntarily, Geraghty Reports, in Decency Drive. Crail Backs Citizens' Unit. Mulroney Asks to get Evidence in Code violations," *New York Herald Tribune*, 13 January 1932, 19; "City Warns Stands to Bar Obscenity," *New York Times*, 13 January 1932, 2.

41 See, for example, "Probe Finds No Fleas on Flea Circus," *Daily News* (New York), 28 April 1932, 39; "Burlesque, Boo! 'Stoo Tame for Bored Patrons," *Daily News* (New York), 13 October 1932, 3.

42 "Jersey Acts Against Magazines," *New York Herald Tribune*, 13 January 1932, 19.

43 "Stay Refused Magazines: Court Denies Injunction Against License Commissioner Ross," *New York Times*, 4 May 1934, 8.

44 United States District Court, Southern District of New York, "New Broad Publishing Co., Inc., Plaintiff Against Warner Bros. Pictures, Inc., Defendant," State of New York, County of New York, In Equity No. 73-365.

45 Thomas & Friedan Defendants, "Notice of Motion," United States District Court, Southern District of New York, 9 February 1933, 4.

46 "Affidavit of Elliot J. Simpson," 10 February 1933.
47 "Back Number Cycle," *Variety*, 14 June 1932, 47.
48 While these volumes of *Gems of Brevities* seemed to gather up issues of the periodical randomly – with no attempt at offering sequences of issues and with identical, unnumbered covers, which made it difficult to differentiate volumes – they nevertheless, with their sturdier covers, have ensured the survival of issues that otherwise might have been torn or allowed to crumble into paper chips.
49 "Literary Market Tips," *Author and Journalist*, April 1932, 18.
50 "Business Records," *New York Times*, 10 September 1932, 27. The history of the Eastern Distribution Corporation is well covered by historians of pulp magazines and comic books. See, for example, Mark Seifert, "Man Who Vowed to Kill the Kill-Joys: Fiction House's John W. Glenister," *Bleeding Cool*, 3 October 2023, https://bleedingcool.com/comics/man-who-vowed-to-kill-the-kill-joys-fiction-houses-john-w-glenister/.
51 Bureau of Social Hygiene, "Commercialized Prostitution in New York City in 1933," in American Social Hygiene Association, Folder 164: American Social Hygiene Association: Vice Investigations, 1930–1934, 2.
52 "Literary Market Tips," *Author and Journalist*, October 1934, 14.
53 Bob Farrell, "New York at Night," *Women's Wear Daily*, 12 January 1934, 18.
54 "New York, Pacific Coast and Detroit Market Letters," *Writer's Digest*, October 1934, 15.
55 "Literary Market Tips," *Author and Journalist*, June 1935, 26; "New York Markets," *Writer's Digest*, June 1935, 25; "New York Market Notes," *Writer's Digest*, August 1935, 16.

Chapter Eight

1 The argument that the Great Depression in the United States hit its lowest depths between 1931 and 1933 is common in histories of the period. See Robert S. McElwaine, *The Great Depression: America, 1929–1941*, twenty-fifth anniversary edition (New York: Crown Publishing Group, 2009), 84.
2 "Clow's New Mag," *Variety*, 25 August 1931, 49.
3 Rian James, "Reverting to Type," *Brooklyn Daily Eagle*, 12 September 1931, 7; Untitled, *Variety*, 29 September 1931, 57.
4 Joseph Bernt, "Ballyhoo," in John McDonough and Karen Egolf, eds., *The Advertising Age Encyclopedia of Advertising*, 133 (New York and London: Routledge, 2002). See, among the many articles covering *Ballyhoo*'s success, "Hooey," *Time*, 14 December 1931, 41.

5 "Strictly Confidential," *Brevities*, 25 April 1932, 2.
6 SGC, "Untitled," *Boloney*, November 1931, 5.
7 "Strictly Confidential," *Brevities*, 25 January 1932, 2.
8 Spellings of Nesbit's name sometimes added a second "t" to her last name or used "Evalyn" for her first.
9 The claim was reported by Louis Sobol in his *The Longest Street: A Memoir* (New York: Crown Publishers, 1968), 334.
10 "Literati," *Variety*, 30 January 1934, 57.
11 *Writer's Digest*, November 1932, 69.
12 "Racetrack Tycoon," *Time*, 28 August 1933, 28.
13 Christopher Ogden, *Legacy: A Biography of Moses and Walter Annenberg* (New York: Warner Books, 1999), 94.
14 "Co-Eds Sell Smutty Literature," *Chicago Hush*, 5 November 1932, 6.
15 "Weekly Editor Arrested," *Editor and Publisher*, 30 July 1932, 38.
16 Ogden, *Legacy: A Biography of Moses and Walter Annenberg*.
17 "Publishers Indicted," *Editor and Publisher*, 26 November 1932, 38.
18 "Brevities Weeklies Quit," *Editor and Publisher*, 3 December 1932, 36.
19 "Baltimore Brevities Staff Fined," *The New York Times*, 19 January 1933, 22.
20 Unsigned, "Literati," *Variety*, 29 November 1932, 52.
21 New York County Clerk's Office, Business Certificate, no. 12336, 10 November 1932.
22 Display advertisement, "To Let for Business Purposes," *The Sun* (New York), 29 September 1900, 9; "Elevator Falls Six Stories: Load of Literary Lights Gets a Bad Shaking Up," *The Sun* (New York), 4 July 1907, 5.
23 "Business Space Leased," *New York Times*, 26 April 1935, 38; "Magazine Rents Larger Offices In West Street," *New York Herald Tribune*, 26 April 1935, 34.
24 *Records of the New York Society for the Suppression of Vice*, container 4, mss 19359, reel no. 2, "Names and Records of Persons Arrested on Complaint of the New York Society for the Suppression of Vice, during the year 1922," 28. See also "'Hot Dog' Too Hot," *The Brooklyn Daily Eagle*, 9 February 1922, 22.
25 United States District Court, Southern District of New York, Bill of Complaint 7-181, Final Order and Decree, "Daily Racing Form Publishing Company, & corporation Complainant, – against – ANNA EPSTEIN, individually, and doing business under the name or style of Daily Racing Tab Co. or Racing Tab Pub Co., TEDDY EPSTEIN and JAMES DAVENPORT," 15 February 1934. Defendants In Equity No. 77–181.
26 See, among many other reports, "3 More Seized in Tipster War; 2 from Boro," *Brooklyn Daily Eagle*, 4 December 1935, 3; "86 Are Indicted in Turf Tipster Racket

Inquiry," *New York Herald Tribune*, 3 December 1935, 1; "2 More Seized Here in Race-Track Drive," *New York Times*, 7 December 1935, 38.

27 No title, *Author and Journalist*, January 1933, 20.

28 Stephen G. Clow, "Atlantic City Goes Pansy," *Broadway Tattler*, January 1933, 1.

29 Ibid.

30 Display advertisement, *Broadway Tattler*, December 1932, 16.

31 Evelyn Nesbit, "Evelyn Nesbit Discusses Our Age of Sex, Gin and Jazz," *Broadway Tattler*, January 1933, 3.

32 "How's Your Dirty Sister," *Broadway Tattler*, January 1933, 12.

33 See Eve Golden, "Queen of the Dead: Bert Savoy," *The Daily Mirror*, 30 October 2012, https://ladailymirror.com/category/queen-of-the-dead/.

34 "City Brevities," *New York Times*, 3 May 1926, 26; "Theatrical Notes," *New York Times*, 2 August 1926, 21.

35 Examples of these columns include "42nd Street," *Scandals*, July 1933, 3; "Along the Main Stem with Noel Meadow," *Broadway Tattler*, October 1933, 3; "Just Gagging Along," *Hot-Cha* 1, no. 2, no date (probably 1933), 27; "Times Square," *Broadway Follies*, September 1933, 38; "Lobby Gossip," *Broadway*, 21 February 1931, 43; "Lounge Lizard," *New York Amusements*, 28 June 1930, 29.

36 Michael Denning, *The Cultural Front* (London: Verso, 1997).

37 Meadow's name appears, without commentary, in the section "Communist Front Organizations," "Fourth Report: Un-American Activities in California," *Report of the Joint Fact-Finding Committee to the 1948 Regular California Legislature*, Sacramento, Ca. 1948, 374.

38 See, among other reports, "Of Local Origin," *New York Times*, 7 September 1943, 20; "Screen News Here and in Hollywood," *New York Times*, 20 April 1942, 17; "Local Screen Notes," *New York Sun*, 21 December 1943, 22; "Of Local Origin," *New York Times*, 10 June 1944, 12.

39 I discuss Meadow's film work and, in particular, his advocacy of a social role for documentary films in Will Straw, "Documentary Realism and the Post-War Left," in Frank Krutnik, Steve Neale, Brian Neve, and Peter Stanfield, eds., *Unamerican Hollywood: Politics and Film in the Blacklist Era*, 130–41 (New Brunswick, New Jersey: Rutgers University Press, 2008).

40 Leonard Lyons, "On Broadway," *Cedar Rapids Gazette*, 27 June 1968, 49. For a late example of Meadow's gossipy columns for *Variety*, see Noel Meadow, "Gotham Potpourri," *Variety*, 6 April 1966, 2.

41 He is also, most probably, the Clifford Mack who, in the 1940s, edited *The Hobo News*, a joke and cartoon paper. See George Pager, "The Hobo News," *New York Folklore Quarterly* 5, no. 1 (Spring 1949): 228.

42 Clifford Mack, "Under the Harlem Moon," *Broadway Tattler*, December 1932, 7.

43 See Will Straw, "Gathering Up the Social: Nightlife Columns in the African-American Press," *Ethnologies* 44, no. 1 (2022): 41–59.

44 Monette Moore, "'Neath the Harlem Moon," *Broadway Tattler*, July 1933, 9.

45 This was perhaps Patricia Rogers, whom Epstein had hired to edit the pulp fiction magazine *Honeymoon Tales* earlier in 1933. See "Market Letter," *Writer's Digest*, May 1933, 42.

46 "Joe Burten," *Pro Football Archives*, last modified 1 January 2025, www.profootballarchives.com/players/b/burt00700.html.

47 See, for example, the mention in Bob Wechsler, *Day by Day in Jewish Sports History* (Brooklyn, New York: Ktav Publications, 2007), 328.

48 "Names and Records of Persons Arrested on Complaint of the New York Society for the Suppression of Vice, during the year 1922," *Records of the New York Society for the Suppression of Vice*, container 4, mss 19359, reel no. 2, 28.

49 Burten and Clow had crossed paths in the 1920s. A column, "Broadway Bunk," in the August 1923 issue of *Burten's Follies* – credited to a "Times Square Night Owl" – featured four items grouped under the heading "According to Clow," and an advertisement for *Broadway Brevities* appeared elsewhere in the magazine. Promotion for other magazines in *Burten's Follies* usually signalled friendly relations or reciprocated favours, and we may assume some form of personal connection.

50 Gerald Jones, "A Yiddish Odyssey: Jews and the Pulps," in Paul Buhle, ed., *Jews and American Popular Culture, Volume 2: Music, Theater, Popular Art, and Literature* (Westport, Connecticut: Praeger, 2006), 241.

51 "Literati," *Variety*, 26 September 1933, 57.

52 Ibid.

53 Unsigned, "Tales of Fairyland: Being a True Story of the Goings-On of the Famous Androgynes of Greenwich Village," *Razzberries* 1, no. 2 (no date), 20–4, 30.

54 For a detailed analysis of Untermyer's boycott campaign, see Richard A. Hawkins, "'Hitler's Bitterest Foe': Samuel Untermyer and the Boycott of Nazi Germany, 1933–1938," *American Jewish History* 93, no. 1 (2007): 21–50.

55 See, for example, "Ford Softpedals Hitler," *Brevities*, 24 April 1933, 1; "Strictly Confidential," *Brevities*, 12 October 1933, 2; "On the Bandwagon," *Brevities*, 30 June 1933, 3.

56 The career of Leo Manso might warrant a book-length study on its own. Prior to working for the Burten magazines, Manso had worked for the New York offices of Hollywood studios on publicity materials, and in early 1934, after leaving Burten, he joined the art department of the film company First Division. In 1943, he was hired by the Simon and Schuster publishing company, where he produced

cover illustrations for their new Pocket Books line. Manso was responsible for some of the most cherished (and collected) of paperback covers of the 1940s, most notably those for crime novels like Dashiell Hammett's *The Glass Key*, Cornell Woolrich's *Phantom Lady*, and S.S. Van Dine's *The Canary Murder*. In the 1940s and 1950s, Manso seemed to be everywhere in New York's commercial art world. He designed and illustrated children's books (like *Wild West* and *Fire House*), painted well-regarded covers for the first American editions of Ian Fleming's James Bond books, drew portrait covers for *Harper*'s magazine, and illustrated small-press limited-run editions of poetry by Robert Frost and the designer P.K. Thomajan.

Amidst all this commercial activity, Manso pursued a parallel career as fine art painter and collagist, working at first within an abstract expressionist style, then finding what he called his own version of impressionism. His work was shown in group exhibitions and the occasional solo show and, ultimately, in a career retrospective organized by the Arts Students League of New York in 1992, the year before he died. Manso is remembered as an important teacher of art; he played a major role in establishing Provincetown, Massachusetts, where he spent his summers, as a key place for art education. While, arguably, Manso's stature in the history of commercial illustration exceeds that he attained in the world of fine art, the lengthy recounting of his life in his 1993 *New York Times* obituary contains no mention of his commercial work.

57 Unsigned, "Lispers and Lesbies Infest Broadway," *New York Life*, October 1931, 16.
58 State of New York, County of New York, 11288 1937 Certificate New York County Clerk's Office.
59 "News Item," WBAP-TV (Television station: Fort Worth, Texas), 17 November 1960, University of North Texas Libraries, Digital Library, accessed 13 November 2017, digital.library.unt.edu/ark:/67531/metadc940250/m1/1/.
60 "Texas 'Obscenity' Indictments," *Variety*, 23 November 1960, 69.

Chapter Nine

1 "New York Society for the Prevention of Vice" was an alternate name for the "New York Society for the Suppression of Vice." The latter name appeared on official reports of the society into the late 1920s, while the former became common in newspaper articles referencing the organization in the 1930s. See, among many histories of the society, Rhonda Evans, "Vice Wars: Researching New York City's Scandalous Censorship Past," *New York Public Library*, 25 September 2017,

www.nypl.org; Paul S. Boyer, *Purity in Print: Book Censorship in America from the Gilded Age to the Computer Age* (Madison: University of Wisconsin Press, 2002).

2 Stephen G. Clow. "The Arbiter of Smut," *Author and Journalist*, November 1934, 9.

3 Ibid.

4 Advertisement, *Author and Journalist*, October 1934, 19.

5 See "Thanks for Sentence," *Toronto Star*, 17 December 1937, 8; "Editor Arrested, Magazines Seized on 'Obscene-Literature' Charges," *Globe and Mail*, 17 December 1937, 7; "Charge Literature Corrupted Morals," *Toronto Star*, 14 January 1938, 7.

6 "Thanks for Sentence," 8.

7 "Charge Literature Corrupted Morals," *Toronto Star*, 14 January 1938, 7.

8 "Charges Dismissed," *Times Colonist* (Victoria, British Columbia), 15 January 1938, 3.

9 "Prohibited Publications," *National Revenue Review*, September 1932, 6.

10 "Stemming the Tide of Obscene Publications," *The National Revenue Review*, January 1933, 4.

11 For examples of the pressure exerted by civic groups, see "Letter from Knights of Columbus, Windsor Council to The Attorney General, Toronto, May 27, 1939," *Department of Attorney-General for Ontario, Complaints: Re: Alleged Obscene Magazines, such as 'Hush' and 'Tattler,'* Government of Ontario Archives, RG 4-32. On the seizure of magazines by local police forces, see "3,000 Copies of Magazines Are Recalled: Police Object to Publications with Snappy Cover Designs," *Ottawa Journal*, 9 February 1939, 1.

12 "Publisher's Annoncement," *Broadway Brevities*, May 1937, 2.

13 Editorial notice, *Broadway Brevities*, May 1937, 3.

14 "Letter from The Crown Attorney for the City of Toronto and the County of York to: W.B. Common, Esq., K.C., Senior Solicitor, Attorney General's Department, Parliament Buildings, Toronto, Ontario, April 6, 1938," Government of Ontario Archives, RG 4-32.

15 "Memo from C. Hope to The Honourable, the Attorney General. Subject: Sex Publications. Date: December 6, 1940," Government of Ontario Archives, RG 4-32.

16 "Letter from The Crown Attorney for the City of Toronto and the County of York to Deputy Attorney General," Toronto, 20 April 1939, Ontario Archives, RG 4-32.

17 Bill quoted in "Import Prohibitions Helpful to Greeting Card Printers," *Canadian Printer and Publisher*, December 1940, 34.

18 The growth of what is now called a "Golden Age" of Canadian pulp magazines and comic books has been the focus of a significant body of scholarship in recent years. See, among many accounts, Caroline Strange and Tina Loo, *True Crime, True North: The Golden Age of Canadian Pulp Magazine* (Richmond, BC: Raincoast Books, 2004); Michelle Smith, "From 'The Offal of the Magazine Trade' to 'Absolutely Priceless': Considering the Canadian Pulp Magazine Collection," *English Studies in Canada* 30 (2004): 101–16; John Bell, *Invaders from the North: How Canada Conquered the Comic Book Universe* (Toronto: Dundurn Press, 2006); and Will Straw, "Constructing the Canadian Lowbrow Magazine: The Periodical as Media Object in the 1930s and 1940s," *Journal of Modern Periodical Studies* 6, no. 2 (2015): 112–33.

19 "New Retail Outlets Lead City's Expansion," *Toronto Daily Star*, 4 November 1940, 26.

20 "Magazines Fined for Newsprint Violation," *The Winnipeg Tribune*, 20 September 1945, 2.

21 Letter, Clayton Ruby to Will Straw, 23 December 2004.

22 Louis Sobol, *The Longest Street: A Memoir* (New York: Crown Publishers, 1968), 334.

23 Ibid.

24 "Stephen Clow Dies at 67," *New York Times*, 7 June 1941, 19. See also "Obituary, 'Stephen G. Clow,'" *Daily News* (New York), 7 June 1941, final edition, 24.

25 "Certificate of Death," Department of Health, Borough of Manhattan. Certificate No. 12502, 9 June 1941.

26 Pete Martin, *Hollywood Without Make-Up* (Philadelphia and New York: J.B. Lippincott, 1948), 90–1.

27 Sobol, *The Longest Street.*

28 See, for example, "STEPHEN CLOW DIES AT 67," *New York Times*, 7 June 1941, 19; "Broadway Brevities' Ex-Editor Dies at 67: Tumor Fatal to Stephen Clow at Bellevue Hospital," *New York Herald Tribune*, 7 June 1941, 10; "Stephen G. Clow," *Daily News* (New York), 7 June 1941, Final Edition, 24.

29 Westbrook Pegler, "Fair Enough" (column), *Los Angeles Times*, 14 June 1941, 2.

30 Ibid.

31 For a useful overview of gossip in American political and social life in the nineteenth century, see Gail Collins, *Scorpion Tongues: Gossip, Celebrity, and American Politics* (New York: Mariner Books, 1999).

Conclusion

1 See, for a lengthy discussion of libel suits against *Confidential* and their relationship to journalistic gossip in a broader sense, Neal Gabler, *Winchell: Gossip, Power and the Culture of Celebrity* (New York: Alfred A. Knopf, 1994), 467–505.

2 To be sure, cases of alleged blackmail by gossip media have continued through the present, though the phenomenon is not widespread. Jeff Bezos, owner of Amazon and the *Washington Post* newspaper, claimed in 2019 that the *National Enquirer* had threatened to publish nude photos of him if he did not cease his attacks on the tabloid. In another episode, that recalls Clow's involvement in the Zelda Crosby affair, prosecutors investigated charges that AMI, the owner of the *National Enquirer*, had collaborated with the Trump organization to buy a story by Karen McDougal, who claimed to have had an affair with Donald Trump, in order to supress its publication. These practices of what is known as "catch and kill" will almost never involve the full purchase of a magazine. See, for a detailed account, "Jeff Bezos Accuses National Enquirer Owner of 'Extortion and Blackmail,'" *The Guardian*, 8 February 2019, www.theguardian.com/technology/2019/feb/07/jeff-bezos-national-enquirer-blogpost-blackmail-claim.

3 *New York Confidential* (1948) was followed by *Chicago Confidential* (1950), *Washington Confidential* (1951), and *U.S.A. Confidential* (1952). Jack Lait died in 1954. In 1956, Lee Mortimer published *Around the World Confidential* and, in 1960, *Women Confidential.*

4 In a famous and widely covered incident, Frank Sinatra punched Lee Mortimer in a nightclub in retaliation for what Sinatra called insulting comments about him in Mortimer's columns. "'One-Punch' Sinatra Floors Columnist," *The Miami News*, 9 April 1947, 7.

5 This is the version of the story offered by Lait and Mortimer in *U.S.A. Confidential* (New York: Crown Publishers, 1952), 253.

6 For claims that television broadcasts of the Kefauver hearings inspired Harrison to begin *Confidential* magazine, see, among others, "The Curious Craze for Confidential Magazines," *Newsweek*, 11 July 1955, 50. Christopher M. Elias offers the more reasonable claim that Harrison was impressed by the sales of the Lait and Mortimer books and sought a way of capitalizing on that success. See Christopher M. Elias, *Gossip Men: J. Edgar Hoover, Joe McCarthy, Roy Cohn, and the Politics of Insinuation* (Chicago: University of Chicago Press, 2021), 135. See also Will Straw, "Urban Confidential: The Lurid City of the 1950s," in David B. Clarke, ed., *The Cinematic City*, 110–28 (London: Routledge, 1997).

7 "Office Memo," Lee Mortimer to Rose Bigman," 13 July 1959, personal collection of Will Straw.

8 Jeannette Walls, *Dish: The Inside Story on the World of Gossip* (New York: Avon Books, 2000), 45.

9 Sobol's column in the 18 February 1967 issue of *Tab International* shared a page with a feature on the "Problem of the Married Bachelor" and advertisements for bondage magazines available by mail order. The column talked about the making of Bonnie and Clyde, comedian Buddy Hackett's move to Hollywood, and Nancy Sinatra's new single, "Sugar Town." Louis Sobol, "New York Cavalcade," *Tab International*, 18 February 1967, 4.

10 Diahann Carroll, "In the Limelight," *National Limelight*, 22 December 1966, n.p.

11 See, for a useful explanation, Katie Robertson, "Murdoch's Pick to Run the *New York Post* Bets on the Web and Celebs," *New York Times*, 23 April 2021, B3.

INDEX

INDEX

INDEX

INDEX